"Finally, a comprehensive book about forensic science by forensic scientists. If you really want to know about the passions and potentials of a career in forensic science, tune in here. In light of issues identified in the recent 'National Research Council's Report on Forensic Science in the United States,' now more than ever we need the insight, advice, and vision of those who have experienced forensic science from its early formative years, through today's multifaceted legal and social challenges, and capable of providing a sound structure for the future of forensic science."
—Professor Tim Palmbach,
chair of forensic science,
University of New Haven

"At the core of criminal investigation is the dedication of forensic scientists in all disciplines and sustained pride in our daily efforts. Our continual path forward includes educating the public, providing quality scientific results, and adhering to the utmost level of ethics and moral standards in relentless pursuit of justice for all those affected by crime. This book will inspire future forensic scientists to move ahead in achieving the same goals as scientists in the field today."
—Traci Harris, forensic quality consultant

"The authors have captured the essence of forensic science—the various types of forensic science, what it takes to become a forensic scientist, as well as a selection of past and current cases . . . that showcase the use of forensic science in solving crimes and securing convictions in the courtroom. A must read for the novice, but enjoyable and instructive for the veteran as well."
—Robert Barsley, DDS, JD,
professor and director,
dental health resource program,
School of Dentistry,
Louisiana State University
Health Sciences Center

THE REAL WORLD OF
A FORENSIC SCIENTIST

THE REAL WORLD OF A FORENSIC SCIENTIST

RENOWNED EXPERTS REVEAL WHAT IT TAKES TO SOLVE CRIMES

DR. HENRY C. LEE
ELAINE M. PAGLIARO
KATHERINE RAMSLAND

FOREWORD BY CAROL HENDERSON
PAST PRESIDENT OF THE AMERICAN ACADEMY OF FORENSIC SCIENCE

Prometheus Books
59 John Glenn Drive
Amherst, New York 14228–2119

Published 2009 by Prometheus Books

Inquiries should be addressed to
Prometheus Books
59 John Glenn Drive
Amherst, New York 14228–2119
VOICE: 716–691–0133, ext. 210
FAX: 716–691–0137
WWW.PROMETHEUSBOOKS.COM

13 12 11 10 09   5 4 3 2 1

Library of Congress Cataloging-in-Publication Data

Lee, Henry C.
    The real world of a forensic scientist : renowned experts reveal what it takes to solve crimes / by Henry C. Lee, Elaine M. Pagliaro, and Katharine Ramsland.
        p. cm.
    Includes bibliographical references and index.
    ISBN 978–1–59102–729–4 (hardcover : alk. paper)
    1. Forensic sciences. 2. Criminal investigation. 3. Evidence, Criminal.
I. Lee, Henry C. II. Pagliaro, Elaine M. III. Ramsland, Katherine M., 1953–
IV. Title.

HV8073.L394 2009
363.25—dc22

2009017839

Printed in the United States of America on acid-free paper

CONTENTS

5

FOREWORD

The title of this excellent book immediately makes one think of the "unreal world" of forensic science—the world of *CSI* and forensic science as entertainment, solving the foulest of crimes with assuredness—and in under an hour. In reality, using forensic science to solve crimes is quite different. It can take days, weeks, or even months to identify and assemble the evidence to solve a crime. Just as the real physical world has three dimensions—length, breadth, and depth—the real world of the forensic scientist has to accommodate the three dimensions of science, the justice system, and information. Shortly before this book was published, the National Academy of Sciences published a report titled *Strengthening Forensic Science in the United States: A Path Forward*, which was critical of the scientific foundation of some of the techniques used in forensic science. The report contains recommendations regarding the need for thorough validation of techniques, citing DNA testing as the benchmark example of a scientifically sound and therefore acceptable technique. The report finds that some traditional pattern evidence, such as tool marks and fingerprints, has not had the same

7

rigorous validation. Science, therefore, is demanding more of its forensic disciplines, which raises the question: *What is forensic science?*

As I pointed out several times during my tenure as president of the American Academy of Forensic Sciences (AAFS) and more recently in testimony before the US House of Representatives Subcommittee on Science and Technology, the nexus between science and law is critical. Forensic science requires reliable and objective testing and interpretation of results to produce evidence essential to the justice system.

The second dimension of forensic science is justice. Unless forensic scientists meet the needs of the justice system—which includes the needs of the investigative phase as well as the adjudicative phase in court—they will not fulfill their obligations to a society that depends on science for the fair and reliable determination of justice. Likewise, unless lawyers understand the realities of science—including the blunt truth that there are no absolutes in science—they will not be able to accord the correct weight to scientific evidence.

The core of the third, and arguably most important, of the dimensions of forensic science in the real world is information. Forensic science is about gleaning information from the silent witness of the scientific test—about learning from others to improve our own abilities to conduct research, teaching, and training, and to be objective and unbiased.

Information is a complex concept: It has a factual basis, an interpretative context, and it depends entirely on the effectiveness of communication. This book demonstrates how information gathering provides a pathway to solving crimes. The focus on information is also the strength and distinguishing feature of this book. It sets aside the rote analysis of evidence and shows how critical thinking is the essential first step in using science to solve crimes. Only then does science allow us to explore the second step: considering the tests that can be best used to address the problem of solving a crime. Dr. Henry Lee; Elaine Pagliaro, MS, JD; and Dr. Katherine Ramsland demonstrate that solving crimes depends on understanding the significance of scientific findings and the ability to communicate those findings to investigators, lawyers, judges, and jurors. The nexus between law and science has been described as an essential alliance as well as a reluctant embrace.[1] Both of our professions constantly evolve and change. This book is an essential contribution to the forensic science and legal communities' understanding of what happens in the real world of a forensic scientist.

Carol Henderson
Director, National Clearinghouse for
Science, Technology and the Law
Professor of Law, Stetson University College of Law
Past President, American Academy of Forensic Sciences

NOTE

1. Sheila Jasanoff, *Science at the Bar* (Cambridge, MA: Harvard University Press, 1997).

Chapter One

THE CRIME SCENE AND THE SCIENTIST

The growth of the discipline of forensic science over the last fifty years has been stunning. Once a small subdiscipline of applied science, forensic science has emerged as one of the most popular career choices today. No one has had a more pronounced effect on the popularity of this field than Dr. Henry C. Lee. The story of Lee and his contributions to this field is in many ways inseparable from the history and development of forensic science itself.

Among the many insights Lee has shared about the day-to-day work of a real forensic scientist is that a key aspect of effective investigation is good teamwork. Among the thousands of cases Lee has investigated, one of the great examples of the type of teamwork that is crucial to the real life of a forensic scientist is the case of Helle Crafts.

The case began when Helle Crafts, a flight attendant for Pan American World Airways, seemed to vanish. Keith Mayo, a private investigator from Newtown, Connecticut, called the local police department on December 1, 1986, to report that Helle Crafts had been missing for the past ten days. Mayo, whom Helle had hired to help her make a case for divorce, surmised that her husband,

Richard, might be involved with her disappearance. He learned that Helle had arrived home just before a major snowstorm hit the area. Richard Crafts had told police his wife had driven to the home of her sister-in-law in Westport, Connecticut, on the following day, November 19. She never arrived and had called no one. Her car was found at Kennedy Airport, in the Pan Am employee parking lot. She was not scheduled to fly on the 19th, but since then had missed two assignments. Friends who generally spoke to her daily had not heard from her, and most people who knew her were aware that her ten-year marriage had been contentious, even abusive.

Richard B. Crafts was a commercial pilot for Eastern Air Lines. When he first met Helle in 1969, he was engaged to someone else, but they dated anyway. They married six years later, after she realized she was pregnant. She quit her job and they moved to Newtown where, over the years, they had three children. Then Helle returned to work at Pan Am. Richard often left without notice for days at a time, and Helle bore bruises from their fights over his extramarital affairs. In fact, Mayo had photographed Richard carrying on with another woman.

Newtown police were acquainted with Richard because, despite his full-time job with the airline, he also worked as an auxiliary police officer and was a prodigious gun hobbyist. He owned several shotguns, handguns, and high-powered rifles. When questioned, he readily confirmed that Helle had disappeared the day after the snowstorm, but he said he had no reason to believe she was upset when she left or that she would not be back. Yet investigators were concerned about several aspects of this case. Helle was a devoted mother who would not have abandoned her young children. One of her friends reported that she had earlier indicated that if something happened to her, it would not be an accident. On an even more disturbing note, in the days following Helle's disappearance, Richard gave several conflicting stories about Helle's absence, including that she had gone to Denmark to visit her ailing mother. The police discovered that Helle's mother was not ill and that she had not seen or heard from her daughter in months.

An interview with the Crafts' au pair, Dawn Marie Thomas, revealed that during a power outage on November 19, Richard had woken her and the children early and taken them to his sister's house. He said that Helle had left earlier, but she was not at his sister's as expected. When Richard picked them up that evening, he told Thomas that Helle had gone to Denmark, although he had initially said he did not know where she was. When she returned to the house in Newtown, Thomas noticed that a piece of carpet was missing from the master bedroom, precisely where she had seen a dark spot the size of a grapefruit the night of the storm. She also thought she saw blood on a mattress and on some towels.

The police asked Richard to submit to a polygraph, which he passed, but when more time went by without any sign of Helle, he was invited in for another interview. He admitted he was embarrassed that he did not know where his wife was. When asked about the rug, he said he had pulled it up to replace it as a surprise for Helle. Earlier, however, he had told Thomas that he had spilled kerosene on it.

For local police, this was the end of the investigation. Pressure from Mayo and concerned friends to solve the case led State's Attorney Walter Flanagan to assign the case to the State Police Western District Major Crime Squad. Mayo went to the dump with the Major Crime Squad and found what he believed was the right piece of carpet. He and the crime squad sergeant took the portion of carpet to the state police laboratory in Meriden, Connecticut, where Henry Lee was the chief criminalist and lab director, and supervising criminalist Elaine Pagliaro was his assistant. The forensic scientists ran tests on the rug, but, to Mayo's disappointment, none of the stains was positive for blood.

The Western District Major Crime Squad continued the investigation on other fronts. When they examined Crafts's credit card records prior to November 19, they learned he had purchased a large freezer and had paid $900 to rent a piece of machinery. He had also purchased a new Ford truck with a special trailer hitch. While Richard had a habit of buying expensive equipment and leaving it to rust on his two-acre property, these multiple large purchases during such a narrow time frame were enough to create suspicion.

They got a warrant to search the Crafts' L-shaped ranch home, breaking in through a back window on Christmas Day while

Richard and the children were away. Lee and Pagliaro supervised the evidence collection. While they did find a freezer, there was no indication it had ever contained a body. Carpets in the bedrooms had been pulled up and discarded, and mattresses from the beds had been placed in different rooms. The investigators realized that Crafts, as an auxiliary officer, knew police work and perhaps had studied it more avidly than most, which could make the investigation difficult. A number of guns were seized, along with fiber samples, towels, and a mattress with apparent bloodstains. In all, Lee's team collected 113 items of potential evidence.

In addition to seizing potential evidence, the lab scientists performed presumptive blood tests throughout the house with the enhancement reagent ortho-tolidine. Some spots tested positive, including those on the mattress Richard had shared with Helle. Several towels in the bathtub also tested positive. Back at the lab, the blood type on the mattress proved to be O-positive, the same as Helle's. But her whereabouts remained a mystery.

There were still more leads to check out. Calling Darien Rentals —a nearby company that had appeared on his credit card statement —detectives learned that Richard had rented an Asplundh Badger Brush Bandit 100—a commercial-grade woodchipper. The thought of what he might have done with it was chilling. They recalled a story from the year before about a man who had put a German shepherd through a woodchipper. They knew that it was of supreme importance to find the actual machine Crafts had rented. If what they feared was true, they faced the possibility that a body could not be recovered.

In the meantime, Detectives Patrick McCafferty and T. K. Brown, checking records, heard a strange story from Joseph Hine, an employee of Connecticut Public Works in Southbury, who had worked on November 20, one of the nights of the storm. Around 3:30 a.m., he had seen a U-Haul truck and a large woodchipper parked along the side of the road near the riverbank. The driver waved him to move on. Hines later returned to the area and saw that the man had been chipping wood. Hines took the detectives to the spot on Lake Zoar, a bulge of water on the Housatonic River.

Fortunately, snow covered the ground, so the detectives could clearly see wood chips scattered along the riverbank, mingled with other substances. A closer inspection revealed light blue fibers and several scraps of paper. When McCafferty and Brown carefully picked up a piece of shredded envelope, they saw a name and address still intact through a cellophane window: Helle Crafts. They immediately called for a search team.

Despite the bitter December cold in Connecticut and the hindrance of sticks and leaves along the riverbank, the search team melted the snow, inch by inch, and found more envelopes addressed to Helle, as well as strands of blonde hair, bone fragments, pieces of cloth, and other items. The painstaking search lasted two weeks and covered two miles, as items were carefully packaged into two dozen bags for the crime lab.

Meanwhile, another team seized the woodchipper Crafts had rented and recovered copies of the rental agreement signed by Crafts. They also collected a record of transactions involving problems with his new truck that had culminated in his rental of the U-Haul vehicle.

Diving teams dressed for extreme cold went into the river, because it was believed that Richard had aimed the woodchipper toward the water, but it proved too cold for even the most experienced to spend long periods of time searching for evidence. One diver soon found a STIHL chain saw with the serial number filed off. The lack of rust indicated that it had not been in the water very long. Scientists examined the various parts of the chain saw for physical evidence, finding fragments of tissue that was later found to be human, as well as several small fragments of blue-green fiber and human hair fragments. As crime scene personnel continued to search the riverbank, several bones (later identified as human) turned up, followed by a tooth fragment, a porcelain dental cap attached to a small chip from a jawbone, part of a finger, and a fingernail with red polish. In the end, the search team recovered 2,660 strands of hair, sixty bone fragments, five droplets of human blood, three ounces of human tissue, a tooth fragment, a dental cap, part of a human skull, one fingernail, one toenail, and part of a finger. In the trunk of Crafts's car, mingled with wood chips, were more hair strands, blue fibers, and a piece of flesh.

The Crafts case epitomizes how forensic science—the study of applying science to legal questions—has progressed from a general investigative discipline to a field with many areas of specialization. Today, there are at least thirty-six specialties and subdisciplines in forensics. (Some of these areas will be discussed in the following chapters.) The subdisciplines include odontology (teeth identification), anthropology (bone and human individual identification), and serology (blood and body fluid typing), among others.

In the Crafts case, crime scene detectives and forensic scientists collected a variety of evidence. Lee assembled a team of top-notch forensic experts to handle the diverse categories of evidence. The team consisted of the following scientists and specialties: Lee, criminalistics; Pagliaro, forensic biology and trace evidence; Dr. Albert Harper, forensic anthropology; Dr. Bruno Frohlich, forensic anthropology; Dr. Gus Karazulas, odontology; Dr. Lowell Levine, odontology; Dr. Alan Reskin, radiology; Dr. Ferdinand Ruszala, forensic chemistry; Dr. Robert Gaensslen, forensic biology; Dr. Bruce Hoadley, wood expert; Dr. John Reffner, forensic microscopy; and Dr. Harold Deadman, forensic hair examination. In addition, experts in the areas of tool marks and fingerprints from the forensic science laboratory also examined evidence and assisted with crime scene searches.

Karazulas and Reskin used X-rays and a detailed dental comparison to prove that the tooth fragment and cap were from Helle's lower jaw. Levine, from the New York State Police Forensic Center, supported this finding using X-rays to analyze the bone chip attached to the partial tooth. To confirm that putting a person through this type of woodchipper would result in pieces of the sizes that were found, the team put a pig's carcass through it. The resulting fragments were similar in size.

On January 11, 1987, the Danbury Court issued an arrest warrant for Richard Crafts. Following an intense standoff, he finally surrendered, and bail was set at $750,000. The working hypothesis was that Richard killed his wife during an argument in the bedroom (where blood was found), had frozen her body, and had dismembered it with the STIHL chain saw. He wrapped the parts in plastic garbage bags, refroze them, and then ran the parts through the woodchipper under the cover of night. He included the blue T-shirt she was wearing the night she was killed and some of her belongings and mail. While it hindered some of his plans, the storm had facilitated others, notably getting the au pair and the children out of the house.

But despite the abundance of evidence, the legal proceedings were complicated. During Crafts's trial, State's Attorney Walter Flanagan put all the detectives, crime scene processors, and forensic scientists on the stand to re-create the incident from the evidence and circumstances—the sequence of events, purchase and rental records, and so on—to establish proof. Forensic scientists went carefully through hundreds of pieces of evidence. They demonstrated that the majority of bone pieces had been cut with a heavy-type cutting edge from a machine with a crushing force, and that the same machine had cut them all. They had found human tissue on one part of the chain saw, and blonde hair fragments and blue fibers in the chain's teeth. Restoring the serial number, they testified that the saw could be traced to Richard Crafts. The fibers were consistent with pieces of T-shirt that looked like Helle's favorite sleepwear. In addition, investigators discovered the purchase of a new freezer that had then been discarded at a dump.

Even with one hundred witnesses and 650 exhibits presented over the course of fifty-three days, it was difficult for the jury to arrive at a consensus. They deliberated for two weeks, but because one juror would not change his mind, they could not render a verdict. This resulted in a mistrial.

The second trial opened on September 7, 1989, with the same expert witnesses and testimony. This jury took only eight hours to return a guilty verdict. For first-degree murder, Richard Crafts received a sentence of ninety-nine years in state prison, and he is currently serving that sentence.

THE CRIMINAL INVESTIGATIVE PROCESS

When an incident call—such as the call Keith Mayo made—comes in to 911 or a police dispatcher, patrol officers are sent to investigate. Sometimes there is a crime scene; other times there are only suspicious circumstances. If necessary, the officers protect the scene and alert their supervisor to send backup personnel. The first responders make sure the scene is safe for police personnel and the public. They note the time of their arrival and record other pertinent observations, such as whether doors or windows were open when they arrived, what they heard, and if there were any odors. Unless they encounter a victim or other injured person at the scene who is in need of assistance, they refrain from touching or moving anything. Paramedics may already be on the way, but detectives, the state's designated death investigator (a coroner or medical examiner), laboratory scientists, and even someone from the office of the state's prosecuting attorney might also be needed. Figure 1.1 outlines the steps in the investigative process.

Modern crime scene response and analysis is a combination of criminalistics and criminology, or analyzing physical and behavioral evidence. Criminalistics is the application of scientific methods to physical evidence such as bloodstains, fingerprints, firearms, DNA, computers, and poison. Criminology involves examining crime scenes for evidence of motive, perpetrator traits, and patterns of behavior that will help in interpreting the evidence and recon-

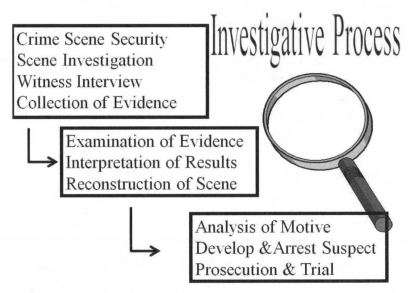

Fig. 1.1. The three phases of the investigative process.

structing the incident. Together these disciplines make accurate reconstruction possible. "Success," Lee likes to say, "lies in how you interpret the results."

Investigators must assume that whoever was at the scene has left something there or taken something from the scene, and probably both. This is Locard's exchange principle. Dr. Edmond Locard, an early forensic scientist in France, was convinced that "every contact leaves a trace," and he relied on this principle when he began his forensic laboratory in Lyon in 1910—one of the first in the world. A devotee of Sherlock Holmes, he relied on logic and careful analysis to connect crimes with perpetrators. His principle postulates that during the perpetration of a crime there is a cross-transference of trace substances between a perpetrator and a victim or crime scene. Locard's principle is still the foundation of criminal investigation. In 1980 Lee further expanded this theory to a four-way linkage theory, as shown in figure 1.2.

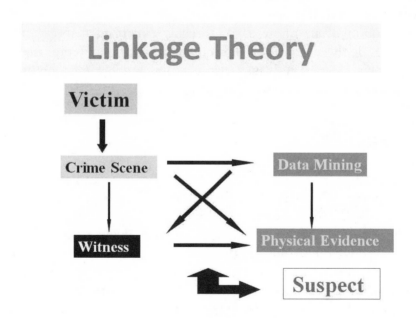

Fig. 1.2. The four-way linkage of evidence, associating a victim with a suspect.

Locard's principle emphasized that when two persons or objects have direct contact, they leave traces of material on each other. But there are many environments in which there is no direct contact; trace evidence can result from airborne or indirect contact, or even through electronic means in e-crime, cell phones, or faxes. The four-way linkage concept is designed to explain the logical process of association for modern criminal investigation. Evidence can be physical, verbal, written, or in electronic form. The crime scene can be a location, a vehicle, a computer, or even something microscopic. The objective of criminal investigation is to link the suspect to the victim, crime scene, and evidence through direct or indirect means.

To preserve the integrity of the evidence, officers must avoid contamination of the crime scene and restrict access to all but the core investigative personnel. The first responder or crime scene personnel must mark the perimeter with tape or a barrier and preserve the defined area. If the crime involves a murder, the death investigator takes over, but, as the Helle Crafts case demonstrates, all crime scene investigation involves teamwork. While that might mean the coordination of many areas of forensic expertise, someone who understands the value of all participants can help to retain the big picture. Dr. Henry Lee is just such a professional: He is one of the world's experts in crime scene reconstruction.

DR. HENRY LEE

Dr. Henry Chang-Yu Lee is one the most knowledgeable experts in contemporary crime scene investigation in the world. His background shows how the road to success involves many different avenues. Born in China in 1938, Lee was only four years old when Chinese communists took over the mainland. To avoid the revolution, his family fled to Taiwan, where his mother raised him and his twelve siblings. When he was in high school, he had hopes of becoming a basketball player, but he soon had to acknowledge that at five-foot-eight, this was not a realistic goal. He decided that all people have dreams, but in the end we must use the talents we have been given to their greatest potential. Real dreams are based on applying these talents as if there were no restrictions to what is possible. As he often says, "Set a limit of no limit!" So Lee looked elsewhere.

He attended the Taiwan Central Police College, graduating in 1960 with a degree in police science. He then became a member of the Taipei Police Department. As the highest achiever in his class, Lee was quickly promoted to the rank of captain. He worked for five years as a police officer and investigator. Watching ineffective police interrogations, he became convinced there had to be a better way to solve crimes. He decided to emigrate with his wife, Margaret, to the United States to further his studies. He often says they arrived with fifty dollars and almost no command of English, but Lee saw an opportunity to learn and prove himself through hard work. Lee attended the John Jay College of Criminal Justice (JJCCJ) in Manhattan, where he became interested in forensic science.

Founded in 1964 as the College of Police Science, JJCCJ is a senior college of the City University of New York and is the only liberal arts college in the country with a focus on criminal justice. When more liberal arts programs were added, the college took a new name, from former New York governor and the first chief justice of the US Supreme Court, John Jay. Internationally recognized as a leader in criminal justice education and research, as well as a training center for law enforcement agencies, the college has provided thousands of students who wish to go into police work, forensic science, public administration, and forensic psychology with a top-notch education.

In 1972 Lee received his Bachelor of Science degree in forensic science from JJCCJ. He went on to get a master's degree at New York University two years later, and was awarded a PhD in biochemistry in 1975. During this time, he worked as a research scientist at the NYU Medical Center, but upon his graduation he joined the faculty at the University of New Haven in Connecticut, where he helped to establish a program in forensic science. He also utilized his police experience and forensic background to help public defenders and police departments to solve cases throughout New England. He volunteered to assist the Connecticut State Police establish a forensic science laboratory, and in 1979 he became the first chief criminalist and director of the Connecticut State Police Forensic Science Laboratory. In 1992 he was elected a Distinguished Fellow of the American Academy of Forensic Science, and he has received numerous honorary degrees in the years since.

In 1998 Lee left the lab when he was appointed commissioner of the Connecticut Department of Public Safety. In 2000 he was made chief emeritus of the Connecticut Division of Scientific Services and a full professor of forensic science at the University of New Haven, where he also instructed students at the Henry C. Lee Institute of Forensic Science. Over the years he has authored or coauthored forty books and book chapters, including *Cracking Cases, Dr. Henry Lee's Forensic Files, Famous Crimes Revisited, Henry Lee's Crime Scene Handbook, Physical Evidence in Forensic Science*, and *Introduction to Forensic Science and Criminalistics*, as well as more than three hundred articles. He has been a key consultant in cases such as the reinvestigation of the Sacco-Vanzetti affair, the murder of Nicole Brown Simpson, the JonBenét Ramsey murder, the John F. Kennedy assassination, and the mystery surrounding the death of Vincent Foster.

Lee also has consulted in many major investigations. He has testified in hundreds of trials and consulted on more than six thousand criminal cases around the world. The Crafts case gave him national prominence as a forensic scientist, but his involvement with high-profile celebrity cases made him a household name—a rare feat for a scientist.

Lee's success as an expert rests primarily on his unique approach to case analysis. Lee understands that while laboratory testing is mechanical, the interpretation of the results is crucial. While science is the basis of objective forensic analysis, he knows how important it is to include the entire case scenario in the evaluation of scientific results. In other words, finding DNA does not necessarily mean anything in itself; it is the way the DNA might fit in with the whole picture of a case that gives it evidentiary weight.

While Lee appreciates the individuality of each crime scene, he also knows that each can be approached using a general principle that will help investigators avoid basic mistakes. Once the general principle is understood, crime scene investigators learn the specifics, developing both a good instinct and a sense of perspective from years of experience. Lee's maxim is to learn from the mistakes of others and avoid making such mistakes in the future.

THE UNIVERSITY OF NEW HAVEN

When Henry Lee was hired by the University of New Haven in 1975, the school had only the barest beginnings of a forensic science program. With the arrival of Lee, the program became organized and focused, and began to flourish. As one of only a few schools at the time that offered both undergraduate and graduate degrees in the field, its forensic science department soon established a reputation for producing students with well-rounded backgrounds, firmly rooted in the sciences. This was a time when most people did not know what forensic science was. The program stressed Lee's philosophy of teamwork and a holistic approach to crime scene analysis and reconstruction.

In the beginning, there was only one plan of study—forensic science. Students with both science and law enforcement backgrounds took the same classes and shared perspectives, learning from each other as they acquired knowledge in each discipline. Every class required a mini research project, in which each student could apply his or her special area of interest or expertise to a forensic issue. This close working environment created a tightly knit community in Connecticut and elsewhere; many of the professional relationships Lee's students developed in school continue to this day.

In the late 1970s, with the help of the popular television show *Quincy*, more people became aware of the work of forensic scientists. Quincy was a well-versed pathologist working with a loyal laboratory scientist, Sam, who conducted tests on evidence that was collected during autopsies. Together they would solve crimes and disease-related mysteries by applying the scientific method—a step-by-step approach to problem solving based on collecting facts from experiments and observations—to these problems. The publicity from the show, as well as several high-profile trials, created an increased interest and enrollment in forensic programs. At the same time, the US Department of Justice was providing funds for training for law enforcement. Many police officers recognized the value of science in their investigations and chose forensic courses to supplement their other criminal justice studies.

Lee's charismatic leadership and the personal interest he took in his students created an exciting atmosphere in which to study. The University of New Haven forensic program soon grew to include a science-based concentration—criminalistics (scientific disciplines practiced in a crime lab)—and an investigation concentration, including criminal investigation, computer crimes, and fire science. Even today Lee can be found at the University of New Haven discussing career plans with students or talking about the latest scientific developments. Student internships now encompass every aspect of current forensic laboratory and investigative practice, with placements in forensic labs, in police departments, in fire marshal offices, in offices of medical examiners, and with private company investigative services. Under Henry Lee's guidance, the forensic science program, which started off with mostly students from the local area, has become an international program. Students have come to the University of New Haven from fifty-two countries to study forensic science, and alumni of the program can be found in almost every state and in diverse countries such as Dubai, Egypt, Saudi Arabia, Taiwan, Croatia, England, Japan, Canada, Singapore, India, and China.

THE LAB YEARS

Lee left a full-time professorship in 1979 to help the state of Connecticut build a world-class forensic science laboratory. At that time the state had a laboratory that was housed in a few refurbished rooms at one of the state police barracks. Laboratory examiners were primarily seasoned police officers, most of whom worked in the identification areas—firearms, fingerprints, documents, imprints, and photography. In addition, there were two troopers who conducted basic microscopical and serological—blood and body fluids—tests. The amount of evidence and the extent of testing necessary for most criminal cases, however, were really too great to be completed by a few people, and before Lee's arrival most of the criminalistics cases were forwarded to the FBI Lab for analysis.

Because he knew science was the future of investigative work, Lee began his tenure at the laboratory by expanding its criminalistics section. Lee also believed the seldom-tapped pool of trained scientists would be the future of the field, so his next move was to hire three scientists with expertise that allowed for the expansion of evidence testing in fire debris, in blood, in enzymes, in microscopy, and in other instrumental testing. The entire criminalistics section of the new laboratory was now composed of Lee's former or current students, who knew his methods and applied his teachings. The forensic science laboratory quickly gained a reputation in the state for insightful and skillful analysis, and its scientists soon were meeting with attorneys and investigators to review cases, investigate crime scenes, and discuss testimony. Lee also initiated training for the Connecticut State Police, prosecutors, and local law enforcement in forensic science and crime scene applications. These successful sessions continue to be annual events.

When Lee became director of the forensic science laboratory, he insisted that defense attorneys have equal access to the laboratory's scientists so they could discuss findings of evidence analysis that might help their cases. Surprisingly, this is not a common practice among many police laboratories. But Lee insisted that science was science; it should not matter who is asking the question because the scientific answer should always be the same. The lab also offered training for public defenders, and soon these attorneys were requesting their own tests be carried out at the laboratory. While the practice has changed somewhat over the years, today the Connecticut laboratories of the Division of Scientific Services carry on Lee's open-door policy. Both attorneys and scientists have found this approach to be a welcome change from previous practices in some other jurisdictions.

During his twenty years as head of the forensic science laboratory, Lee analyzed evidence in all local cases of importance. This often involved not only interpreting laboratory analyses, but visiting crime scenes and reconstructing the events of those crimes. Some cases involved reexamination of evidence from crimes committed years before, such as his study of the Martha Moxley homicide. That case involved the murder of a fifteen-year-old girl who left home to go to a neighbor's Halloween party on October 30, 1975, and never returned. When her body was found near her backyard the next day, the number of possible suspects was limited because she lived in an exclusive community in Greenwich, Connecticut, with its own security force and restricted access. More than a decade after Moxley's death, Lee began to reexamine each piece of evidence. He reviewed photographs of the crime scene. He read accounts of witnesses. In time, as new techniques such as DNA analysis were developed, additional tests were performed on the evidence. While these results did not point to one individual, they did serve, in some cases, to rule out possible suspects. When Lee testified at the trial of Michael Skakel, who was charged with the crime, he was able to show the jury how the patterns at the scene and the injuries to Martha told the story of what had happened and how it had happened. A short time after the case was given to the jury, they arrived at a verdict of guilty.

The Skakel trial was one of many cases in which science and logic were brought to criminal investigation. In a more recent case, a number of women were found strangled in various locations in Hartford. A single person was linked by DNA evidence to all the areas where the bodies were found, leading the police to believe they were looking for a serial killer. DNA profiles were developed and searched against the Combined DNA Index System (CODIS), a national DNA database. A "hit" identified a man named Mark Johnson as the source of the DNA. Because the DNA was isolated from different types of evidence, such as cigarette butts and a soda can at the scenes, and none was found directly on the victims, there was some concern that the suspect could not be linked conclusively to all of the crimes. It was Lee who provided the necessary linkage of the cases. By applying logic and pattern analysis, he showed that it was highly unlikely that the same individual's DNA would be found randomly on objects at three different crime scenes. He further showed that the locations and patterns of the scenes and the positions of the victims' bodies logically related these cases to each other using the four-way linkage theory. Logic was the crucial link that brought a serial killer to justice.

These are just two of many crimes that were solved by the application of scientific principles by Lee and his protégés during his tenure as chief criminalist at the Connecticut Forensic Science Laboratory. While the laboratory analyzed hundreds of cases when Lee began his tenure at the lab as chief criminalist, in 1998, the year he left the laboratory to become commissioner of the Department of Public Safety, the laboratory received more than five thousand cases from the state police, local law enforcement, federal investigative agencies, and at least ten other states.

THE INSTITUTE

Established in 1980, the Henry C. Lee Institute of Forensic Science at the University of New Haven is a leading institution in the arena of public safety and forensic science. The institute is pledged to advance forensic science through training programs and research. It links students, investigators, scientists, attorneys, and other professionals in addressing the emerging scientific and social issues in the field, as well as demonstrating the latest forensic technologies.

Looking at the history of criminal justice around the world, it is clear that many cases were not handled properly. The physical evidence often was not collected, was collected improperly, got contaminated, or was distorted. To improve the handling of cases, Lee took a three-pronged approach in the work of the institute:

1. *Education.* The institute runs regular advanced crime scene symposia, inviting detectives from all over the country to learn the latest techniques. The annual Markle Symposium draws thousands of police officers, students, and other professionals together for two days of presentations on a designated topic, such as high-profile crimes or serial killers. The institute also stresses the need for practical experience. Law enforcement and laboratory personnel take classes that build specific practical skills necessary for proper crime scene investigation. Courses such as basic and advanced crime scene investigation, bloodstain pattern interpretation, latent fingerprint development, specialized photography, anthro-

pology, and others are offered regularly. Students in all of these courses review "evidence" placed in rooms set up as crime scenes. Attendees are thus provided with the practical experience they need through actual hands-on exercises and critiques by both fellow students and seasoned practitioners. For example, in the shooting reconstruction course, students shoot up a car and then study the bullet holes in the glass and car body; they then learn how to use the bullet trajectories and cartridge case ejection patterns to determine the shooter's likely position. After Lee joined the state forensic laboratory, he noticed how difficult it was for students to gain practical experience in the field. To meet this need, he set up the institute, which accepts cases from those unable to pay a consultant's fee. Working on these cases, students acquire solid forensic working experience.

2. *Research*. The activities of the research laboratories include crime scene investigation, biometric identification (identification of persons and remains using biological evidence), tele-forensic communications (long-distance communication of evidence or test results using modern technologies), and cybercrime prevention. Scientific research at the institute also includes botanical DNA analysis, bone and bloodstain typing, nonhuman DNA testing, and analytical techniques for weapons of international terrorism. In 2003 the National Institute of Justice (NIJ) awarded the institute $2 million to set up a national crime center that provides crime scene training for law enforcement personnel from all around the country. In 2005 the NIJ issued another grant to establish a national cold case center that will assist police departments in the investigation of unsolved homicides and other major cases. Most recently, the institute received a grant award to set up a national forensic crisis management center for the purpose of aiding small to medium-sized police agencies in handling major forensic issues. These educational programs provide police with topical educational opportunities and the chance to learn the most important concept—the team approach.

3. *Logic*. Lee uses a logic tree approach for decision making in case analysis, instead of what he views as the "shotgun" (that is, hit-or-miss) approach. Using a logic tree, the investigator first examines the crime scene or evidence to try to determine the perpetrator's modus operandi and the physical and pattern evidence to determine what happened, where it happened, how it happened, and when it happened. Then the investigator develops a hypothesis, or a guiding principle, that can be tested as new evidence is found or new information is learned. Logical thinking must always be applied. Once the hypothesis has been tested and found viable, the investigator can form a theory about the incident under investigation. Lee stresses that scientists and crime scene investigators must be careful not to develop tunnel vision, picking and choosing only the evidence that supports their hypothesis. Many so-called cold cases may have been easily solved at the time of the incident if police had followed up on all leads, including scientific evidence that eliminated the prime suspect. A good forensic scientist must be objective and interpret *all* facts and evidence to arrive at the best and most logical conclusion.

THE *CSI* EFFECT

When Lee started in forensics, most people had no idea what the discipline involved. Now a large number of people are interested in the subject. When asked about this phenomenon, Lee says proudly, "Our classes are overflowing and we attract some of the best future scientists in the nation!" There have been several studies about the effect this awareness has had on what people expect to happen in a case.

CSI: Crime Scene Investigation is an internationally popular television series about a team of crime scene investigators in Las Vegas, with spin-off programs set in New York and Miami. The original series started late in the fall of 2000, and by 2001 it had become a major success. For several years, *CSI* and its spin-offs have been the most popular shows in the United States. This inspired more series in the forensic arena, including *Without a Trace*, *Cold Case*, *Bones*, *Crossing Jordan*, and *NCIS*.

U.S. News & World Report attributes *CSI*'s influence to its ability to attract 60 million viewers to a presentation of science that is "sexy, fast, and remarkably certain." But even when the show is not "sexy," it has a way of demonstrating a step-by-step process that makes viewers feel knowledgeable about forensic science.

These programs purport to offer the public an education about forensic science and investigation, but many professionals believe they have had an adverse effect on the legal process. First, the story lines of these programs rely on a mix of fact and fiction, and most viewers cannot distinguish one from the other. Viewers also come to expect that the type of evidence found on TV shows will be present in most, if not all, cases. Sometimes, attorneys claim, jurors look for better results than can actually be produced or techniques that may not exist when examining the evidence. Many jurors expect that DNA will be present in every case. Thus, they might translate testimony from imperfect or technologically unsophisticated investigations into "reasonable doubt" and decline to convict. Because of this, many professionals in the legal system are disturbed by the so-called *CSI* effect. They believe that, thanks to these programs, people on juries believe they know more than they actually do about forensic science and investigation.

While increased jury awareness about forensic science has helped to make evidence handling and investigative practices more accountable, it sometimes sets the evidentiary bar so high that legal professionals despair. Few police departments are equipped with the high-tech gadgets and experts that the television shows have portrayed, and attorneys find themselves at pains to correct misperceptions.

Another problem is that on these TV shows, issues are oversimplified and investigation is made to appear quick and easy. Scientists often become involved with investigator and police responsibilities. There are no backlogs or understaffed labs. In addition, the investigators seem always to be right, which makes trial procedure appear to be more or less moot. These shows pay little attention to human error, and viewers gain the impression that the use of science and technology always brings with it absolute certainty. In reality, most of these procedures rely on interpretation, and even well-meaning scientific experts can make mistakes.

Science evolves, and some approaches that were once believed to be scientifically valid now fall short of that standard. For example, an FBI Lab expert claimed in 1995 that the analysis of lead content in bullets proved that a man had murdered his mistress. He was convicted and sentenced to life in prison. But in 2005 the FBI Lab discarded the analysis of the chemical composition of bullets as flawed—and two years later the "expert" was revealed as a fraud. The convicted man had spent twelve years in prison based on "science" that wasn't scientific at all. But there was no way for jurors to make that distinction.

Yet the *CSI* effect is not necessarily to blame. Before this show, there were others: *Perry Mason* and *Quincy* were both highly popular programs that purported to show how the legal and investigative systems worked. Both were fiction, and both were flawed in ways similar to the crime shows of today. Even newspapers and TV news programs package their versions of crime investigation, often distorting it by concentrating on tests that are cutting edge and not routine procedures. The focus is on cases solved by high technology, such as the latest DNA analytical method or computerized fingerprint searches, giving the impression that such procedures commonly solve crimes.

One of the first reports on the *CSI* effect, written by psychology professor Tom R. Tyler, was published in 2006 in the *Yale Law Journal*. Tyler noted that the real "effect" was that there were a higher number of acquittals, which supported calls for reform in the legal system. For example, as the public became more aware of objective scientific evidence, juries were not willing to convict someone based on eyewitness testimony alone. When they perceived incompetent or incomplete crime scene processing, they would not find a verdict of guilty.

Washtenaw County Circuit Court judge Donald Shelton and two researchers from Eastern Michigan University agreed. They decided to learn from jurors themselves whether they were affected by watching crime TV shows. While jurors in the general Ann Arbor/Ypsilanti, Michigan, area do not compose a random sample for the entire nation, the study, which used 1,027 subjects, was the first to examine what jurors actually thought. The study found that jurors did expect significant scientific evidence in trials—but less because of television than the impact of living in an advanced technological age. Shelton calls it the "tech effect": Jurors expect that modern technology will be utilized in investigations, especially when investigating serious crimes. Television shows such as *CSI* may well have some influence, but the effect has been positive as well as negative: As more interest has arisen from the public in forensics, so has funding from Congress and avenues for training investigators have increased.

SO YOU WANT TO BE A FORENSIC SCIENTIST

The great popularity of shows like *CSI* has created an unprecedented interest in the forensic science profession. The number of forensic science programs in the country has grown from a handful to hundreds in a relatively short period of time. Nineteen of the programs offered by colleges and universities have been accredited by the Forensic Science Education Programs Accreditation Commission (FEPAC), and many unaccredited programs may be found as part of chemistry or biology departments at universities across the country. The large number of options available inevitably raises numerous questions in the minds of prospective students seeking an appropriate program and career pathway.

The first point to bear in mind is that actual crime scene investigators are primarily police officers. Individuals who work crime scenes typically have trained at a police academy and put in several years as a patrol officer before being assigned to the specialized unit. Many police departments will also consider individuals who have specific training or degrees in crime scene investigation or forensic science when making assignments to crime scene units. There is also often on-the-job training in specific procedures and techniques employed by that organization. A few departments and organizations, such as the Las Vegas Police Department and the North Carolina State Bureau of Investigation, hire "civilian" crime scene investigators, but these positions are limited in number.

Some forensic science laboratories participate in crime scene investigation; some may even be in charge of the scene investigations of major crimes. In addition, death investigators often come from medical examiners' offices. These professionals usually follow a more typical college-based career pathway.

Another thing to remember is that the requirements for a career in forensic science differ depending on which specific field of forensic science you wish to pursue. Here, we will look at the general requirements for work in a typical crime laboratory today; in each chapter, where various fields of forensics are examined, the particular course of study practitioners of that field often follow or professional organizations recommend will be noted.

Lastly, it is important to remember that forensic scientists, no matter in what discipline, are first and foremost *scientists*. As such, they must have appropriate background and training in the physical sciences. At a minimum, forensic labs today require a bachelor's degree in an applied or physical science. This is because the application of the scientific method learned in this course of study helps to ensure that proper techniques are applied to the evidence and quality control measures are followed. (There are some exceptions to this rule for examiners in firearms, fingerprints, or documents with a long history in their discipline.) In addition, a good liberal arts education is a plus, since forensic practitioners often work with varied evidence that comes from many different sources. Because forensic scientists work within the legal system, it is also a good idea to have some understanding of the legal process and the training both police and attorneys undergo. Forensic students today often participate in internships or research programs that provide hands-on experience and exposure to the actual work of practitioners in their particular field.

Many practitioners do not major in forensics in school but instead choose a specific scientific discipline, such as molecular biology or chemistry, as their major area of concentration. This path provides a solid background in the science that will be the basis of the practitioner's focus. A forensic DNA analyst with a degree in genomics or molecular biology will be an asset to the laboratory, having developed skills and experience with the very tests that will be performed and having the theoretical knowledge to understand, troubleshoot, and analyze complex issues. Some individuals who take this route minor in forensic science; others do not. Some may develop forensic perspectives from internships or by taking graduate courses in forensic science and criminal investigation. Fortunately, there is more than one way to learn the basics needed to be a skilled forensic practitioner.

A good criminalist also needs to be a good communicator. Scientists who work at a crime lab or as private experts must write reports, explain their findings to nonscientists such as attorneys, and testify in court. Experience in oral presentation is a great advantage in forensics, and specialized courses in public speaking or teaching may be useful.

Above all, forensic scientists must have unquestionable integrity and unwavering objectivity. If at any time the validity of the scientific results can be questioned, the evidence loses its value. No scientist can work within the legal system for long if the parties involved in a case cannot rely on that scientist's results.

While the actual work of a forensic scientist is very different than what is portrayed in the media, the interesting aspects and the rewards of the real work done by forensic scientists are many. The preparation for this profession may be varied, but all scientists bring to their casework a unique combination of training and experience that together create a broad and diverse workforce in the service of justice. As Henry Lee's career shows, hard work, determination, creativity, the scientific method, and logic all have a significant role to play in the fascinating field of forensic science.

Chapter Two

FORENSIC SCIENCE IN HISTORICAL PERSPECTIVE

As Dr. Henry Lee has observed, "There have been many twists and turns in forensic science since it began in China hundreds of years ago." To fully appreciate the field of forensic science, an understanding of its history is in order. The story of Dr. John Webster and George Parkman is a case in point.

George Parkman left his home in Boston to collect rents and speak to Dr. John Webster at Harvard Medical College about an overdue loan. He did not expect a positive outcome because Webster always had excuses. Then Parkman went missing. The last time anyone saw the fifty-nine-year-old was at 1:30 p.m. on Friday, November 23, 1849, on the steps of the college. When he failed to return home, a police inquiry led to Webster, who claimed he had repaid the loan and Parkman left, although no one saw Parkman exit the building. Just to be sure, investigators performed a quick search of Webster's lab, but they turned up nothing unusual. The businessman's disappearance was a mystery.

However, Webster soon began to act out of character, which aroused the suspicion of the building's janitor, Ephraim Littlefield. So the janitor decided to drill through a wall into the pit for Webster's privy—the only unsearched place in the building. When he broke through, he saw human remains: a pelvis, a dismembered thigh, and the lower part of a leg.

Webster was arrested and his lab was searched more thoroughly. In a tea chest, police discovered another human thigh and a human torso. In the furnace lay charred bone fragments, including a jawbone with artificial teeth. A unique indicator that tied the remains to the hirsute Parkman was an abundance of body hair. Attorney General John Clifford realized he would have to count on medical experts to prove the remains were those of the missing George Parkman. Otherwise, with no body, he had no basis for prosecuting a case.

A grand jury ruled that Webster should be tried for murder, and, although he protested his innocence, the trial began on March 19, 1850, with Judge Lemuel Shaw presiding. Representing Webster were Pliney Merrick and Edward Sohier. Clifford described how he believed Parkman had been killed, how his skull had been fractured, and how his various parts had been removed and burned. Then Dr. Jeffries Wyman, an anatomist who had identified charred bones from the furnace as originating from the skull, neck, face, and feet, drew a life-size skeleton to illustrate how these parts fit a frame the size of Parkman's. Dr. Winslow Lewis, a physician, used Wyman's drawing to show an opening in the thorax region that might be a stab wound.

The defense attorneys challenged these attempts to make a definitive identification, stating that the parts found could have come from a lab specimen. They also sought to establish that the so-called stab wound was a postmortem cut from a routine dissection and that, for a stabbing incident, there was too little blood at the alleged crime scene.

Dr. Oliver Wendell Holmes, dean of the medical college, testified that someone with knowledge of human anatomy and dissection had done the dismembering. He also explained that a wound between the ribs would not necessarily produce a lot of blood, and that the remains were "not dissimilar" to Parkman's build. Following him, Dr. Nathan Keep, Parkman's dentist, testified that the jawbone with the false teeth was that of George Parkman. He recognized his own handiwork from three years earlier, and while the gold fillings had melted, there were still some identifiable characteristics of the remaining portion of the jaw. To make the teeth, he had used a wax mold of the man's uniquely protruding jaw, filling it with plaster. Displaying this item, he was able to demonstrate how it resembled the pieces of jawbone found in the furnace. The loose teeth from the furnace fit perfectly into his exhibit.

While this testimony was impressive, Dr. Willard Morton, a dentist for the defense, said that nothing about the jawbone from the furnace offered individual identification. George Parkman had a protruding jaw, yes, but so did other men. Morton produced a few false teeth of his own making and he showed how they, too, fit Keep's mold. In rebuttal, three more dentists testified that an artist knows his own work, backing up Keep's testimony.

Faced with the difficult circumstance of having no definitive identification, the judge instructed the jury that in order to make a decision they needed only a reasonable degree of certainty regarding the identity of the remains. On the same evening they began to deliberate, they had a verdict: Webster was guilty of first-degree murder and should be hanged.

As he awaited his fate, Webster confessed that he had killed George Parkman but claimed he had done it in self-defense. This seemed to many merely a last-ditch effort to save himself. The sentence stood and he was hanged on August 30, 1850.

EARLY FORENSIC MEDICINE AND THE RISE OF SCIENCE

Solving this early case involved the coordination of several scientific specialties, along with careful observation and measurement based on deduction from physical laws. The aim of science is to approach facts with a method that can be replicated under controlled conditions. Science is not necessarily about certainty; the goal is to devise a testable hypothesis that best fits the full array of facts without distorting them. The story of forensic science joins the historic narratives of both science and the law. Advancing that evolution were persevering men and women who found more truth in the scientific method than in religion, myth, or superstition, and who took risks to ensure their work would be taken seriously.

Science did not emerge as a player in the legal arena without a struggle, and its success was often assisted by cultural shifts. The earliest legal medicine treatise was written in the sixth century by a Chinese doctor named Sung Tz'u. His original work has been lost, but a copy of his treatise published in China in 1247 still survives. During the Renaissance, educated men saw the value of objective experimentation and measurement, exploring the human body to learn more about its function. In 1560 the first scientific society was organized in Italy, and by 1642 the University of Leipzig offered a course for doctors in forensic medicine. Still, as of that time there were no formal organizations dedicated to the scientific detection of crime. This changed in Europe because of a unique man named Eugène François Vidocq, a former criminal who pioneered undercover investigations in Paris in the early 1800s and formed the world's first detective force, the Sûreté. As he succeeded in catching criminals, he also invented a number of forensic techniques, such as matching bullets to guns, handwriting analysis, and undercover investigative methods.

It was the field of toxicology that made the most dramatic progress in forensic science during this era. In Spain, Mathieu Orfila published the first systematic treatise on known poisons and consulted on several criminal cases in 1813. Since toxicologists could not yet measure the actual amount of poison present in human tissues, prosecutors had to rely on building a convincing circumstantial case. This issue inspired scientists to improve their methods, while other toxicologists developed qualitative tests to determine the presence of alkaloids. Yet a problem surfaced: An alkaloid that mimicked the test reactions for vegetable alkaloids might develop naturally in the body after death. When challenged in court by savvy defense attorneys, toxicologists realized they must devise even more sensitive tests. For every stride in forensic science, there was a dogged attorney to challenge it, but such a dialectic offered benefits to both sides. Scientists who met the challenges presented in courts of law provided procedures and evidence that could be used by attorneys to prove their cases on a basis that was more objective than witness testimony or speculation. As new sciences emerged to play a part in the courtroom, their lessons became invaluable.

The impressive resolution of several sensational trials helped to persuade the judiciary that science was essential to the pursuit of justice. Still, those scientists who hoped to improve the judicial process had to learn to make their work understandable to ordinary people. In 1836 Scottish chemist James Marsh tried to prove that he had detected arsenic in the organs of a potential murder victim, but the case failed because he was unable to explain it easily to the judge and jury. Undaunted, he invented a device that was more visually instructive, and in a similar case, the jury returned a guilty verdict.

By midcentury, Ludwig Teichmann of Poland had invented the first crystal test for hemoglobin, which proved the presence of blood, and Richard L. Maddox had developed dry plate photography, a technique that proved highly practical for photographing inmate mug shots. In Germany in 1859, Gustav Kirchoff and Robert Bunsen founded the field of spectroscopy by developing a prism-based device that made it possible to study the spectral signature of chemical elements in gaseous form. It would eventually become integral to the instrumental analysis of trace evidence.

While science was improving methods of investigation and prosecution, it was clear from the increasing crime rate that a new approach was needed to process and identify criminals who repeated their crimes (recidivists). Alphonse Bertillon, a file clerk for the French police, organized the chaotic collection of police files in Paris and developed a technique for studying recidivism. As offenders were arrested, he took fourteen measurements, from the length of the foot to the width of the jaw, recording them on cards. He then arranged the cards into a classification system based on assumptions derived from mathematics and anthropology: the adult human bone structure does not change, and the chance of two adults having the same value for all fourteen measurements was less than 4 million to one. In 1883, after measuring almost two thousand men, Bertillon succeeded in identifying a repeat offender strictly by these measurements. After this, many police departments used Bertillon measurements to prove the identity of felons upon arrest. This technique was part of anthropometry (measuring the human body for scientific purposes), known more precisely as Bertillonage, and it quickly became *the* method used throughout Europe and America for identification.

Yet problems arose when others had difficulty replicating Bertillon's method. It would soon be supplanted by another technique that had already received considerable attention from people in several different countries. In 1880 Scottish physician Henry Faulds, who had discovered how to use powders to make fingerprints visible, successfully used fingerprints to eliminate a suspect as the perpetrator in a burglary and help convict the true offender. Other researchers discovered that an individual's fingerprints did not change over time. Moreover, getting a set of prints from an arrested suspect proved much easier than taking all their bodily measurements.

The first trial that included fingerprint evidence in its crime reconstruction occurred in Argentina in 1892. Francesca Rojas accused a man named Velasquez of stabbing her two children to death. He protested his innocence, and even a round of intimidation and torture did not produce a confession. In the meantime, rumor had it that Rojas had a young lover who resisted marrying her because of her children. Then Juan Vucetich, who knew something about the European theories on fingerprints and had formulated his own system of identification, went over the crime scene and found a thumbprint in a spot of dried blood. He compared this pattern with the prints of both suspects and identified the mother as the person who had placed her thumb in the blood. It was she who had murdered her children. She confessed, was convicted, and was sentenced to life imprisonment. Still, investigators in Europe and America continued to use the unwieldy Bertillonage method.

By this time, the age of Sherlock Holmes had arrived. Ever since this character had been introduced in 1887 in A Study in Scarlet, the popularity of the fictional freelance investigator had grown with the reading public. They were inspired by the idea of a detective who relied on deductive logic and empirical methods to solve difficult crimes. The series of stories by Sir Arthur Conan Doyle created a role model for real-life detectives, and this, too, had an effect on the merging of science and crime investigation.

Austrian lawyer Hans Gross opened the Imperial Criminological Institute at the University of Graz, offering it as an institute for police science that called for a collaboration of diverse specialists. In 1891 he published Criminal Investigation, the first comprehensive description of the use of physical evidence in solving crime, which influenced the methods of England's "murder squad"—a group of detectives who brought new methods to law enforcement. By the end of the century, they were categorizing criminals by modus operandi and emphasizing the value of preserving crime scenes and properly handling evidence. In France, Alexandre Lacassagne, a professor of medicine at the University of Lyon, demonstrated that the grooves on a spent bullet could be matched to the spiraling in the barrel of the gun that fired it. Paul Jesserich made the same discovery in Germany.

Lacassagne also influenced the direction of forensic medicine as he improved methods for examining wounds and physical changes after death. He was also concerned with identifying human remains. In a difficult missing-persons case, he believed that a corpse recently dragged up from a river in another town might be the man he was trying to find. Because the corpse's hair was darker than the missing man's, police had dismissed the possibility. But after examining the corpse's bones, teeth, and physical dimensions, Lacassagne believed they were wrong. Surmising that body fluids released during decomposition might alter hair color, he washed the corpse's hair and found that the color was lighter than had first appeared. Thus, the corpse was identified, and Lacassagne proved the victim had been strangled. He further assisted in successfully tracking down the perpetrators.

The early 1900s brought a flurry of scientific invention for forensic purposes. Pathologist Karl Landsteiner first detected distinct human blood groups in 1901. In Germany the next year, Paul Uhlenhuth devised the precipitin test, which helped investigators distinguish primate blood from that of other animals.

In 1902 R. A. Reiss created the first academic curriculum in forensic science at the University of Lausanne in Switzerland, and shortly thereafter, the science of personal identification underwent a dramatic change. The 1903 case of Will West at Leavenworth Penitentiary in Kansas marked a turning point. In the prison at that time were two men, one named Will West and the other William West, with almost identical physical measurements. However, one characteristic did distinguish these two men: fingerprints. Anthropometry, already losing ground, fell out of fashion.

Sir Francis Galton had already published a book about the method of fingerprint identification, in which he proposed that prints bore three primary features: ridges, bifurcations, and ridge endings. From these features he was able to devise sixty thousand classes. Galton had worked with Sir Edward Henry, the head of Scotland Yard, who had created a classification system based on five pattern types and established the Central Fingerprint Branch. In the United States, based on expert testimony about a fingerprint left in wet paint at a crime scene, an appeals court declared that fingerprint technology had a scientific basis.

In France in 1910, Edmond Locard set up the first forensic police lab, using scientific analysis on the minute particles considered trace evidence (dust, soil, seeds, fibers, and so on) to solve crimes. Locard's unique endeavor would motivate many more. Inspired by the Sherlock Holmes stories, Locard bought microscopes, studied forensic techniques, and developed his evidence transfer theory (see chapter 1). Few people listened to him until he took on a case in 1911 that required him to prove that fine dust that came from counterfeit coins was present in a suspect's pocket. His success in that case poularized the analysis of trace or amounts of materials to link suspects to crimes.

Other investigators at the time did not yet rely on microscopes, but that trend soon shifted. The microscope was the first scientific tool to be used in a murder case in the United States, when a Massachusetts homicide was solved by the microscopic analysis of threads on a coat. Millionaire George Marsh had been shot to death and his body dumped along an embankment. A few yards away, an investigator picked up a swatch of material with a button fastened to it. A landlady offered information about Willis Dow, whom she had observed studying the victim's house with binoculars. Dow's landlady had a coat Dow had left behind in his rooms, with all the buttons removed. Investigators sent the coat to a textile school, where Professor Edward Baker microscopically compared fibers from a hole on the coat with the torn piece of material from the scene. The thread colors and raw ends appeared to match. Then a pistol was found in a canal near the crime scene that was traced to a man named William Dorr in California. An abandoned car found in Boston was registered to a Willis Dow, also from California. The "W. D." initials of both names seemed too coincidental. Persistent detectives traveled to the West Coast, learned that Dorr was the nephew of Marsh's heir, and that he had left California just prior to the murder. Based on descriptions and circumstances (Dorr had tried to become a beneficiary of the heir's trust fund and Marsh had been warned about him) the police deduced that Dorr was Dow, and proved their case. Dorr was convicted and executed.

Great strides were made in scientific research and applications during the first decades of the twentieth century. Such developments were also evident in forensic investigation during the same period. During World War I, Albert Schneider developed a vacuum apparatus to collect trace evidence. Following the war, investigator Luke May demonstrated the value of striation marks for comparisons between specific tools, such as screwdrivers or chisels, to determine which specific tool could be linked to markings found at crime scenes. More contributions to forensic science were to come. Charles E. Waite cataloged all American and European guns in terms of construction, date of manufacture, caliber, number and twist of lands and grooves, and type of ammunition used. He observed that no type of gun was identical to any other and was able to scientifically determine which type had fired a specific spent bullet. As his work progressed, his associates devised the invaluable comparison microscope, used to make side-by-side comparisons, and the helixometer, used to examine gun barrels. Then an incident occurred in Massachusetts in 1920 that would draw on this new knowledge. The trial of Nicola Sacco and Bartolomeo Vanzetti for murders committed during a robbery made national headlines because of the political implications of trying these self-proclaimed anarchists. To give scientific weight to evidence in the case, Waite compared the bullets from the shootings to guns seized by investigators. His conclusion that one of the bullets was definitely fired from Sacco's gun provided significant proof to the authorities of the pair's guilt.

One sensational incident brought forensic science to the attention of the public: the 1932 kidnapping of Charles Lindbergh Jr. from his home in Hopewell, New Jersey. Although kidnappings were more common in those days as a source of quick cash, the elder Charles Lindbergh was a national hero as a result of his historic nonstop solo flight from New York to Paris in 1927. So this kidnapping outraged the nation. Ransom notes arrived demanding money, which was paid in marked bills, but no baby was forthcoming. Two months later the child's remains were found in the woods just a few miles from the Lindbergh home, and it took police two years to track down the man they believed was responsible. Bruno Richard Hauptmann was in possession of a large sum of the ransom money, and despite his protests that he had received the money from a now-deceased business partner, he was arrested and tried. Based on several areas of forensic expertise, including wood analysis and handwriting comparisons, Hauptmann was found guilty and executed. Many years later, Hauptman's wife maintained that her husband was wrongfully convicted. Henry Lee and a panel of experts reexamined the wood evidence from the ladder used to gain entry into the Lindbergh home and the boards from Hauptmann's attic. The wood grain from both sources was indeed a match.

There were many forensic chemical and biochemical discoveries in the years that followed the Lindbergh case. Applications of blood grouping techniques to blood and body fluid stains were implemented, adapting the findings of medical scientists such as Dr. Karl Landsteiner. By 1937, Walter Specht had developed luminol, which detects latent bloodstains that criminals may have tried to wash away. The following year, at the University of Kharkov in Ukraine, N. A. Izmailov and M. S. Shraiber introduced simple thin layer chromatography, used for separating and analyzing chemical compounds. In 1940 Vincent Hnizda pioneered the forensic analysis of ignitable fluids, laying the foundation for arson research.

In contrast to the nineteenth century, forensic science made rapid strides in the early twentieth century, often thanks to men who showed how intuition, persistence, and broad scientific knowledge complement the scientific method in solving difficult cases. After World War II, discoveries and developments such as the transistor, the structure of DNA, computers, and many others revolutionized the way scientists worked and the problems they researched. Rapid development in all aspects of science, including forensic science, followed each new discovery. The expansion of the forensic field and the shift from forensic generalist to specific areas of expertise during the last part of the twentieth century was due in large part to this growth in scientific knowledge and capability. Computerization has also allowed scientists to share data with many laboratories and to communicate instantly with scene investigators.

EARLY FORENSIC INVESTIGATIONS

The evolution of modern crime scene investigation in the United States began in California after the turn of the twentieth century. In 1916 August Vollmer established a school on the campus of the University of California, Berkeley, to educate investigators. He was the first police chief to require that his officers earn college degrees. He had educated himself on the published works of forensic investigative techniques that were popular in Europe and founded Berkeley's Crime Prevention Bureau, for which he established a strict code of conduct. His department was the first to utilize the analysis of blood, soil, and fiber in solving crimes. He also developed a fingerprint classification system, established a call box system, and later equipped squad cars with radios. In addition, he supported Sergeant John Larson's invention of a systolic blood pressure device called the cardio-pneumo-psychogram, intended to detect when a person was lying. Leonarde Keeler, another Berkeley recruit, made the apparatus portable and then refined it into a device that more closely resembles the modern polygraph.

Also in Berkeley, a chemist named Edward O. Heinrich gained a reputation as a "wizard" who had mastered a number of forensic methods and could tackle any crime. In 1916 he became the chief of police in Alameda, California, where he took the unprecedented step of training his investigators in scientific procedures, and three years later he accepted a post in San Francisco as a handwriting expert. By the 1920s, investigators from other states and countries brought their difficult cases to him. A 1923 train robbery in Oregon that involved masked men, explosives, and several murders had stumped local law enforcement. So they sent Heinrich the evidence left behind: a pair of gunnysack shoe covers, a revolver, and a pair of greasy denim overalls. After his examination, Heinrich told investigators the overalls had been worn by a left-handed Caucasian lumberjack in his twenties who worked in the Pacific Northwest. Heinrich asserted that the lumberjack would stand no taller than five-foot-ten and weigh 165 pounds. He also had small feet for his size, light brown hair, and a habit of fastidiousness.

How did Heinrich get so much information from these items? He pointed out that the stains on the overalls were not car grease but pitch from fir trees, and their size, along with the shoe covers, had provided the suspect's height and weight. Tiny wood chips in the right pocket indicated the position the man took when cutting a tree. Since the overalls buttoned on the left and there was more wear on the left-hand pocket than the right, it stood to reason the person who wore them was left-handed. Hair shafts caught on an overall button indicated his race, possible age, and hair color, while fingernail clippings in one pocket affirmed his tendency toward neatness. Even more interesting was a receipt for registered mail overlooked by earlier investigators: It was burrowed deep inside the narrow bib pocket, and magnification had revealed a number.

This evidence led to the three D'Autremont brothers, missing since the incident, one of whom was a left-handed lumberjack the right size and age. Evidence from the brothers' personal effects matched evidence on the overalls, and strands of hair and fibers from items in their homes were consistent with evidence from the scene. A knapsack found days later near the train tunnel yielded minute grains of dust like that on pine needles taken from the overall pocket. In fact, the knapsack had been mended in the same manner and with the same type of thread as a worn area on the overalls.

Heinrich also turned his skill to the revolver, which the investigators had deemed worthless, since only part of the serial number was legible. He found a hidden serial number on the inside of the gun, which led to a sales slip that had been signed with an alias. The handwriting, according to his expert analysis, was that of Roy D'Autremont. After a long manhunt that lasted several years, the youngest brother was finally caught, creating press coverage that led to the apprehension of the other two. All three brothers confessed and were sentenced to life in prison.

Heinrich relied on Locard's theory that all criminals leave clues, which decreases the pool of possible suspects, and his procedure was to reconstruct the crime by visualizing the habits and actions of the criminal. He was aware that the forensic arena during the 1920s was in a state of chaos, with charlatans touting themselves as experts, and he hoped to improve this situation. He learned everything he could about forensic chemistry, handwriting analysis, ballistics, and trace evidence investigation, and was among the first investigators to use strings to compute bullet trajectories. As a result, he became one of the greatest forensic scientists of the early twentieth century, a living encyclopedia of the natural sciences, with a reputation that reached across the country and abroad. His formula relied on answering five questions—what, when, where, why, and who—and his specialty was ferreting out minutiae at a crime scene that others overlooked—including the bad guys. "The smaller the detail," he said, "the more likely it is that the criminal has overlooked it."

In another case, Heinrich introduced a new type of evidence into the courtroom. When John McCarthy, foreman for the Vallejo Street Department in Vallejo, California, went home on December 19, 1925, he was shot in the chest. A .38-caliber bullet was recovered at the scene. As he was dying, McCarthy said again and again, "I fired Colwell." The police believed he was referring to fifty-nine-year-old Martin Colwell, a local ruffian with a criminal record for assault. McCarthy had dismissed Colwell from a street labor gang, and during one of Colwell's drunken binges he'd threatened revenge. When police arrested Colwell, they found a .38 revolver in his pocket with one chamber empty. He had three more bullets on his person, and a box of ammunition taken from his home had four bullets missing. Colwell could not account for the missing bullet, but he protested that he had been drunk at the time of the incident. He remembered nothing.

The gun and bullets were sent to Heinrich, who test-fired one bullet from Colwell's pocket, several from his ammunition box, and others from an unrelated batch that was the same caliber. Examining the test bullets under a stereoscopic microscope along with the recovered bullet that had killed McCarthy, Heinrich found convincing similarities that led him to believe Colwell's revolver had fired the fatal bullet. Colwell was arrested.

As the trial approached, Heinrich strove to produce photographs that showed the tiny rifling scratches on the bullets in a side-by-side comparison as a single three-dimensional image. He experimented over and over until he was able to successfully click his two cameras simultaneously over the dual microscope lenses. No court officers had ever before seen such an image, in which the photographs of two different bullets seemed to perfectly merge, and they thought it was impressive. As Heinrich made his presentation to the jury, he called the marks the weapon left on the spent bullets a "bullet fingerprint." Jury members asked to look into the microscope to see for themselves what Heinrich had observed. Spotting a unique opportunity to teach laypeople the methods of science, he allowed them to look through the oculars. They asked Heinrich to re-shoot the photographs right there in front of them. He accepted the challenge, taking the negatives to a nearby darkroom. He replicated his laboratory feat, convincing the jury, and so Colwell was convicted.

Henirich was a well-versed generalist. He educated himself in every area of forensic investigation, pushing himself to become an expert in as many areas as he could. He firmly believed in the value of education, especially to broaden his own expertise. Even as the field of forensics was branching into increasingly more specialized areas, he embodied the value of knowing about a wide range of methods, including the use of logic for case reconstruction. There would be few investigators in the future quite like him.

FORMATION OF THE FBI

During an Illinois legal case in 1886, the Supreme Court ruled that the states had no ability to regulate interstate commerce, so the Interstate Commerce Act was enacted by Congress the following year to establish the federal government's jurisdiction over interstate activities, including interstate law enforcement. However, few actual federal investigators were employed until after the turn of the century. In 1908 the attorney general created a small group of special agents within the Department of Justice after Congress passed a law preventing the loan of Secret Service agents to his department. In

March 1909 the newly appointed attorney general named this group the Bureau of Investigation. The bureau was renamed twice again, finally settling again in 1935 under its permanent name: the FBI. Its first official director was J. Edgar Hoover, who, during his tenure of almost forty-eight years, was instrumental in forming the Scientific Crime Detection Laboratory in 1932.

The FBI came to public prominence during Prohibition (between 1919 and 1933) and the 1930s gangster era. Special agents captured or killed celebrity criminals such as John Dillinger, George "Baby Face" Nelson, and George "Machine Gun" Kelly. Hoover extended the field offices and professionalized the organization, establishing the Identification Division for the centralized storage of fingerprint records.

In 1967 the FBI started the National Crime Information Center (NCIC), a computerized index that permitted state and local jurisdictions access to FBI archives on such items as license plate numbers and recovered guns, as well as the ability to post notices about wanted or missing persons. It also provided a way to coordinate certain types of national investigations. The FBI also instituted a plan for the Automated Fingerprint Identification System (AFIS), which was finally established in 1975.

In the late 1970s, the FBI also established the criminal profiling unit at Quantico for a better approach to the investigation of serial crimes. This unit dealt with such offenders as Wayne Williams (the Atlanta Child Killer), David Berkowitz (Son of Sam), and Richard Trenton Chase (the Vampire of Sacramento), whose crimes required specialized behavioral analysis.

By the mid-1980s, the FBI had developed a national computer database called the Violent Criminal Apprehension Program (VICAP), which was slated to become the most comprehensive computerized database for the investigation of homicides nationwide. Police departments around the country were invited to enter information regarding solved, unsolved, and attempted homicides; unidentified bodies in which the manner of death was suspect; and missing-persons cases involving suspected foul play. The FBI then set up the National Center for the Analysis of Violent Crime (NCAVC) and the Combined DNA Index System (CODIS), which stores DNA profiles from every state. During this time the FBI was also instrumental in developing the DRUGFIRE system, which is a computerized database of bullet and cartridge case evidence against which firearms evidence from unknown sources could be compared.

Today, with a budget in the billions, the FBI keeps a wide range of crime statistics, oversees programs for combating terrorism and cybercrime, offers one of the world's most advanced forensic laboratories with enormous databases, and now is responsible for collecting foreign intelligence. In addition, it has an impressive behavioral analysis unit that investigates serial crimes and child abductions.

PROFESSIONAL ORGANIZATIONS

In 1948, two scientists met at the police academy in St. Louis, Missouri, to discuss the First American Medicolegal Congress. They believed that dialogue among toxicologists, biologists, chemists, criminalists, and other members of the scientific community who worked in the legal arena would assist the forensic field in becoming more interactive. This conference would mark the first international multidisciplinary effort to ground an organization in forensic science. Dr. Rutherford B. H. Gradwohl, director of research at the St. Louis Police Department and director of his own private medical lab, offered financial support. Dr. Sidney Kaye, former assistant director and toxicologist at the St. Louis Police Research Laboratory and at the time with the Office of the Chief Medical Examiner in Virginia, agreed to be the secretary/treasurer and co-planner. The group's legal counsel was Orville Richardson, a St. Louis attorney.

The pair envisioned scientists and investigators from different forensic disciplines interacting as colleagues, finding personnel to fill job openings, helping to resolve problems, and brainstorming solutions to unresolved crimes. In addition, they supported training for more personnel in such sorely lacking areas as chemistry. The conference opened on January 19, 1949, with 150 participants present. Later that year, considering the meeting to have been a rousing success, several members discussed an appropriate name for the fledgling organization. The final choice was the American Academy of

Forensic Sciences. The founders hoped to set and sanction ethical and procedural standards for their participation with law enforcement. Today, the AAFS is an international multidisciplinary organization of over six thousand members that provides leadership to advance the application of science to the legal system. Just as the founders hoped, its journal and annual conference encourage the collaboration of disciplines from its ten primary sections. The organization is committed to promoting education, accuracy, precision, and specificity in the forensic sciences. Members also meet to discuss issues of admissibility of scientific evidence and testimony.

Today, a number of professional organizations promote continued education and understanding in various disciplines within forensic science. These include, among others, the International Association for Identification (IAI), the Association of Firearm and Tool Mark Examiners (AFTE), and the International Association of Forensic Sciences. In addition, regional associations of forensic scientists have been formed to promote interaction among forensic scientists within the same area of the country, since these practitioners may have similar interests and issues. Managers have also formed organizations such as the American Society of Crime Laboratory Directors (ASCLD) to assist in the proper oversight of forensic laboratories and to discuss technological developments and common problems.

JUDICIAL ISSUES— ADMISSIBILITY AND EVIDENCE HANDLING

In 1923 the District of Columbia Court of Appeals issued an opinion that became the first guideline for the admissibility of scientific evidence. In *Frye v. United States*, the defense counsel tried to enter evidence about a device that scientifically measured an individual's blood pressure to determine whether he was telling the truth. The court ruled that in order to be admissible in court, "the thing from which the deduction is made must be sufficiently established to have gained general acceptance in the particular field in which it belongs." In addition, the information offered had to be beyond the general knowledge of the jury. This *Frye* standard became general practice in most US courts for many years. Over the decades, legal experts have criticized the *Frye* standard for excluding theories that are unusual but well supported.

In many jurisdictions, the *Frye* standard has been replaced by a standard cited in the Supreme Court's 1993 decision in *Daubert v. Merrell Dow Pharmaceuticals, Inc.*, which emphasizes the trial judge's responsibility as a gatekeeper. The Court ruled in *Daubert* that "scientific" means "grounded in the methods and procedures of science" and that knowledge is more reliable than subjective belief. The judge's evaluation must focus on the methodology, not on the conclusion, and also on whether the scientific evidence applies to the facts of the case. In other words, when scientific testimony is presented, the judge must determine whether the theory can be tested, whether its rate for potential error is established, whether it has been adequately reviewed by peers, and whether the procedure has attracted widespread acceptance within a relevant scientific community. The judge also must decide whether the opinion is relevant to the issue in dispute. As part of their findings, judges also may have to determine whether a procedure that is generally scientifically acceptable was applied correctly in a particular case.

Many attorneys look to these guidelines to try to separate so-called junk science from work based on scientific principles and performed with controls in place for screening confounding variables, with established scientific methodology and with appropriate precautions. It also falls upon the court to decide whether the science is good and whether the person conducting the testing is inaccurate or unqualified. These standards apply to all areas of science, including the behavioral sciences.

* . *

Forensic science has come a long way over the last two hundred years. In the chapters that follow, we will examine some of the subdisciplines of forensic science in greater detail, look at some of the challenges forensic science has faced, and discuss what the future might hold for forensic science practitioners.

Chapter Three

THE SCIENTIFIC METHOD IN FORENSIC EVIDENCE EXAMINATIONS

N o one has emphasized the importance of applying the scientific method to forensic work more than Dr. Henry Lee. He has often stressed the significance of the scientific method in all phases of a forensic investigation to assist in maintaining an objective scientific viewpoint. To illustrate this point to a group of students at a special symposium, Lee recalled a particular case.

The local FBI agents were ready to start the search and make the arrest. The organized crime task force had identified a site where the bodies of several missing persons had been buried. An informant had told investigators that this location could be linked to the local boss of a crime syndicate. By the time the FBI and the state police arrived, it was clear that the owner of the property had been tipped off. The crime scene patterns showed that the floor of a garage and the earth below it had been disturbed. The evidence that the investigators had hoped to find was gone—or was it? Crime scene equipment, such as ground-penetrating radar and metal detectors, was brought in. Forensic scientists from the medical examiner's office and the forensic lab were also called in.

Crime scene personnel soon began digging and placing earth

onto a screen for sifting. Slowly, small bones began to appear on the screens. Scientists—including an anthropologist, a chemist, and a trace evidence examiner—helped scene personnel identify significant evidence. A slow, methodical search was carried out. Soon fragments of hair were found, mixed with some white powdery substance. Back at the lab, the chemist identified the powder as lye. And the hair, according to the hair and fiber analyst, was human, with roots that showed it was in scalp tissue as it decayed. After many hours searching the scene, numerous small bones were identified— two hyoid bones (the U-shaped bone in the neck region), three left "big toe" bones, and several additional metatarsals, metacarpals, and phalanges (the small bones of the hands and the feet). Since the area had never been used as a cemetery, the presence of these human remains was significant.

The forensic anthropologist confirmed the human origin and types of bones. Based on the bones found, he could tell that the remains of at least three persons had been buried in this area. Lab tests confirmed the bones were human, but attempts to obtain DNA profiles were unsuccessful; the lye had destroyed the DNA molecules. However, the laboratory was able to establish the blood type of the bones tested: Two were type A and one was type O. Hospital records showed that two of the missing men police believed had been killed by the crime syndicate had these blood types.

Arrests were made and a trial followed. Because no complete bodies were found, the defendants believed they could not be convicted. But, along with nonscientific investigative information, forensic science had proven that at least three persons had been buried in that garage, that the blood types of those persons matched those of the presumed victims, and that the other portions of the bodies had been moved prior to the scene search. Lye had been used to aid the decomposition of the bodies, which further indicated criminal activity.

While it may seem a simple matter to find out the type of sample and some of its individual, unique characteristics, the proper search for and analysis of evidence requires careful application of the scientific method.

THE SCIENTIFIC METHOD

All science is based on careful observation and the stepwise testing and evaluation of data. This process is called the scientific method. There are many different ways to describe the steps scientists go through to reach their conclusions, but all contain the following basic procedures:

1. *Careful observation.* All scientific discoveries begin with keen observation of the scientist's surroundings. Gregor Mendel, the monk who did pioneering work on genetics, noticed the different colors and heights of his pea plants. Marie Curie found a piece of film that had been exposed while stored in a drawer, leading to the discovery of a new radioactive element and the nuclear age. What made these people and others like them outstanding scientists is the fact that their observations started them thinking and asking questions. They began to make associations. Noticing different things that are over-looked by most people starts an organized thought process in the true scientist.

2. *Formation of a hypothesis.* After careful observation, the scientist uses her education and experience to begin to create a hypothesis, an idea about what caused the observed phenomenon. This is basically an educated guess. Sometimes these guesses are later proved wrong, as they are based on a limited number of facts and observations, but they serve as a starting point for further study.

3. *Continued observation and testing.* Next, the scientist must test the new hypothesis. She collects data through more observation and conducts experiments, hoping the data will support the hypothesis. The amount of data that must be collected varies depending on the nature of the problem and the type of experiments that are conducted. Eventually the scientist determines that there is enough preliminary scientific data and evidence to begin to draw conclusions about her data.

4. *Evaluation.* After further testing, the scientist evaluates the data that are collected. She must use a critical eye to look at

the results to see if the hypothesis is supported by the data. The scientist often reports these data and the hypothesis at professional meetings so that other scientists can assess the work that has been done. Sometimes, the testing shows the original guess was wrong, and the scientist must reformulate the hypothesis.

5. *Formation of a theory.* When sufficient testing has been conducted, if the hypothesis remains supported by the information gained and the testing is reproducible by others, the scientist develops a theory that can be adopted to explain not only the particular problem but also similar problems in similar situations. Continued testing and data collection by other scientists may uphold the theory, or, as new information is collected and evaluated, the theory may be disproved or modified over time.

THE FORENSIC METHOD

The forensic examiner must be a good scientist. As such, he must be observant and disciplined, no matter what his area of expertise. He must be inquisitive, always asking the questions what, where, when, how, who, and sometimes—but not often—why. He must collect data and question his hypotheses. By making detailed observations, he is able to show others the steps he used to test the evidence and reach his conclusions. Above all, the forensic scientist must embody the objective observer. At no time can personal belief or bias enter into his evaluation of data or the conclusions he reaches. If a forensic scientist follows the model of the scientific method, he can achieve each of these goals.

The forensic scientist applies a modified form of the scientific method in crime scene and laboratory work, as shown in figure 3.1. In forensic investigation, the stepwise testing and evaluation must be done if the result is going to be reliable. The work done both in the lab and at the crime scene is methodical and based on well-recognized principles and procedures. Because the forensic scientist does this work as part of a legal process, additional rules and responsi-

Scientific Method	Forensic Method
• Observation	• Recognition
• Hypothesis Formation	• Documentation
• Data Collection	• Identification
• Data Evaulation	• Data Collection
• Hypothesis Testing	• Comparison
• Theory Formulation	• Individualization
	• Reconstruction

Fig. 3.1. The forensic method compared to the scientific method.

bilities, which will be discussed later in this book, apply when testing evidence. The basic components of the forensic method include:

1. *Recognition.* The forensic scientist observes a crime scene or objects and must determine what is, in fact, evidence. If a shirt has been submitted to a forensic lab for testing, the scientist does not know how long the shirt was worn, who wore it, or what that person did while wearing it. For example, there could be stains, fibers, or hairs present that have nothing to do with the crime. On the other hand, those stains, fibers, or hairs could have been transferred from or to another object involved with the crime, so they may be very important in a case. A good forensic scientist will observe the objects and patterns that are present and form an idea about what the material is, how it got there, and how it may be related to the case.

2. *Documentation and collection.* All scientists take detailed and careful notes. The forensic scientist must do the same. In some cases, the basis of the case—the evidence—cannot be removed easily. Footprints on a cement floor or bloodstain patterns on a wall are two examples. In these cases, evidence must be photographed, measured, sketched, and documented so scientists can review and interpret the patterns at a later

date. The fact that the forensic scientist works within the legal system is another reason he must take detailed notes. Legal proceedings often take a long time, and the scientist must have enough information to remember each item and each test performed at the time of the trial. The history—the chain—of evidence that details who handled a piece of evidence and what was done with it must be shown so that the court can rely on the data. Many practitioners have found that the more documentation they have, the greater the understanding of that evidence by others.

After thoroughly documenting it, the scientist will collect and preserve the evidence. Evidence must be kept in such a way that it is not altered or destroyed. This is a scientific requirement as well as a legal one. A scientist can interpret test results properly only if he knows there has been no change to the chemical or physical nature of the material since the tests were conducted.

3. *Identification and comparison/individualization.* At the laboratory, the scientist conducts experiments to determine precisely what the evidence is and how it was produced. This is the data creation and evaluation part of the process. These tests involve a number of different techniques, such as microscopic, serological, immunological, chemical, and instrumental analysis. Once it is known what a material is, the forensic scientist often must determine the possible source of the material. This process is called comparison. Comparison may take place by searching a library or database of known materials, such as paints and DNA, or by using a particular source for comparison, such as a victim's or suspect's fingerprints. If the scientist can link the evidence to one—and only one—original source, that is individualization. If there is a group of possible sources, the scientist can eliminate other materials that are not of similar makeup. In other words, evidence can be classified, but not associated with one and only one origin.

4. *Conclusions and reconstruction.* The forensic scientist then looks at the data and writes a report that outlines the find-

ings and the conclusions that can be drawn from the analysis and comparisons. Conclusions might include whether a suspect could or could not have left a particular DNA profile (the specific types at the locations tested in a DNA sample) or fingerprint. Sometimes the scientist looks at all of the data and the crime scene and arrives at conclusions about what occurred and when or how it happened. This reconstruction of the incident scene and related events—the theory of what happened—can be crucial in cases such as a motor vehicle accident, homicide, bridge collapse, and many other types of incidents. Materials that are commonly referred to and analyzed for crime scene reconstruction are shown in figure 3.2.

5. *Interpretation and testimony.* Forensic scientists are often asked to explain the significance of their findings or the scientific theory and techniques used in their tests. If necessary, they give testimony in a court of law about the tests and their significance.

Fig. 3.2. Materials used for a crime scene reconstruction.

LOGIC TREES

No matter what the task, the forensic scientist must be objective, thorough, and logical. There are many stories of crimes that remain unsolved because a haphazard approach was taken to the investigation of a crime or because the scientist did not consider other factors of the case when performing a particular test. These mistakes can be avoided when examining a crime scene or a piece of evidence if the scientist takes an organized approach. While the details may vary from crime to crime or based on a particular piece of evidence, there are common threads that scientists can look for and basic principles they can apply. Each investigation involves recognition, identification, and individualization. A final step, reconstruction, may also be required. For example, all fire investigations should determine the point of origin, path of the fire, and potential cause, which should be the focus of pattern documentation and interpretation of results of analysis. Using this approach, the crime may be solved quickly.

Lee developed a process of diagramming common features of crimes by devising a series of logic trees. These logic trees are examples of how crimes should be investigated. These are intended as a starting point and are not meant to present all aspects of a particular crime; they were designed to help practitioners devise a thorough, stepwise approach to an investigation. Investigators might avoid common mistakes by referring to these logic trees often. As more is learned about a specific incident and scientific testing is conducted, the details and branches can be added to the trees.

The best way to see how logic trees are used in an investigation is to apply the process to a case scenario. The following are some examples of particular types of crimes and the logic trees that may help investigators identify important evidence and prevent mistakes.

Logic Tree 1: Death Investigations

A young woman was last seen jogging in a park. When she did not return home, her mother notified the police. A search was conducted, but the woman was not found. Several months later, skeletal remains were found in a wooded area several miles from the jogging

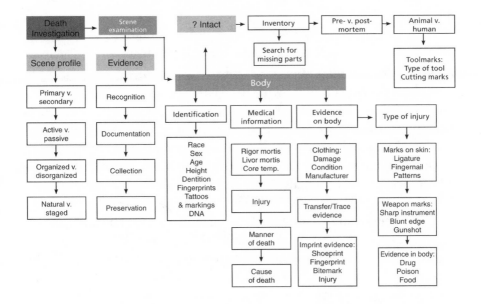

Fig. 3.3. A logic tree for death investigations.

path. Because the clothing at the scene matched the description of what the young woman was wearing when she disappeared, a tentative identification was made. Even though the crime had possibly occurred months earlier, the scene was carefully and methodically searched. All possible areas of access and pathways around the body were searched. Items of possible importance were collected as physical evidence. Photographs of the area were taken and scene maps created. Insect larvae and casings from around the body were also collected. Examination of the crime scene at this point using the logic tree may provide important information to investigators. They should ask themselves: Does the scene appear organized or disorganized, planned or unplanned? Is this a primary scene (the original site of the crime) or a secondary scene (the location to which evidence or the body was moved)? Was the scene in a natural state or was it staged?

In this case, the autopsy found that the woman died from blunt trauma to the skull. Each area of damage to the bone was carefully documented and searched for trace evidence. The skull was reassembled to determine how many fractures were present. During this process, the overarching question was the identity of the victim. Identification of the body is crucial in any death investigation. If the pathologist has some idea who the victim is, as in this case, dental records may be used for confirmation of identity. If the victim is truly unknown, other anthropological examinations and mitochondrial DNA analysis may provide some clues to the identity of the victim. Once the cause of death is determined, the surrounding circumstances point to whether it was a homicide or accidental death. Could the skull injuries have happened during a fall? Was an object of a particular shape indicated by the fractures? The answers to these questions may be found during the autopsy. The presence of various insect larvae and casings help entomologists to estimate the time of death. These samples may also show whether the victim has been moved or if drugs were present in her body.

Examination of the scene in this case indicated that the victim's body may have been moved to the wooded site. Each item of her clothing was examined for trace evidence and biological stains. Several types of hairs were found on the victim's clothing. Scientists had to determine whether the hairs were animal or human. If human, were they similar to the victim's hair? If animal, could they be from a pet or an animal that lives in woods? If foreign human hairs are identified, DNA analysis may be required to search for a possible suspect. Biological stains were also found and tested. The DNA profiles developed may lead to individualization of the source of those materials. Fibers on her jacket were found to be carpet-type nylon. These carpet fibers did not match any materials in the victim's home or her car. This could indicate that her body was transported from some other place or in a car to the location where it was found. Trace evidence often serves as circumstantial evidence that supports the facts of the case or its reconstruction.

Some of the evidence collected from the area surrounding the body will inevitably be unrelated to the crime. Certainly whenever a crime occurs in a public area, this will be the case. The forensic scientist must evaluate the importance of each item, and all results must be reported, even if they appear to contradict the hypothesis that has been developed regarding the crime. In some cases the forensic practitioner will formulate a new hypothesis based on the information gained from analysis. In other cases, the scientist will determine that the results do not warrant a change in the direction of the case. Ultimately, the importance of this unaccounted-for result or evidence is up to the jury to decide at the time of trial.

Investigators in this case found that the woman had recently broken up with her boyfriend. He was questioned and volunteered to give a DNA sample for comparison to the biological material found on the victim. The DNA profiles from the boyfriend matched the evidence. Fibers from the boyfriend's car and home were also collected. Because the park was a secondary scene, investigators looked for evidence of injury (bloodstains, tissue), patterns (cleaning, blood spatter), and other indicators of a struggle or attack in the boyfriend's home and car. No evidence of a struggle was identified, but a patterned carpet was found in the boyfriend's garage that had recently been washed. Even though attempts were made to eliminate the bloodstains, small quantities of diluted blood were found, which matched that of the victim. Some of the multiple types of fibers removed from the victim were microscopically similar to the evidence. As happened in this case, the number and type of scenes related to one crime may expand as the investigation proceeds. If the body is transported, the vehicle(s) used constitute a scene. There may be intermediate areas to consider as well, such as places where the suspect cleaned up or disposed of incriminating evidence.

Logic Tree 2: Sexual Assault Investigations

Sexual assault is the most common crime committed against persons. National recommendations for the collection of evidence from victims of sexual assault have been developed to assist in the investigation of this type of crime. These guidelines also include information for the medical treatment of victims at health-care facilities. When the victim of sexual assault is living, he or she may provide valuable information about the facts of the incident and the identity of the rapist. Sometimes, however, the victim has no memory of the incident or cannot recall details. This may be a result of the psycho-

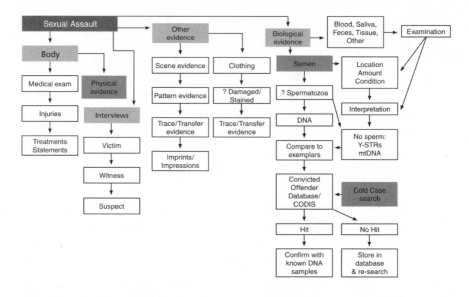

Fig. 3.4. A logic tree for sexual assault investigations.

logical trauma of the rape or because the victim was drugged by the rapist. Without thorough collection and proper analysis of the evidence in such cases, it is extremely difficult to determine whether the victim was actually given a drug.

Last year, a college student leaving the local mall was invited to join a few acquaintances at a local hangout. Because it was a school night, she ordered only a cola and started to play pool with a small group of people. The student remembers nothing after that until she woke up in a strange room. There were no other persons around. The student was partially clothed and had bruises on her arms. With no recollection of how she got there or what had happened, she was unsure what to do.

In such a situation, if the victim calls the police, she will be brought to the hospital for a medical examination. The victim may also choose to go to the hospital herself and, with the help of medical personnel and a sexual assault counselor, decide whether she will report the crime to the police. In either case, the victim will receive any medical care necessary. Her injuries and bruises will be measured and documented, and at the same time, physical evidence will be collected that may provide proof that the crime of sexual assault occurred. That evidence may also provide links to the individual(s) who committed the crime. Because many of the drugs used to facilitate sexual assault—so-called date rape drugs—are quickly broken down in the body, it is crucial to collect blood and urine samples as soon as possible. A forensic toxicology laboratory can test these samples and identify any number of chemicals that may have been used. Physical evidence in the form of swabs from the victim will usually be examined for the presence of semen. If present, the spermatozoa may provide some indication as to how recently the semen was deposited. DNA can be extracted from any semen or other biological fluid that is found. DNA profiles developed from the fluid may be used to include or exclude possible suspects. The DNA profiles may also be entered into the National DNA Identification System (NDIS) to identify the source of the DNA.

In addition to the swabbings collected from body cavities, other samples are also included in the sexual assault evidence collection kit. Hairs, fibers, and other trace material collected from the victim's body may provide additional links to a perpetrator or primary scene. For example, grass and leaf parts collected from a victim's body may be used to support the case that the crime occurred outside. Additional samples may include dried body fluid stains or other materials near bite marks, blood, or fingernail scrapings.

The victim's clothing should also be collected and examined at the laboratory for biological stains, trace evidence materials, and patterns. The transfer of hairs or fibers from the perpetrator to the victim's clothing is common, especially if there has been a struggle. If the assault occurred outside, there may be grass or soil stains where the clothes came in contact with the ground. There may be patterns of damage such as tears, stretched portions of fabric, or torn-off buttons.

In this case, the victim awoke in an unfamiliar location. This area should have been considered a crime scene and checked for the presence of fingerprints, trace evidence, patterns, shoeprints, or other significant evidence. While not usually associated with sexual assault cases, the identification of latent fingerprints that can be linked to an individual may be powerful evidence, with or without accompanying DNA profiles. Unfortunately, the police did not follow the logic tree approach in this case. Physical evidence was not collected and preserved, and this became another cold case that remains unsolved.

Logic Tree 3: Drug and Poisoning Investigations

Some of the most difficult cases to investigate are those involving poisons or drugs. In the case of an overdose that leads to death, the medical examiner and toxicologist will collect samples of tissue to be tested for the presence of common street and prescription drugs. If the drug that caused the death is not common or does not produce readily identifiable symptoms, it may be very difficult to determine the specific chemical used. Thus, investigators should collect all drug containers, prescription medications, and suspicious materials at the scene.

A young boy was brought to the hospital with extreme gastric pain. His mother, who worked in the hospital's clinical laboratory,

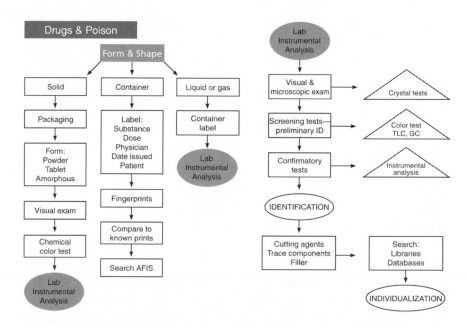

Fig. 3.5. A logic tree for drug investigations.

said he vomited several times so she brought him to the hospital. A series of tests showed an inflamed digestive system, but no particular cause was noted. After a few days in the hospital the boy appeared better and was sent home. The doctor gave the mother a prescription acid blocker and told her to feed the child a bland diet. Within a few weeks, the child was back at the hospital. The mother would not leave the child's side. This pattern repeated several times. Because the boy again became better at the hospital, the doctor suspected he might be ingesting a toxic material while unsupervised at home. An extensive toxicological analysis of the boy's stomach contents was conducted. Extracts of the fluids were made and instrumental testing for the presence of poisons, toxins, and biological contaminants were carried out. Several screening tests, which often are used to eliminate possible drugs and toxins, were not possible because of the nature of the sample. In addition, scientists examined the solid materials in the stomach contents, and tests showed the presence of lead in samples from the boy.

With the chemical agent identified, it was then necessary to search for the possible source of that agent. Investigators searched the home, but could not find a source of lead in the house. Toys were screened for lead, with negative results. The cabinets were locked and too high for the child to reach. The mother was questioned and, based on her behavior and the lack of indication of any other source of the lead, she was later arrested for endangering her child. Forensic scientists examined the child's stomach contents and found small particles of white paintlike material.

Some chemicals, such as arsenic, are deposited in hair and tissue samples over time. These deposits can be detected by instrumental analysis, and the forensic toxicologist can estimate the amount of chemical and the times when it was administered. If drugs are suspected, investigators search for powders and pills that might be in the medicine cabinets and in drawers of the house. These drugs would provide scientific leads and help laboratory scientists determine which tests to carry out. Since lead was found in the specimens in this case, the forensic scientists returned with the police to reinvestigate the scene, hoping to identify possible sources of that metal. In several rooms small bite marks were noted on the windowsills.

These windowsills were submitted to the lab for analysis. Under a fresh coat of white paint the lab found layers of older paint that contained lead. The child's biting the windowsill had caused lead poisoning. His mother was subsequently released.

Because medical personnel recognized a pattern, they called in the police. Careful investigation into the possible sources of the chemical through forensic analysis helped to identify that a crime had not been committed.

Logic Tree 4: Shooting Investigations

Shootings are becoming more common events in today's society, according to the most recent Uniform Crime Report. Almost 50 percent of all violent crimes in the United States involve firearms. Shootings may be assaults, such as drive-by incidents, or may be associated with other crimes such as robberies. Certainly a shooting investigation often involves examination and comparison of bullets or cartridge cases. If no gun is available for comparison, the projectile or casing can be entered into the National Integrated Ballistics Information Network (NIBIN) to link the shooting to other crimes or weapons that

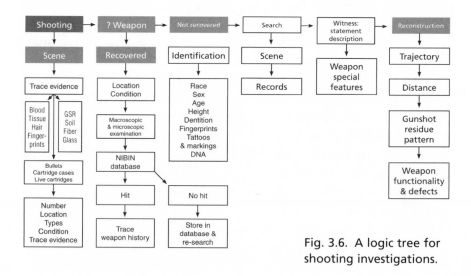

Fig. 3.6. A logic tree for shooting investigations.

have previously been examined at the laboratory. The clothing and hands of suspects will be tested for gunshot residue.

In a recent case, a teen was sitting in his living room when a bullet passed through the screen window and into his back. He was rushed to the hospital, where the bullet was removed and turned over to the police. Investigators searched the area around the house and found two bulletlike holes in the siding and two spent cartridge cases near the gutter on the street. Trajectories for the two shots were estimated using a laser and were documented with photographs. Measurements of the locations of the evidence and the angles of bullet impact were taken. Based on the trajectories and the absence of gunshot patterns, the approximate location of the shooter at the time of the incident was determined.

The laboratory's firearms unit examined the bullets recovered from the victim and from the house as well as the cartridge cases. These tests showed the shots had been fired from the same weapon, most likely a 9mm semiautomatic handgun. These bullets and casings were entered into NIBIN. A hit was obtained: The bullets matched those fired in two other drive-by shootings involving a gang rivalry.

In addition to the firearms evidence, the area was searched for other types of trace and pattern evidence. Some cases involve searching for fingerprints, hairs, blood, and other biological materials. There may also be video surveillance records that can be checked, such as in a convenience store robbery. In this case, tire tracks were found at this scene, where it appeared a vehicle sped away from the area. These tracks were photographed and measured, and the pattern of the tracks was searched against a database that indicated a Firestone brand tire. Because the NIBIN hit indicated gang involvement, local gang members were questioned, and the police noted that Firestone tires similar to the pattern at the scene were on the suspect's car. Ultimately, two members of this gang were arrested for the assault of the teen, who was shot "by mistake" as the two were hanging out of a car window shooting at a passing vehicle.

Logic Tree 5: Enhancement of Pattern Evidence

Logic trees can also be designed to assist the examiner in the identification and analysis of physical evidence. It is often desirable to enhance patterns and materials noted on evidence or at a crime scene. Enhancement refers to a process that makes details more visible without altering or damaging the original pattern or object. As this example involving pattern enhancement shows, it is important to consider the effects of each step on any subsequent steps in the enhancement process. One also has to consider the effects of chemicals on other procedures, such as DNA testing.

A woman found her mother dead on the kitchen floor with multiple stab wounds when she arrived for a planned visit. Examination of the area around the body using visible light techniques showed several faint bloodlike smudges and possible imprint patterns. The next step in the process involved examining the area further using an alternate light source. The use of alternate light of various controlled wavelengths often provides details of patterns that are not readily seen in visible light. In this case, no additional detail emerged in the area of the imprints, but the blood around the body appeared to have been cleaned. After the condition of the victim and the floor

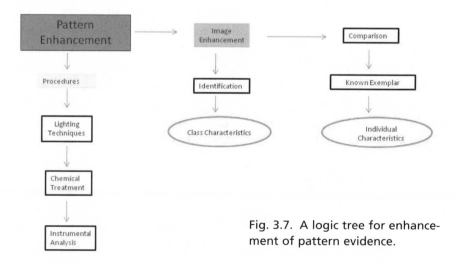

Fig. 3.7. A logic tree for enhancement of pattern evidence.

were thoroughly documented, the blood enhancement chemical tetramethylbenzidine (TMB) was sprayed on the floor. This chemical reacts with small amounts of blood and turns blue. Several footwear patterns were noted after this enhancement. The identifiable patterns were from Puma brand athletic shoes, as determined from the details developed. Investigators photographed these footwear patterns because they were on a surface that could not be removed and submitted to the laboratory.

When investigators searched the surrounding area, they found a pair of Puma sneakers in a trash barrel behind a local store. These shoes had the same class characteristics, the same size and design, as those that formed the patterns at the crime scene. The sneakers were compared to the scene photographs by an expert at the laboratory who was able to make an individualization and determined that the patterns were, in fact, made by the shoes from the trash barrel. Samples from the soles of the shoes tested positive for blood, and a DNA profile of this blood matched that of the homicide victim. Additionally, human and animal hair were found inside the athletic shoe. After reviewing the list of store employees, police noted that one of the employees was a recently released career criminal. When he was questioned, he voluntarily gave police hairs and a DNA sample. The hair in the shoe was similar to this suspect's sample. With sufficient evidence to obtain a warrant, police found items that likely came from the victim's home. One of these items had a faint fingerprint in blood, which was also enhanced and compared to fingerprints of the suspect. The fingerprint matched the suspect's and the blood matched the DNA of the victim. Faced with the evidence, the suspect confessed to the murder.

Enhancement reagents can provide valuable information to investigators by showing the presence of evidence that may otherwise be overlooked. Because these chemicals may permanently change the nature or appearance of evidence, their use must be guided by knowledge and logic.

PHYSICAL EVIDENCE

As discussed in chapter 2, numerous television shows and movies about forensic science and crime scene investigation have become very popular during the past few years. These shows often deal with what is referred to as physical or scientific evidence. Physical evidence is material of a tangible or observable nature that may provide a fact relevant to the truth of what occurred or a fact that may need clarification in a case. It can be solid, liquid, or gas. It can be a single object or a pattern. Physical evidence—evidence to which analytical procedures and the scientific method are applied—has become a critical part of many legal proceedings. In fact, some criminal and civil attorneys today will not proceed with a case unless there is scientific evidence to present to a jury. Because of the expectations created by the media, if no significant physical or medical evidence exists in a case, attorneys often call experts to testify as to why there is no such evidence. This commonly occurs in sexual assault cases where there is a lack of semen and DNA or physical injuries.

The examiner or crime scene investigator encounters various types of physical evidence. Physical evidence may be classified in many different ways, and the method of classification often depends on who is collecting the evidence or using it. A classification scheme may be based on the nature or composition of the evidence, which may assist in determining the origin of the evidence. For example, pattern evidence would require an answer to the question: What object or action created this pattern? Evidence is also commonly grouped by the type of testing that will be done at the laboratory, such as DNA analysis, firearms, fingerprint comparison, tool mark comparison, and so on. Classification by this method can be useful when considering the value of the evidence, but may result in the loss of evidence that can be tested in more than one way.

It is also useful to consider the nature of the incident when identifying and analyzing evidence. Incidents such as accidents, arson, medical malpractice, and sexual assault, for example, each require certain actions to be proven or excluded, which may be indicated by physical evidence. This, in turn, helps the practitioner to assess the significance of each piece of evidence as it is identified and to determine the scope of the incident. In addition, classifying evidence by the type of crime or event relies on previous experience and national standards to assist the practitioner when she evaluates victims, injuries, or scenes. Different types of evidence may be handled in specific ways or be observed only at specific times.

One classification method divides evidence into general types that include transient, pattern, transfer, conditional, and associative evidence.

1. Transient evidence is, as its name implies, temporary. Examples of evidence in this category include smoke, maggot and insect growth, color of bruises, and odors. Forensic practitioners may have to depend on witnesses to identify transient evidence, unless there are video or surveillance tapes that make a permanent record of it.

2. Pattern evidence can be produced by any number of objects and actions. Some examples of pattern evidence include blood spatter, burn patterns, gunshot residue patterns, and glass fracture patterns. Patterns may be used to support a witness's statement, associate an individual or object with an incident, or provide leads.

3. Transfer evidence is a general category in which an exchange of material occurs when two objects, two people, or an object and a person come in contact with each other. By definition, this is a large category of evidence, which includes things such as fingerprints and footprints, as well as small materials like fibers and hairs. Transfer evidence can be almost anything; it is the action of exchange that puts evidence in this category.

4. Conditional evidence is often important in criminal and civil litigation. It points to or depends on specific conditions surrounding an incident. For example, conditional evidence may relate to the accidental discharge of a firearm, the condition of the wires of a coffee pot, or a person's mental condition.

5. Associative evidence is another large, general category. This type of evidence is often easily recognized and is used to associate a person, object, or place with an incident. This type of

evidence can often be traced to an individual by use of a registered number or other identifier. Examples of associative evidence include bar codes on merchandise, credit cards, VIN numbers, serial numbers, and ID cards.

The proper identification, collection, and evaluation of evidence are critical for justice to be served in modern legal proceedings. Since evidence is the basis of all scientific and legal investigations, it is important to consider the value of potential evidence as soon as possible in the process. The practitioner can organize evidence—and the investigation—most easily by classifying evidence as it is sought, found, and collected.

The proper identification, collection, and maintenance of appropriate evidence can be very valuable in the course of an investigation. Information that can be gained from evidence includes identification of the elements of an incident; identification of a perpetrator or another person of interest; exclusion of an individual as the source of the evidence; proof or disproof of witness or party statements; association of objects or persons with the scene, the crime, or each other; and additional information or investigative leads.

Lee has pointed out several key roles physical evidence plays in criminal investigation:

1. *Provides information on the corpus delicti (the body of the crime).* The basic facts that show that a crime has occurred are often based on physical evidence. The weapon with the victim's blood on it, a broken window at the scene of a ransacked house, and a chemical accelerant found in charred remains at the point of origin of a fire all point to the nature of the crime.

2. *Provides information on the modus operandi (the mode of operation).* Physical evidence may show patterns of behavior in the way crimes are carried out by the same individual, for example, patterns of entry in a series of burglaries. Serial rapists sometimes take a piece clothing or jewelry from the victim after the assault, which then may be linked to this person by DNA found in the objects. Physical

evidence is sometimes the only way investigators can link cases; for example, cartridge cases left at the scenes of several drive-by shootings may be used to prove that the same gun was used in all the incidents. The knowledge that these cases are alike can also provide additional investigative leads when investigators combine information from each of the incidents.

3. *Links a suspect with a victim.* Association of a victim with a suspect is the most common use of physical evidence, especially in violent crimes against persons. Transfer of hairs, tissue, blood, fibers, and other materials are examples of evidence used for this purpose.

4. *Links a person with a crime scene.* Physical evidence can also associate a person with a place. Blood left on a broken window at a burglary, for example, can place a suspect at the scene through DNA analysis. Shoeprints or clothing left behind at the scene may also allow an association.

5. *Supports or disproves the statement of a witness.* In some cases, physical evidence can be used to show whether a person's statements are reasonable or untruthful. For example, if blood on a dented fender is shown to be deer blood, this supports the claim that a suspect in a hit-and-run crime hit an animal and not a person.

6. *Identifies a suspect.* Fingerprints found at crime scenes are commonly used to identity suspects. Recently, the value of DNA analysis of items such as cigarette butts and "touch" DNA (DNA left on an object from contact, such as handling a weapon) testing have been used to identify a potential suspect by matching the result from the evidence to profiles stored in various databases.

7. *Provides investigative leads.* As noted earlier, physical evidence is often the starting point for a criminal investigation. Each item of evidence may point the investigation in several directions, and each of these directions leads to additional physical evidence. For example, red paint chips left at the scene of a hit-and-run will lead to a car on which evidence of impact with the victim may be found.

8. *Identifies unknown substances.* The nature and identity of physical evidence is not always apparent. For example, a white powder sent in a letter to a senator may be an infectious agent, a harmful chemical, or a completely benign substance. The identification of this powder is critical to the proper handling of the evidence and the safety of citizens. If the powder is found to be baking soda, investigation will proceed with the assumption that it was a hoax or a harmless error, rather than as a potential terrorist activity.

9. *Determines the cause of an incident.* Physical evidence may help to determine whether the cause of an incident is natural, accidental, or intentional. For example, a fire may be determined to be accidental in nature if the laboratory determines the kerosene heater that was the source of a fire contained gasoline, which caused the heater to explode.

10. *Reconstructs a case.* Physical evidence is extremely valuable for crime scene reconstruction. Evidence such as cartridge case ejection and bullet trajectories can be used to determine the victim's and shooter's locations and positions. Blood drops can be used to determine the impact force, the number of blows, and the location of the individuals involved.

COLLECTION AND PRESERVATION OF EVIDENCE

No matter what classification method is used to help identify evidence or interpret a result, that evidence is of little value if it is not properly collected and preserved. As numerous cases have shown, evidence that is well maintained can provide conclusive results even decades after it is collected. The discriminating power of DNA analysis and its potential to exonerate those who are falsely charged or convicted have been well publicized. If, however, a sample is not properly packaged and maintained, that evidence could be lost forever. In fact, if evidence is improperly handled, contamination can occur that alters the evidence to the extent that analysis could provide false associations or false exclusions. This is particularly true in the collection and preservation of biological evidence.

Forensic evidence must be "reliable" and its integrity must be unquestionable or its value is lost. Errors in collection and packaging that lead to questions about the evidence can usually be easily avoided. In general, physical evidence should be packaged to prevent changes to the evidence that may interfere with or alter test results. When the scientist applies logic and practical experience to preserve the evidence, test results on that evidence will be scientifically reliable.

FORENSIC TESTING METHODS

Of all the skills used by the forensic scientist, the most important and valuable is the ability to make accurate and complete observations. Detailed examination of an item or a crime scene is vital to the proper identification of evidence and its analysis. A good forensic scientist will note subtle differences in color, texture, size, and density of stains, and these patterns must be fully documented. The importance of careful observation cannot be overstated. For example, at times the pattern of a stain is more important than any DNA result that is obtained. If a husband claims he attempted to assist his injured wife, finding her DNA in bloodstains on his shirt is not surprising. If the bloodstain pattern in which her DNA is found is consistent with blood that impacted the husband's shirt, however, such a pattern could not have been created by a husband holding his wife, which would be a contact, transfer bloodstain. If the forensic scientist only does a DNA test and fails to observe and document the stain pattern, however, there is no information to contradict the statement of the husband. Similarly, if a suspect in a self-defense shooting claims his shirt was cut when he was attacked, the scientist's observation of sharp, cut ends to the threads at the damaged area of a shirt will support his story. If the lab examiner only tests for gunshot residue on the shirt, however, this important evidence will go unrecognized.

Visual and microscopic examination of physical evidence can be a slow, painstaking process. But it often is one of the most important steps in an investigation. In addition to the actual location and size of any significant markings, stains, and damage, the location and amount of trace materials should also be noted. It is seldom known at the beginning of an investigation what is and what is not important evidence, so the forensic scientist must observe and note as much of this detail as is reasonable, even if the information ultimately does not prove useful to the investigation. Only after detailed visual examination and documentation can the scientist proceed with the next steps.

Once the evidence has been properly examined and documented using notes and photographs, the scientist should remove any trace materials on the evidence and keep these for later testing. Determining which stains or materials to test is the next step. This decision often involves both science and art. The practitioner must think about what the patterns indicate. She also must consider which elements of a crime need to be proved in the case at hand. If evidence will be consumed or permanently altered by the testing to follow, the scientist should carefully consider whether such testing is necessary. This is one of the instances in which the forensic process differs from that in other scientific fields because it may be decided by more than science alone. If the choice is to conduct the tests, the scientist should consult with the appropriate legal authority before using all of a sample, to ensure the rights of the individual accused of the crime are protected.

Scientists who work in forensic laboratories or at crime scenes test materials using many different techniques. In general, they employ physical, chemical, or biological methods. There are also database-assisted procedures, which increase the speed of an analysis or the types of information that can be obtained from testing.

1. *Physical methods.* Physical analysis methods include visual inspection and visualization techniques. Hands-on work such as dusting for latent prints or the use of alternate light sources may be considered part of this group of tests. In the laboratory, physical matching (jigsaw puzzle matching), photographic methods, and microscopic techniques are examples of this kind of testing.

2. *Chemical methods*. Chemical analysis includes both traditional wet chemistry and the use of instrumentation. Field tests for chemicals ranging from suspected explosives to drugs help to provide probable cause for searches or arrests. These chemical-screening tests also may be used to narrow the possible nature of materials being examined in the lab. Instruments (gas chromatograph, mass spectrometer; UV, visible light, or infrared spectrophotometer; scanning electron microscope; capillary electrophoresis; and so on) are then used to separate or identify the components in these materials. At times, such as in DUI or toxicology cases, it is important to know the quantity of the chemical present. Additional instrumental tests may be necessary to develop this information.

3. *Biological methods*. Biological analysis consists of both screening and confirmatory tests for a vast array of biological materials. Screening tests for blood, such as those using phenolphthalein or luminol, provide valuable information about which stains may contain blood, and if the scene has been cleaned up, these field tests may also provide information about the patterns of blood that remain. Traditional serology (blood) and immunology (antibody-antigen) tests may be applied to identify or classify a biological sample. Enzyme-based tests are conducted for identification and classification of many materials—ranging from drugs to proteins—in the forensic lab. DNA- and RNA-testing techniques are often applied to determine the specific source, or individualize, these substances.

4. *Database-assisted methods*. Testing sometimes produces results that are not immediately useful in forensic investigation. The chemical profile of a complex mixture may not be easily interpreted. A DNA profile or latent fingerprint may not match known persons in a case. Computerized databases can be used to help investigators in such cases. For example, searching paint databases may identify the make and model of a car based on paint found at the site of a hit-and-run. The DNA from a bone sample may match the DNA of a missing person on file in CODIS + mito. Extensive files of mass

spectra, which are molecular patterns of chemicals, can be searched to identify an unknown white powder and determine whether it is harmful. Databases also exist for comparison of tire and footwear impressions, barcodes, serial numbers, VIN numbers, law enforcement photographic identification files, and other data. Various means are available to analyze hard drives and electronic storage media to reveal information that has been deleted or to search for illegal images.

Scientists use these different lab methods to determine the class or individual characteristics of the evidence and, when appropriate, to compare those characteristics to those of materials of known origin. Class characteristics are those that place an object or material within a related group; for example, class characteristics are used to group drugs that have similar chemical properties or tires that have similar tread designs. Individual characteristics are used to identify the unique source of a material or pattern, such as fingerprints or DNA.

Sometimes a potential source of an item or pattern is identified. If that occurs, a K sample, or "sample of known origin," is collected. The same tests used on the evidence are then used on the known sample, and the results are compared. Sometimes the materials are compared directly with each other, as in the case of microscopic hair comparisons. When this comparison is complete, the scientist can sometimes draw conclusions about the possible source of the evidence material: The known may be excluded as the source, the known may be included as a source (or as *the* source, in the case of individualization), or the results may be inconclusive.

Many modifications to these methods and techniques exist that cannot be covered in detail in this discussion. Some of the specific methods and procedures will be discussed in more detail in later chapters.

RELIABILITY OF EVIDENCE

In addition to the scientific requirements, the forensic practitioner must also satisfy certain legal requirements for evidence. Forensic evidence must be *legally* reliable. One way the integrity of the evidence is shown in court is by providing proof of the facts surrounding the collection and testing of evidence. The scientist must also show the court that the evidence has not been altered. No matter when or how evidence is collected, an evidence seal is one of the most important ways to demonstrate the integrity of the physical evidence. An evidence seal is a closure on an evidence package that prevents loss of the evidence and indicates whether the container has subsequently been opened. The seal is usually dated and/or initialed at the time of collection.

A chain of custody for each item of evidence is another way this proof is shown. Police and crime scene technicians use forms and labels to collect complete "chain of custody" information. The chain of custody usually begins when an investigator locates or receives physical evidence. The evidence must be marked as to how it was found and where it was located prior to collection. Any documentation of an item of evidence should begin with a description of the item, the date, the time, and the location at which it was found. The case or identification number must be noted, as well as a number that identifies the item itself. The initials or signature of the person collecting the evidence must also appear in the chain of evidence. Any subsequent transfer of that evidence is also documented as part of the chain of custody. This paper trail following the evidence provides a clear history of how the evidence was handled and by whom.

Another way in which evidence can be shown to be reliable is by documenting that it has been handled and stored properly. Procedures will be in place to limit changes in the evidence quantity and quality. Most of these procedures are part of the quality control and quality assurance programs in a forensic science lab. But the forensic scientists must be aware at all times of the general principles involved to limit evidence changes. A good forensic scientist also knows the effects a particular test may have on any later analyses of a piece of evidence. The court must be convinced that the procedures used were not only generally reliable, as outlined by the laboratory, but applied appropriately in the case at hand. If questions about the handling of evidence in a particular case are raised, a scientist may be asked about the methods used, precautions taken to limit contamination or loss, or who else had access to the evidence.

Reliability is more than a matter of simply using the latest techniques or the correct instruments. It is more than having the right facts or information in the notes. Ultimately, the quality of the evidence and the results is determined by the scientist. If he is observant and disciplined, the established protocols will be followed correctly and significant features of the evidence or scene will be properly documented. If he is inquisitive, valuable evidence will not be overlooked, nor will there be many unanswered questions related to the scientific analyses carried out in a case. Sometimes an observation or question that comes up requires additional experiments. Sometimes new tests or applications must be developed. If the forensic scientist is dedicated, these challenges are welcomed.

Unlike other scientific practitioners, forensic scientists work in association with the legal system. Some may be tempted to take sides in legal cases. But if the forensic scientist is objective, the evidence will speak for itself. The scientific facts, with all their value and limitations, will be presented to the trier of fact. The forensic scientist should have no concerns other than quality results and appropriate interpretation of the data in a particular case. This is how the scientist truly serves justice.

Chapter Four

DEATH INVESTIGATORS

D eath investigators perform critical work when investigating a suspicious fatal crime scene. In cooperation with their team members, they strive to determine the cause and manner of death, bloodstain patterns, and the circumstances surrounding a death. Dr. Henry Lee often recalls a particular case where the significance of the death investigator stood out.

On December 9, 2001, a 911 dispatcher received an emergency call from a home on Cedar Street in Durham, North Carolina. Novelist Michael Peterson identified himself and shouted, "My wife had an accident. She's still breathing." He explained that she had fallen down the stairs. Paramedics and police units responded, finding Kathleen Peterson, a forty-eight-year-old executive with Nortel Networks, sprawled on her back in the well of a stairway, blood spatters covering the staircase and walls around her. She had no pulse. Peterson, who had blood on him, was walking in circles, sobbing.

Although medical examiner Dr. Kenneth Snell initially decided that the death was consistent with an accident, chief medical examiner Dr. Deborah Radisch subsequently learned from the autopsy that there were multiple lacerations on Kathleen's scalp. She advised officers to look for a long rodlike implement that might have caused these lacerations. Kathleen also had bruises on her face and head, and her manner of death was ultimately determined to be blunt force trauma to the head that was inconsistent with a fall. Thus, the case was deemed a homicide.

Looking for evidence to try to reconstruct the incident, the police seized Michael Peterson's computers and more than sixty other items from the home. They also videotaped the scene and collected the clothing Michael had worn that night, but they failed to find a rodlike implement that might be construed as the murder weapon.

Michael hired attorney David Rudolf to represent him. He was then arrested and released on $850,000 bond. Investigators learned that in 1985, while living in Germany, Michael and his first wife had been friends with Elizabeth Ratliff, who had also taken a fatal fall down a flight of stairs. At the time, the authorities concluded she had died from a stroke; Michael had been the last person to see her. District Attorney Jim Hardin Jr. believed that incident was no accident, and he ordered Ratliff's remains to be exhumed. Radisch reexamined her body, resulting in a new finding of homicide in that case. Michael Peterson was now associated with two women who had fallen down stairs to their deaths, which seemed more than a little coincidental.

Michael Peterson's trial for first-degree murder began in July 2003. Hardin, joined by Assistant District Attorney Freda Black, insisted that Michael had battered Kathleen to death with a fireplace blow poke that had mysteriously disappeared from the home, and had then fabricated the story that she fell. Hardin stated that he did not need to prove a motive, but hypothesized that Michael had earned little that year from his writing and the couple had been spending beyond their means. Killing Kathleen would bring a $1.8 million insurance payout, sufficient to settle debts and continue a lavish lifestyle. During the trial, Hardin suggested another motive: Kathleen, eleven years younger than Michael, may have learned about her husband's attempt to arrange a secret homosexual liaison and argued with him over it.

Reconstruction of the incident involved experts primarily in pathology, neuropathology, biomechanics, and bloodstain pattern analysis. Under cross-examination, crime scene technician Dan George admitted to a number of errors in processing the scene and allowing it to become contaminated. Key items had not been taken into evidence, important areas were not photographed, people who did not belong there were allowed to wander through, and a few items were mishandled. Notes were brief or nonexistent, and the investigators had caused some contamination.

The defense team insisted Kathleen's injuries were consistent with a fall, not a beating. They suggested that as a result of the fall, she had experienced an episode of hypoxia from head injuries related to the fall. Because she had been drinking heavily that evening as the couple sat around the pool, when she slipped and fell, she could not help herself get up. Peterson, who remained by the pool, could not hear her. So she struggled there, expelling blood all over the stairwell as she coughed and fell again, hitting her head several times.

Since there was no evidence of violence between the Petersons and good evidence that Michael and Kathleen had experienced a warm relationship, Rudolf pointed out that it was unlikely that Michael would just start beating his wife, even during an argument. Kathleen allegedly knew about Michael's bisexuality, and while she might have been angry, it would hardly amount to a motive for such a brutal attack.

The key factors in the trial were the amount and placement of the different types of blood spatter patterns (some ten thousand individual spatters) and the nature and number of lacerations on Kathleen's skull. While police claimed to have discovered, using luminol, bloody footprints going from the body to a utility sink and other places, they had failed to take photographs. Also at issue was whether Michael had done other things to cover up his connection to the crime as his wife lay dying rather than calling for immediate assistance, and why there were blood spatters inside the hem of his shorts.

Radisch, the prosecution's expert on Kathleen's injuries, had performed both Kathleen's autopsy and the second autopsy on Elizabeth Ratliff. Radisch described the similarities between the two deaths and said that based on her experience with wounds, she believed that Kathleen had been beaten to death, because the wounds were too numerous to have occurred during a fall. She stated that Kathleen also bore defensive wounds on her hands, as well as broken cartilage in her throat.

Peter Deaver, a blood spatter expert from the North Carolina State Bureau of Investigation, had run simulation experiments. He cited three distinct blood patterns indicating that Kathleen had been bludgeoned with a weapon: blood spatter on the adjacent hallway wall as high as nine feet was possibly cast off from a weapon being raised to hit again; blood on the door molding indicated that Kathleen had been standing when she received at least one of her injuries; and eight drops of blood inside Michael's shorts offered proof that he was standing close to her when she was hit. Additionally, a bloodstain pattern on the stairs indicated that the weapon was placed there. Deaver concluded that Kathleen had been assaulted by someone using a fireplace blow poke.

Several forensic experts, including medical examiners Dr. Werner Spitz, Dr. Michael Baden, and Dr. Cyril Wecht—all of whom believed the death was not a homicide—testified for the defense. Dr. Jan Leetsma, a forensic neuropathologist, indicated that the speed of the fall and the angle of the head, among other factors, could cause death without leaving the effect of a contrecoup injury, expected from a blow to the back of the head. He testified that during his career, he had examined 257 beating deaths, and he believed Kathleen's injuries were inconsistent with a beating. In his estimation, she had sustained four blows, not seven, and concluded that a beating death with a blow poke was inconsistent with his findings, but a fall down stairs was not inconsistent with what he saw.

Dr. Henry Lee testified that the blood spatter was consistent with a finding of accidental death. He contended that Kathleen's repeated coughing and breathing as she struggled could have caused a lot of blood to spray on the walls. There was a lack of the cast-off patterns and damage to the adjacent surfaces expected in a bludgeoning using a forty-inch blow poke in such a confined area. Further, activities conducted by the state's crime scene investigators had altered the original bloodstain pattern. Lee disagreed that the marks of blood high on the wall in the adjacent hallway indicated cast-off from a weapon, and he bolstered his testimony by coughing and spitting diluted ketchup onto a piece of white poster board to show the resulting patterns were similar to those found at the crime scene.

Dr. Faris Bandak, a biomechanical research scientist, testified that Kathleen had experienced a ground-level fall. He used Kathleen's height and weight, along with the dimensions of the staircase and stairwell, to calculate the incident and showed the jury a computerized animation of what had occurred. Bandak disagreed that an implement such as a blow poke could have caused the injuries.

The prosecution claimed that the murder weapon, the fireplace poker, was missing, but Rudolf produced a poker found a few days earlier in the Petersons' garage. The dust-covered implement clearly had not been used in a beating death.

Hardin's closing argument emphasized the fact that the victim had sustained thirty-eight separate injuries to the face, skull, back, hands, and wrists, for which he said that even two separate falls could not account. He reminded jurors that the two staircase deaths associated with Peterson were linked, and repeated his notion that Kathleen had grown angry over a homosexual liaison.

Rudolf repeated what his experts had said, reminding the jury of the problems with the processing of the crime scene. The jury deliberated for six days, and on October 10, 2003, Michael Peterson was convicted of first-degree murder. He received life in prison without parole, to be served at Nash Correctional Institution.

Michael appealed, stating that judicial errors prevented him from getting a fair trial, but in 2006 the state appellate court refused to overturn the conviction. One dissenting judge noted that there was insufficient evidence to prove Ratliff had been murdered and insufficient similarity between the deaths to even include the Ratliff case in the trial, but this official was in the minority.

This case illustrates the importance of death investigation. There is no doubt that Kathleen died of blunt trauma to the head. The question is whether that trauma was the result of an accidental fall or intentionally inflicted by her husband, Michael. Science is not always black and white. In this case, prosecution experts and defense experts had different opinions about the cause and manner of death. If a crime scene is not properly documented and noted and the physical evidence is not collected or preserved, subsequent examinations and interpretations can prove difficult.

DEATH INVESTIGATION PROCEDURES AND AUTOPSY

Death investigation involves reconstructing an incident to determine whether the manner of death was the result of a homicide or suicide, an accident, natural causes, or undetermined. A reconstruction is the process of determining the events and actions that occurred during the death event, including the examination and interpretation of physical and behavioral evidence. This process follows the basic scientific method, which is the formulation of a hypothesis against which evidence is tested. Experience, sound logic, and careful observation are necessary for an accurate reconstruction. The goal is to determine what happened, how it happened, when and where it happened, and who was (or was not) involved.

When a crime is initially discovered, a call goes out to authorities—generally via 911. A dispatcher notifies patrol units close by the scene. A uniformed police officer arrives and decides whether other personnel (a homicide or arson unit, for example) are needed. The officer notes the time and writes down pertinent observations, but refrains from touching or moving anything. If the suspected perpetrator is present, the officer makes an arrest. Otherwise, the officer secures and controls the scene.

If a body is present, the coroner or medical examiner decides when and how to protect it and move it to the morgue. This official also determines whether there is reason for an autopsy, or a post-mortem medical examination, for an official report. A partial autopsy examines only part of the body (for example, an injury to the head), while a selective autopsy may involve only a specific organ, such as the heart or the brain (if there is evidence of a specific cause of death, such as a heart attack).

The body is photographed, both clothed (if it was clothed when found) and unclothed. All trace materials on the body should be documented, photographed, and collected. Then the body is X-rayed, weighed, fingerprinted, and measured, and any identifying marks are recorded. Old and new injuries are noted, along with tattoos and scars. Trace evidence, such as hair and fibers, is collected from under the fingernails. The wrapping sheet, along with clothing and trace evidence, is sent to the forensic lab for analysis. Anything wet must be air-dried and properly preserved.

Once the body is clean and free of all hindrances (clothing, ligatures, jewelry), it is laid out on its back on the steel autopsy table, with a stabilizing block placed under the head. The pathologist then makes a Y incision, which is a cut into the body from shoulder to shoulder, meeting at the sternum and then going straight down the abdomen into the pelvis. A saw or lopper cuts through the ribs to remove the ribcage. Next, the examiner takes a blood sample to determine blood type and then removes the organs to weigh them. Samples of fluids are taken from the organs. Then the stomach and intestines are slit open to examine the contents. Samples are taken of everything that seems relevant to the case. Finally, the head and face are examined. After the physical examination, tissues from various organs are sent to the toxicology lab for further analysis.

In some cases, a body might not be present—for example, when someone is missing and presumed dead—and so the investigation might involve the search for a body. In other cases, examiners may attempt to identify a found body and determine the cause and manner of death. The investigation might also involve the identification and analysis of skeletal remains or an exhumation to look for evidence that might have been overlooked before a body was buried.

HISTORY OF DEATH INVESTIGATION

The earliest systematic death investigators on record developed their profession in China. During the thirteenth century, they codified several centuries' worth of practices involving death incidents. In 1247, Sung Tz'u, a Chinese lawyer, offered a compilation of this advice in one of the oldest extant works of forensic techniques, *Hsi yüan chi lu* (*The Washing Away of Wrongs*), basing his ideas on observation, experience, and logic. "Among criminal matters," he wrote, "none is more serious than capital cases; in capital cases nothing is given more weight than the initially collected facts; as to these initially collected facts, nothing is more crucial than the holding of inquests."

Sung Tz'u was a national scholar and a judicial intendant. He documented the differences among victims of poisoning, hanging, self-immolation, and other conditions. Thorough, meticulous, and clinical, his manual served death investigators for seven centuries. During his era, it was decreed that in the event of a complicated death, an inquest—*chien-yen*—was to be carried out, after which a high official would do a *fu-chien*, or more detailed inquest. At the time, civil servants oversaw the negotiation of legal disputes; often they had no training, so handbooks such as the *Hsi yüan chi lu* helped them to learn about death scenes.

A popular anecdote from this forensic text features a group of men laboring in a ditch, where one worker killed another. The victim was later found by the roadside, covered with sickle wounds. Since he still had his personal effects, it seemed unlikely that he was attacked by a thief, so it was suspected that the perpetrator knew him. The victim's wife indicated that another man had asked to borrow some money and was angry when he was refused, so he became a suspect. However, during the inquest no one would confess, and further questions turned up nothing more, so the magistrate ordered all the male villagers to gather before him with their sickles. Some eighty men arrived and laid down their implements. In time, the flies came, attracted to blood and specks of flesh, and the sickle on which they alighted revealed the killer. He was the same man who had wanted to borrow money. Confronted with the physical and circumstantial evidence against him, he confessed.

The early anatomists who dissected corpses for medical research gained a bit of support when Charles V of the Holy Roman Empire decreed in the 1500s that medical expertise be relied upon in all trials involving suspected murder or abortion. The anatomists were the ones who noticed how things like rigor mortis (the temporary rigidity of muscles after death) and algor mortis (the cooling of the body temperature after death) worked, and to this list they also added the progressive changes in coloration known as livor mortis or lividity (blood settling at the lowest point of gravity).

In the late 1700s, French physician Pierre Nysten recorded the changes in rigor mortis from flaccid to stiff to flaccid and formulated Nysten's law, stating that the process begins in the face and neck and moves downward through the body. Even decapitation, he discovered, does not seem to change this. In England, Dr. John Davey developed a scientific time clock using thermometers to measure diminishing body temperature. However, as forensic pathologists—as they were then called—learned more about the conditions of death and the variables involved, they grew less confident of these formulae. (As Lee says, "Every time there is a rule, there is an exception in death investigation.")

THE US DEATH INVESTIGATION SYSTEM

Death investigation in the United States today is carried out by coroners and medical examiners. The coroner system derives from the British Charts of Privileges, which listed an office of "crowner" or tax collector. In 1194, the judicial circuit under the rule of King Richard recorded in the Articles of Eyre that crowners would be elected as the *custodes placitorum coronæ*, or the keepers of the king's pleas. Coroners summoned inquest juries for people who were seriously wounded or had died from "misadventure." Eventually the office evolved into that of a death investigator. Beginning in the nineteenth century in the United States, some states recast the position of coroner as that of a medical examiner, who was usually a physician.

The duty of any death investigator is to determine the cause and manner of death, and, if possible, the time of death and the facts surrounding the death. A coroner generally brings a discovered body to a forensic pathologist for an autopsy, unless a treating doctor acknowledges that the individual was ill and the death was from natural causes or an obvious accident. Because they have a medical background, medical examiners can perform autopsies on their own.

The first step in a death investigation is to identify the deceased. Sometimes his ID is found nearby or he can be identified by next of kin, but other times the body itself serves as the means for identification. Generally the teeth, which endure longer than soft tissue, offer a means for identification using dental records when there is some indication who the decedent might be. If no records are available, a scar, distinctive mole, tattoo, or deformities shown by X-ray might be of assistance. A forensic artist may also make a drawing or sculpture of the face. In addition, DNA typing results can be compared to known samples, samples from presumed relatives, or databases.

Dr. Thomas Noguchi, the former chief medical examiner/coroner for the county of Los Angeles, California, is a US death investigator who has risen to the level of celebrity. Often called the "Coroner to the Stars," he determined the cause and manner of death in such high-profile cases as Marilyn Monroe, Sharon Tate, John Belushi, Natalie Wood, and Robert F. Kennedy. After emigrating from Tokyo to the United States, he became deputy coroner in 1961, and after his tenure as chief medical examiner, he taught at the University of Southern California and UCLA. He may also have been the inspiration for the popular television series *Quincy*.

More recently, Michael Baden, Cyril Wecht, and Werner Spitz have earned renown in the field of pathology. Baden was the chief medical examiner of New York City from 1961 to 1986, and is currently codirector of the New York State Police Medicolegal Investigation Unit. He has taught at several colleges and medical schools and served as chair of the Forensic Pathology Panel of the US Congress Select Committee on Assassinations, which investigated the murders of John F. Kennedy and Martin Luther King Jr. He has also been involved in high-profile cases, including the trials of O. J. Simpson, Claus von Bülow, and Byron De La Beckwith, the assassin of Medgar Evers, and the identification of the remains of the Romanov family.

Wecht earned an MD from the University of Pittsburgh and a JD from the University of Maryland. He was formerly the chair of the Department of Pathology and president of the medical staff at St. Francis Central Hospital in Pittsburgh, Pennsylvania. In 1965 Wecht undertook an analysis of the Warren Report on behalf of the American Academy of Forensic Sciences. Then, in 1972, he was the first non-government forensic pathologist permitted to observe and study the Kennedy autopsy materials preserved in the National Archives. He was appalled to discover that certain key items were missing, including Kennedy's brain. He stood firm in insisting that one bullet alone could not have caused all the wounds present in Kennedy and Governor John Connally, who was riding with Kennedy when he was shot.

Spitz was born in Stargard, Germany (now part of Poland), the son of physicians. As a young man he worked during the summers in the pathology department at the hospital where his parents were employed. In 1953 he graduated from the Hebrew University Medical

School in Jerusalem. During his seven years at the coroner's office in Jerusalem, Spitz recalls that he saw only one homicide. When he moved to Baltimore in 1960 to serve as deputy medical examiner, he saw four hundred homicides during his first year! In 1972 Detroit's Board of Commissioners offered Spitz the position of chief medical examiner for Wayne County. Spitz created a coroner's system in Wayne County that serves as a model for medical examiner's offices around the country. Many of the pathologists who trained under Spitz went on to become medical examiners in other districts. In 1988 Spitz left Wayne County to work as chief medical examiner in Macomb County. He retired from the county in 2004 and now concentrates on consulting work. Spitz has served on committees investigating the assassinations of President John F. Kennedy and Martin Luther King Jr., and has offered expert testimony in several high-profile cases, including the Preppy Murder Trial in New York, the California Night Stalker case, and the wrongful death lawsuit against O. J. Simpson.

BLOODSTAIN PATTERN ANALYSIS

One of the foremost authorities in the discipline of bloodstain analysis was Dr. Paul Leland Kirk, who was a professor of biochemistry at the University of California, Berkeley. In 1937 Kirk helped to develop Berkeley's criminalistics program, eventually working with August Vollmer and chairing the criminalistics department.

In 1955, after Sam Sheppard was convicted of killing his wife, Marilyn, in Bay Village, Ohio, Kirk visited the crime scene, the upstairs bedroom of the Sheppards' home. According to police reports and other records Kirk reviewed, Marilyn's body had been found bludgeoned to death on the bed, and there were blood spatters throughout the room, blood smears on the sheets where she lay, and a blood trail leading through the house. Sam claimed to have been asleep on a daybed on the first floor when he heard Marilyn yell for him, whereupon he rushed up the steps and grappled with an intruder, who got away. When it was learned that Sheppard was having an affair and Marilyn had decided to divorce him, the motive seemed obvious and the jury convicted him.

Twelve years later, defense attorney F. Lee Bailey succeeded in getting the conviction overturned in a landmark case concerning pretrial media influence. Kirk testified that the killer had been left-handed, which would exclude the right-handed Sam, and said that the blood spatter found on Sam's watch was a transfer stain resulting from incidental contact with Marilyn's body when he tried to find her pulse. In addition, Kirk stated that a spot of blood found in the bedroom where the murder took place came from someone other than Sam and Marilyn. It was type O, the same as Marilyn's, but contained other characteristics that eliminated her as its source. To determine this, Kirk had performed an unprecedented test, claiming that one of the stains reacted more slowly than the others to the blood-typing chemicals. Thus, he concluded that the slow-reacting stain was type O blood from a source other than Marilyn. His analysis was instrumental in Sam Sheppard's acquittal.

Kirk coined the term "blood dynamics" to describe the scientific approach to bloodstain pattern analysis, stating that no other type of investigation of blood yields information as useful as an analysis of the blood distribution patterns. At the scene of a violent crime where blood is spilled, the shape, size, and position of the stains—blood spatter—can assist investigators in reconstructing what occurred.

It is important to understand that the heart is still pumping in a wounded but still living person, so blood will leak or spray out, depending on the nature of the wound, and the behavior of blood in flight tends to remain uniform. When blood flies through the air, the pattern in which it lands can determine its track, as well as the location and position of the weapon that inflicted the wound. When it is layered, one spatter atop another, it can also provide an estimate of how many blows were struck.

The most essential aspects of the bloodstains at a scene are the size of the spots and the velocity of the drops at impact with a surface. Blood may be dripped out, sprayed from an artery, oozed out through a soft tissue wound, smeared, or flung off a weapon raised to strike another blow. In the 1930s, Scottish pathologist John Glaister classified blood splashes into distinct categories based on the energy needed to disperse it and on projectile angles, which many experts still rely on today. For example, circular marks come from blood ejected with relatively little force, while irregular, crenellated marks are made by blood flying at a good clip. Elliptical blood drops strike a surface at an angle, and their degree of elongation can help to calculate the angle from which they came, while splashes with long tails come from blood flying through the air and hitting a surface at an angle of 30 degrees or less.

Since blood generally moves in a straight trajectory with a slight arc, and since a fine mist indicates more force than large droplets, bloodstain patterns can assist investigators in reconstructing the positions and the means by which the victim and suspect interacted—and possibly struggled—through a crime scene.

Lee has also examined bloodstain patterns, helping to solve a scandalous cold case involving the murder of a nun. In June 2003 a woman wrote to the Catholic diocese in Toledo, Ohio, claiming that several local priests were involved in satanic ritual abuse. Her letter prompted an investigation of Father Gerald Robinson, a murder suspect in a 1980 case in Tiffin, Ohio, that was still unsolved. Despite his denial that he was near the chapel at the time of the murder, Robinson was arrested on April 23, 2004. In his home, police found more than one hundred photos of corpses in caskets and a book on the occult in which passages about satanic rituals were underlined.

The murder itself was quite disturbing. Around 8:00 a.m. on April 5, 1980, a nun found the elderly Sister Margaret Ann Pahl strangled and stabbed in the chapel at Mercy Hospital, where she worked. Only an hour earlier, Sister Margaret Ann had eaten breakfast and gone to prepare the chapel for Easter services. Her killer had wrapped a cloth around her neck and pulled it tight enough to force her necklace to make an impression in her skin and to break the hyoid bone in her throat.

The murder appeared to have a ritualistic element, because a series of stab wounds supposedly took the shape of an upside-down cross. Nine distinct puncture wounds—three times the Holy Trinity—crossed her chest over the heart, but she had also been stabbed twenty-two more times along her left side, including her neck and jaw. The weapon, a pointed and relatively flat item with a four-sided edge, had been pressed against her dress and her forehead, as if in a symbolic gesture of anointment.

Additionally, in what seemed a calculated humiliation, the killer rolled her dress up to her chest and yanked down her girdle, underwear, and pantyhose, giving the appearance of sexual assault. However, no semen was found during the autopsy.

Robinson responded to the alarm and claimed to have been in the shower when the police questioned him about his activities around the time of the killing. The police had already heard his name mentioned as a potential suspect, and it seemed odd to some that while his quarters were nearby, he had not heard any screams. A few days later, a cleaning woman went into Robinson's quarters and noticed his letter opener—shaped like a sword, nine inches long, with a slightly curving, four-sided blade. It had a ribbed metal handle, knuckle guard, and a medallion featuring the US Capitol building. Compounding the suspicion was the fact that he apparently had a strained relationship with the nun, chafing at taking orders from her.

During the initial interrogation, Robinson said someone had confessed the murder to him. When the detective expressed surprise at this violation of trust, Robinson quickly said he'd fabricated it under pressure. When police searched his quarters, they found the letter opener and confiscated it. Although the coroner had determined the wounds could have been made with scissors similar to a pair missing from the sacristy, she thought something sharper had been used on the victim's face. Suspiciously, the letter opener proved to be devoid of fingerprints and had been freshly polished. A test showed a tiny amount of blood present beneath the medallion, but the quantity was too small for further testing at the time.

All the evidence went into police storage, including the letter opener and the stained altar cloth that had been placed on top of the victim during the stabbing. The case went cold, but was reopened in 2003. In May that year, the remains of Sister Margaret Ann were exhumed. The bone of her left jaw retained a shallow impression of the murder weapon, and the deputy coroner removed that section so it could be examined by local forensic anthropologists Drs. Frank and Julie Saul, who declared it consistent with the shape of the letter opener. Bone trauma expert and forensic anthropologist Dr. Steven Symes, from Mercyhurst College, came to a similar conclusion, saying the letter opener could not be ruled out.

Lee examined the crime scene and autopsy photographs as well as the bloodstained altar cloth, and surmised that the killer had attacked the nun from behind, strangling her into unconsciousness. As she fell to the floor, still alive but unconscious, he stabbed her in the face and neck, and through the altar cloth covering her upper body. Her heart had probably stopped, which accounted for so little blood at the scene. Lee thought the assailant had cut a deliberate pattern in her chest with the stabbing instrument. He also examined the letter opener, the shape of the stab wounds, and the size and shape of the holes pierced through the altar cloth, and accepted that the instrument could have been the murder weapon. A bloody pattern on the altar cloth was chemically enhanced, and the pattern was found to be similar to the dime-sized medallion on the letter opener. The ten-foot cloth had other blood-stains as well, and one mirrored the ribbing on the letter opener's handle. Another looked like the slight curve of the long blade.

The trial opened on April 17, 2006, when prosecutors played the video-recorded police interrogation from Robinson's arrest. There was little content, but when left alone, Robinson mumbled, "Sister." Defense attorney John Thebes managed to get the coroner to admit that the wounds could have been made by a pair of scissors like those missing from the sacristy. He also pointed out inconsistencies in the accounts given by some of the witnesses and dismissed the investigation as shoddy and politically contaminated.

One theory about motive was that Robinson had shortened the Good Friday services that year and Sister Margaret Ann had been distressed to the point of tears. It was possible they'd had an argument that had set him off, and after the crime he had fabricated a confession from a fictitious suspect and lied about being in his quarters. The strongest evidence—and the trial's centerpiece—was the infamous letter opener.

The jury went to deliberate, and on May 12, 2006, they returned a guilty verdict. Robinson was sentenced to a mandatory term of fifteen years to life.

Since this was a cold case involving examination of skeletal remains rather than a fresh autopsy, the forensic anthropologist played an important part. Let us now turn to a consideration of the role of forensic anthropology in death investigations.

FORENSIC ANTHROPOLOGY

In 1932 the FBI set up the first government crime lab in Washington, DC, and soon the agents discovered the resources at the nearby Smithsonian Institution. It was clear that the scientists at the Smithsonian were qualified to consult on the skeletal remains of victims that might otherwise go unidentified. As the demands grew, and many states asked for assistance from university-affiliated anthropologists, these experts honed their methods for detecting past injuries, noting indicators of illness or occupation. In 1972 the Physical Anthropology Section of the American Academy of Forensic Sciences was established.

Forensic anthropology is the application of the science of physical anthropology to the legal process. The identification of skeletal, badly decomposed, or otherwise unidentified human remains and body parts, such as from airplane accidents or major disasters, is important for both legal and humanitarian reasons. Forensic anthropologists generally work with forensic pathologists, odontologists, and homicide investigators to point out evidence of foul play and assist with time-of-death estimates. Among the most prominent figures in this field was Dr. Clyde Snow.

In 1968 Snow became the head of the Department of Forensic Anthropology at the Office of Aerospace Medicine, Civil Aerospace Medical Institute. He earned renown from skeletal confirmations of the victims of serial killer John Wayne Gacy and of former Nazi doctor Josef Mengele. He also pioneered a computer program in 1979 to assist in the identification of the 273 fatalities of American Airlines Flight 191. He helped to establish the science of forensic anthropology, which already had a basis in work done during the nineteenth century.

Many other well-known contemporary forensic anthropologists—including Dr. Douglas Ubelacker, Dr. Albert Harper, and Dr. Bruno Frohlich—have also contributed a tremendous amount of knowledge and experience to this field.

Much of what occurs in forensic anthropology comes from the area of osteology (the study of bones), although some forensic anthropologists specialize in body decomposition and entomology

Identification of Human Remains

- Are the remains human?
- Are the remains recent?
- To whom did the remains belong?
- What is the estimation of age?
- What are the determined sex, race, and stature?
- What were the manner and cause of death?
- What was the means of death?
- What facts can be related to the death?

Fig. 4.1.

(the study of insects). The human body has 206 bones, collectively weighing about twelve pounds for the average male and ten pounds for the average female. To determine characteristics of the bones, they are laid out on an osteometric board, which holds the bones in place in the desired orientation and allows measurements with calipers. The basic identifying factors investigators evaluate are sex, age, race, previous trauma, stature, body type, evidence of disease, and the cause of death. Figure 4.1 lists the questions forensic anthropologists try to answer while examining bone specimens.

ENTOMOLOGY AND THE BODY FARM

Forensic entomology, or the use of insect analysis in law enforcement, was first introduced into Western courts in 1850 in France. A mummified infant was discovered between the walls of a building undergoing renovation, and suspicion fell on the couple who resided there. But other couples had lived there before them, so Dr. Marcel Bergeret constructed a time line based on the insect activity on the corpse. Using logic and data from studies in biology, he established that the infant had been placed between the walls two years earlier—before the current couple had moved in. Thus, they were exonerated and another couple was arrested.

This case inspired widespread interest among pathologists, notably Edmond Perrier Mégnin in France, who regularly visited morgues and cemeteries and who recorded eight distinct stages of necrophilous insect infestation. He wrote a book on forensic entomology, published in 1894, which identified the progression of insect activity that assisted in postmortem interval estimates over the course of three years: egg-laying blowflies, beetles, mites, moths, and flies that liked fermented protein.

Once flies lay their eggs, the biological clock begins. By looking at the most mature species present on the body when it is found, entomologists work backward to determine how long it took the insects, under those conditions, to reach that stage. That becomes the measurement of the minimum time since death. As a corpse decays, it emits odorous chemicals such as cadaverine and putrescine, which blowflies can detect from miles away. These flies often find a corpse within minutes of death and lay their eggs, and the eggs make the corpse attractive to other species. As different chemicals emerge with postmortem changes, other insects such as carrion beetles arrive, along with predators and parasites of the flies and beetles. Ants consume the fly eggs and beetles eat the newly hatched maggots. Wasps may lay eggs among the maggots, or eat them. Finally, spiders use the body as a habitat to prey on other insects, and moths may decimate clothing. If they survive all the predators, maggots consume the flesh for some two weeks before leaving it, and they leave trails behind them.

Insect activity can yield information about a diverse number of factors, from whether the corpse has been moved to whether the deceased took drugs or was poisoned. The insects may even yield important evidence such as DNA when tested for remains of what they have ingested from the body.

As law enforcement learned of the possible uses of insect study, they began seeking assistance from entomologists of varied backgrounds. In 1984 several forensic entomologists began meeting informally, eventually deciding to form a certifying board. This board was finally incorporated in the state of Nevada in 1996 as the American Board of Forensic Entomology. Several of these entomologists have gained national prominence in sensational cases, but none has been more extensively showcased than Dr. William Bass III, a forensic anthropologist with a specialty in entomology and the founder of the Forensic Anthropology Center at the University of Tennessee at Knoxville, also known as the Body Farm.

A strange case set the wheels in motion for this facility to exist. One day, Bass was asked by investigators to estimate the age of a skeleton that was in the apparently disturbed grave of William Shy, a colonel in the Confederate army during the Civil War. Bass said the remains were those of a white male between the ages of twenty-four and twenty-eight, and that he had been dead approximately a year. Bass conducted additional tests on the remains at his laboratory and soon discovered—from the age of the material in the clothing and from its fashion—that his estimate was dramatically inaccurate. The corpse, which was in relatively good condition because it had been embalmed, turned out to be that of Shy himself, dead and buried since 1864. Investigators concluded that someone had opened the grave and casket to steal effects of value from the corpse.

Given how little science had been done on the postmortem interval, Bass knew that someone had to start a serious study of this subject, so he asked the university where he worked to give him a small plot of land and obtained the unclaimed cadavers of several homeless men. As the corpses lay exposed to the elements, buried, or placed in water, they provided a vast amount of information about how bodies decompose under diverse conditions. As research progressed and the researchers expanded in number and specialization, the Body Farm became a center for training and consultation. Even the FBI has trained many agents there. Figure 4.2 shows Bass and Lee during a training session at the Body Farm.

Researchers at other institutions, such as Dr. Wayne Lord and Dr. M. Lee Goff, have also studied different aspects of insect activity and interactions of body temperature, environment, and soil on decomposition and insect life cycles. Scientists analyze soil samples because by-products of decomposition generally seep into the ground. This means that a scientist can determine how long a body was lying in a particular area or whether it was moved—and when that occurred. Due in part to the many specializations that have developed from this research, another forensic discipline, forensic taphonomy, was born that combined a number of death investigation activities.

Fig. 4.2. (*Top*) Dr. Bill Bass with Dr. Henry Lee at the Body Farm.
(*Bottom*) Dr. Henry Lee at the Body Farm conducting experiments
on decomposition.

FORENSIC TAPHONOMY

The human body goes through several stages during decomposition. Signs of early-stage decomposition are bloating, skin slippage, and bacterial discoloration under the skin. The corpse will discharge a foul odor, and as expanding gasses inside the tissues burst through, the eyes and tongue bulge out and the internal organs and fat begin to liquefy. During this stage, insects consume the tissues, the remains become increasingly more skeletal, and the head or limbs may disarticulate. Climate has an effect on decomposition rates for bodies buried or dumped outside, with cool temperatures having a preservative effect and thus creating a longer decomposition period. Many different disciplines—biology, entomology, anthropology, and pathology, as well as botany, geology, and climatology—may be necessary to conduct a thorough investigation into the circumstances surrounding decomposed human remains.

The science of forensic taphonomy is the discovery, recovery, and analysis of human remains in a context that has legal ramifications. The term "taphonomy" derives from the Greek words for burial, *taphos*, and laws, *nomos*. This discipline deals with the complex factors involved in the history after death of physical remains and the ways in which death-related processes have affected them. Taphonomy is primarily concerned with the death event, the modification of soft tissue through decomposition, the subsequent bone exposure to external agents, and the event of discovery and collection. If there is an injury to the bone, for example, the death investigator must decide whether it occurred before the incident that caused death (antemortem), immediately prior to death (perimortem), or after death (postmortem). This involves understanding the processes to which the bone was exposed, such as animal activity, as well as how specific types of damage appear in the bones of a living person versus the bones of a deceased person.

Bass was called to look into a gruesome series of murders around Knoxville, Tennessee. On October 20, 1992, a hunter came across the bruised and bound decomposing body of a prostitute who had been missing for a week. They associated her with a convicted rapist, whom the streetwalkers called the Zoo Man because of his propensity to take women behind the zoo for torture and sex.

Nearly a week after the first victim was found, police scouting the area came across two more bodies. One was fresh, but one had been there for quite a while, and animals had pulled her from her original site, leaving a greasy residue on the ground. Then, on October 27, the skeletonized remains of a fourth victim were discovered in the same general vicinity. Arrested and interrogated, the Zoo Man confessed to all four murders, but the court later ordered the charges tossed out. The cases remain open.

Because the women's remains were found outside in various states of decomposition, the taphonomic analysis required a number of different areas of expertise. While these bodies were all found above ground, many death investigations require the exhumation of remains buried in shallow or deep graves, or under rocks. The procedure may be used to check historical records, to locate an individual in a mass grave, to prove that the correct person is in a grave, to reexamine the deceased for something that was originally missed, to identify a missing person, or to conduct a war crimes investigation.

It is important to note that this has been a general overview of death investigation. Complicated cases often involve scientists from other disciplines. Each incident has its own specialized demands, but in general the death investigator needs to determine what must be done to obtain the most accurate incident reconstruction that satisfies both scientific and legal requirements.

WHO ARE DEATH INVESTIGATORS?

As evident from the different aspects of death investigation discussed, death investigators may have any of a number of backgrounds. Medical doctors, academics, forensic scientists, police officers, and others may all play a role in the process. Many medical examiners have death investigators on their staff. In addition to the general education and experience required to be a forensic scientist outlined earlier, these death investigators must have additional expertise in medicine, crime scene investigation, entomology, or a related specialization. Consequently, they are often forensic nurses, former police officers, or persons who have received a degree in criminal justice or forensic science and have had internships with coroners or medical examiners. It is the job of the medical examiner, death investigator, or homicide detective to collect investigative information and physical evidence that is used to determine the cause and manner of death. Because of this, these staff members must be well trained in the collection and preservation of evidence and in the proper protocols to search medical and personal records of the decedent. Experience conducting other types of investigations or knowledge of medical procedures and drugs is vital for a through and accurate evaluation of the scene and evidence. Forensic nurses, practicing a specialized area of nursing requiring an advanced degree, are trained in both of these areas.

Some death investigators also employ technicians who assist with basic tasks during the investigation process. These persons may have some basic training in science or related fields; some are medical assistants. Other training that is valuable to the death investigator is a background in photographic techniques and digital imaging. Many medical examiner offices hire photographers who document death scenes or autopsies and who are familiar with digital X-ray equipment.

Chapter Five

FINGERPRINT EVIDENCE

A number of lawyers have contended that fingerprints are useful when the actual fingers are studied, but cannot be reliable when dealing with latent fingerprints left behind at a crime scene. Dr. Henry Lee has heard these arguments many times. The potential for error, the problems with unconscious bias, and the mistakes made by fingerprint experts when comparing latent prints to suspect prints are all issues regularly raised when evidence is being challenged. Some of the arguments might be valid in some situations, especially if poorly trained examiners were carrying out the tests. But Lee has seen the value of fingerprint analysis when conducted by qualified and honest examiners. Many cases would have remained unsolved if fingerprints could not be used to identify possible suspects and link an individual to a crime. Some of the most difficult cold cases have been solved when fingerprint databases were searched for a match to crime scene evidence. So, Lee can easily attest to the value of fingerprint analysis.

In 1984 Anthony Golino, a New Haven, Connecticut, businessman, was arrested and charged in the 1973 murder of Penney Serra, based partially on a statement made by his estranged wife.

Several key crime scene items bore type O blood, different from Serra's type A, but Golino's blood was not tested, so he was detained in prison until the eve of his trial. The prosecutor sought a court-ordered blood test, which was performed by Lee and Elaine Pagliaro, of the Connecticut Forensic Science Laboratory. The results indicated his blood was also type A; Golino could not have left the blood at the crime scene and was not the killer. More years passed and John Serra, Penney's father, kept the case alive, placing numerous ads in the local papers and making regular phone calls to the prosecutor and the police. He asked Lee to personally take over the case.

The facts of the case were well known to Lee and his colleagues. On a humid summer day, July 16, an employee of the Temple Street Garage in downtown New Haven returned from lunch to find the body of Concetta "Penney" Serra on the bottom steps of the tenth-floor stairwell. She had been stabbed to death, killed by a single deep stab wound to the heart. Penney, who worked as a dental hygienist, was only twenty-one years old. She had borrowed her father's Buick Electra 225 that day, taking it into the parking garage, and her killer apparently followed her inside. When her body was found, her feet were bare and the bottoms were badly soiled.

It appeared to the police investigators from a blood trail more than three hundred feet long that her killer might have attacked her near her car, which was parked erratically on the eighth floor, and chased her to the stairwell and up to the tenth floor. (However, a serological analysis would offer a different scenario.) The car yielded potential evidence as well. There was blood on a door handle; the gas pedal, carpet, and steering shaft; a tissue and tissue box found inside the car; and the driver's side floor, as well as on interior and exterior trim. A purse in the front seat with a pair of shoes identified the victim, and the license plate helped police to locate Penney's father. On the same floor, investigators found a colored rag similar to those used by mechanics and a bloodstained white envelope.

Under the direction of Nicholas Pastore, a chief inspector with the New Haven Police Department, further investigation located a set of car keys with wet blood on them, dropped on the floor on the seventh level, along with a bloodstained white handkerchief that also bore dried paintlike stains. Another blood trail was found going as far as the fifth level.

Fingerprints were lifted from the tissue box and the car's interior, and a bloodstained ticket turned up with the parking attendant, who said he had taken it from a man with a foreign accent who appeared to be injured on his left hand. The attendant had asked if he could help, but the man declined assistance before driving off in an erratic manner.

Several witnesses had seen a thin man with long dark hair chasing a young woman who resembled the victim. They were on levels five and six, as well as on the eighth level, and one person remembered that the girl was barefoot.

Blood from the primary and secondary scenes indicated that Penney's type-A blood was present only in the area where she was stabbed. The rest was type O, which suggested that Penney's assailant was wounded during the attack and it was he who made the blood trail. But given the primitive state of blood analysis in 1973, this did not help them to identify a suspect.

John Serra told police that dental invoices from an Albanian immigrant, found in the car after the attack, had not been there when he had loaned it to his daughter that morning. However, this potential suspect protested his innocence with a solid alibi. Since he also had blood type O, he remained on the suspect list. Penney had worked at a dental office, however, and it was reasonable to believe she could have had the invoices in her possession.

Penney's former fiancé had an alibi, but he also would remain a suspect for many years. At the time, there were no other viable suspects. For years the New Haven Police Department compared the lifted prints against thousands of fingerprint cards on file, but failed to find a match. For more than a decade, the case went cold.

In 1989 each item of physical evidence was resubmitted to the state forensic science laboratory and reexamined. Lee and other law enforcement officials orchestrated a reenactment of the crime, starting on the seventh floor, where the attacker had apparently parked his car. The review of the evidence included the tissue box from Penney's car with a bloody thumbprint, the bloody handkerchief with traces of paint, a wig found on the upper level of the parking garage, and the bloodstained parking ticket. Samples of the bloodstains from the trail and the car were also tested. The car keys had been lost, but the wig contained a few human hairs. The investigating team noted that Penney's blood was found where her body lay, and the blood trail was the blood of her assailant. Examining where it was left, they surmised that he probably sustained a cut to his left hand, which had then dripped as he moved. He chased Penney from her car on the ninth floor, killing her in the stairwell on the tenth floor before going back to her car. Inside, he stanched the flow of blood from his wound with a tissue from the tissue box, which he left behind the driver's seat, providing one readable thumbprint. He drove Penney's car to the eighth level, where he left it parked at a slant before returning to his own car on the seventh level. In his haste, he dropped the keys and handkerchief there and drove out of the garage, leaving blood on the parking ticket. From the time stamp, it was clear that he had entered the garage immediately after Penney.

Enhancing the fingerprints allowed investigators to utilize a new tool that was not available during the initial investigation. The latent print images were digitized, entered into a computer, and passed through filters and grayscale programs to produce the clearest images. These images could then be viewed as enhanced photographic reproductions on a high-resolution monitor and searched through the Automated Fingerprint Identification System. However, despite the use of this new technology, no match was found. While this was disappointing, the investigators realized that the thumbprint would remain in the system in the event that the killer's prints were entered later in connection with some other incident. Lee predicted this case would one day be solved. Sadly, John Serra died three years later, just before that day came.

In 1999, fifty-six-year-old Edward R. Grant was arrested and charged with the murder of Penney Serra. His fingerprints were entered into AFIS because his fiancée had filed assault charges against him. (The charges were later dropped.) In 1997 latent print examiner Christopher Grice reentered the Serra evidence into AFIS and found that on twelve points of comparison, Grant's fingerprint matched that of the bloody fingerprint found on the tissue box taken from Serra's car. In addition, the descriptions from two witnesses matched Grant's 1973 appearance, and he did not have an alibi. A DNA analysis confirmed that the blood from the dropped handkerchief and a tissue in Serra's car was Grant's. The paint on the handkerchief was found to be chemically similar to paint used at the auto body shop where Grant worked. He was a complete stranger to Penney Serra; she had just been at the wrong place at the wrong time.

Although Grant's motive remained unclear (it was suggested by some to be attempted car theft), the forensic evidence against him was strong. Pagliaro testified about the state of blood typing in 1979, as well as the advances in serology and DNA analysis that had been made in the interim. Grice described the fingerprint comparison. Other criminalists testified specifically about how the new analyses applied to this case, stating the odds, conservatively, as at least 300 million to one that the blood from the trail in the garage and on several items in Penney Serra's car was that of Edward Grant.

Despite Grant's attorney's attempt to challenge the science, chain-of-evidence handling, and evidence storage conditions, on May 28, 2002, Grant was convicted. He received a sentence of twenty years to life.

In January 2008 Grant appealed to a panel of five justices on the Connecticut Supreme Court, on the grounds that the authorities had failed to provide sufficient evidence to justify the search warrant by means of which they had acquired a sample of Grant's blood. He called it an unjustified invasive search of his body, arguing that the tissue box found in the car was "movable evidence" and could have been handled by him elsewhere in some unrelated context. In April of that year, however, his conviction was upheld.

This case demonstrates the importance of fingerprint evidence in investigations. It also shows the importance of the initial observations and thorough examination of the crime scene and physical evidence, without which this case may never have been solved.

THE HISTORY OF FINGERPRINT IDENTIFICATION

Several ancient societies recognized the individualizing value of the ridged patterns present in human fingerprints. The earliest datable prints were left in Egypt about four thousand years ago. In China, prints were relied on to authenticate an artist's work, legal contracts, and documents. An example of one such ancient document is shown in figure 5.1. In the third century BCE, finger- and thumbprints showed up on official documents used in business and court dealings, and there is a record of a Roman attorney during the first century CE using a palm print to show that a suspect was framed.

Centuries later, scientists first noted the value of using fingerprints in criminal investigations. Several researchers took an interest in the ridge patterns on certain areas of human skin, and in 1798 J. C. Mayor of Germany suggested that they might be unique. By 1823, Professor Johannes Purkinje had classified nine basic fingerprint patterns. Twenty-five years later, William Herschel recognized

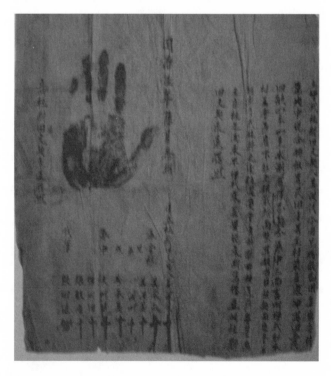

Fig. 5.1. Latent fingerprints applied to an ancient Chinese document to verify the author.

the individuality of fingerprints and began using them for contracts. He also fingerprinted prisoners for identification purposes.

By 1880, the observant Scottish physician Henry Faulds had discovered that the perspiration and other secretions from fingerprints left on surfaces could be made visible with powders. He used a fingerprint found at a crime scene to both eliminate a suspect and implicate the perpetrator. Other researchers discovered that fingerprints were unchanging over time, and after superficial injury even healed back to their original pattern.

In 1892 Sir Francis Galton published the first book about the forensic utility of fingerprints, proposing that prints bore three primary features and from them he could devise sixty thousand classes. Independently, Sir Edward Henry started his own fingerprint classification system in India, which was published in 1900. When he became assistant commissioner of police at Scotland Yard, he established its Fingerprint Office. In 1902, the first British conviction based on fingerprint evidence was obtained, and Henry's ten-print system was a major influence on those now used around the world.

Henry separated fingerprints into two basic groups: value patterns (whorls) and nonvalue patterns (arches and loops). With assigned values for different fingers, he formed codes for each set of prints. Thus, prints were filed according to numeric codes and could easily be retrieved for comparison. However, the system was limited in that it required all ten prints for accurate identification, while crime scenes often turned up only a few, or even just one. Single-print systems were developed years later.

A sensational court case was needed to confirm the utility of fingerprinting, and Britain got one in 1905. An employee entered Chapman's Oil and Colour Shop in Deptford, near London, and found owner Thomas Farrow lying dead under a chair and his wife dying upstairs. The cash box on the premises was empty. At this point, Chief Inspector Frederick Fox and Assistant Commissioner Melville Macnaghten from Scotland Yard's Criminal Investigation Department (CID) took over. Aware of the unique value of fingerprints, Macnaghten used his handkerchief to pick up the cashbox. On the underside of a metal tray, he spotted a clear impression of a thumbprint. He turned the tray over to Detective Inspector Charles

Collins, who was in charge of the CID's fledgling fingerprint division. From witness reports, they developed strong suspects in Alfred Stratton and his younger brother, Albert. Collins then got a match from the thumbprint to the elder Stratton.

At first the trial did not go well, which made the thumbprint identification all the more crucial. When Collins showed the jury enlarged photographs that illustrated how the thumbprint from the scene matched that of the elder Stratton on eleven points of comparison, it was impressive. He stated that he had been working for more than four years with files that numbered more than ninety thousand prints. Despite the defense attorney's attempt to undermine this testimony with its own expert, it took the jury just two hours to accept the fingerprint interpretation as definitive. Both men were convicted of the murders and were hanged.

In the United States, a jury first heard such testimony when Thomas Jennings was tried in 1910 for the murder of Clarence Hiller. Although circumstances were suspicious, only the fingerprints from four fingers left in wet paint on a porch railing conclusively linked Jennings to the crime. Four experts all agreed that these fingerprints were a match to Jennings. After his conviction, he appealed on the basis that the fingerprints should not have been admitted because there was insufficient proof to show this type of testing was reliable. The appellate court examined information from several treatises on fingerprints and declared that fingerprint technology had a scientific basis.

The International Association for Identification (IAI), founded in 1915, is among the oldest and largest forensic associations in the world. Once called the International Association for Criminal Identification, it offers seven certification programs in the areas of latent print analysis, bloodstain pattern analysis, crime scene analysis, footwear examination, forensic art, forensic photography, and "tenprint fingerprint." Its objectives include bringing professional examiners together, keeping them up to date, encouraging research, and providing training.

In 1924 Congress established a national depository of fingerprint records at the FBI, which took custody of more than eight hundred thousand fingerprint files from various prisons. Today the FBI Fingerprint Division contains millions of fingerprint records.

HOW FINGERPRINTS WORK:
CLASS VERSUS UNIQUE EVIDENCE

A key issue in solving crimes is the need to make close or definitive matches between evidence and suspects. Certain items—such as shoeprints, fibers, and soil—are generally known as "class evidence." This means an item can be grouped with like items, but because any given class item is just one of several possibilities, its evidentiary value is less impressive than when it can be associated with a specific individual and only that individual. The more unique a piece of evidence tied to a suspect is, the more likely it will have substantial value to the prosecution of the crime. A size-ten shoeprint impression, for example, might narrow the suspect pool to men wearing that size and style of shoe, but a cut mark on the sole can link it more definitively to a specific shoe and its owner. Class evidence adds weight to other circumstances, but only unique evidence can truly match a suspect to an item.

Fingerprints and DNA are the gold standard for unique or individualizing evidence. The examination of fingerprints, known more technically as dactyloscopy, is based on the fact that the smooth, hairless surfaces of hands and soles of the feet are covered with patterns of raised papillary, or friction, ridges. Those on the pads of the fingers, thumbs, and palms form patterns so unique that they can be used for individual identification. These friction ridges form in the inner layers of the dermis in a developing fetus and remain unchanged throughout life.

Present on top of these ridges are tiny sweat pores that exude perspiration, which combines with amino acids and adheres along the ridges. Thus, fingers, thumbs, and palms can leave readable impressions. Some agencies are even building databases of impressions from the soles of the feet. When a suspect in a crime is brought in, his or her fingerprints are rolled in black ink to reproduce the ridge patterns. Prints from both thumbs and all eight fingers are placed on ten-print cards, as seen in figure 5.2. Electronic fingerprint systems that scan the fingers of a suspect and store the information digitally are now widely in use. The fingers are numbered one through ten, starting with the right thumb; the left thumb is number

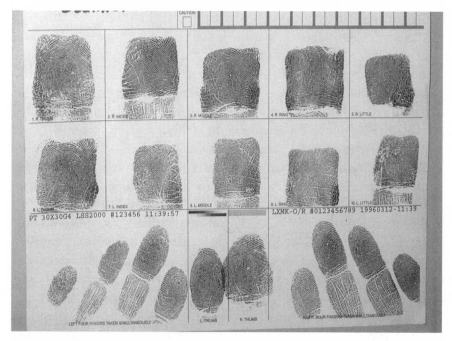

Fig. 5.2. A ten-print card used by law enforcement and other investigative agencies.

6. Then they are coded, along with descriptions of any extra, missing, or uniquely scarred fingers.

Prints left in ink, paint, or blood are called visible or patent prints; latent prints are invisible, except with the use of certain procedures or lighting conditions; plastic prints are those left in soft surfaces, such as warm wax. The impression might be whole or partial, but even a partial print can be sufficient to provide a lead and make a match. Its purpose may be to prove a case against a suspect in a crime, identify an unknown body or a victim of a mass disaster, assist a victim of amnesia, or even eliminate someone from consideration as a suspect. It can also be used to possibly determine whether someone has been arrested previously and to identify a fugitive or international terrorist. Taken properly, fingerprints can last a long time and assist in solving cases many decades old.

The characteristics that make a fingerprint unique are called minutiae, and identification via fingerprints relies on the detection of the patterns of minutiae and a comparison of their relative positions on a reference print. Examiners compare where the ridges start and end on a finger, where they split, and where and how they join, as well as where dots and other unique structures are located.

While patterns are unique to individuals, fingerprint patterns can be divided into eight basic types, based on specific features. Plain arches are ridges that run across the fingertip and curve upward in the middle; tented arches show a spike. Loops, which flow inward and then curve out again in the direction of origin, have a delta-shaped divergence and are either radial (toward the thumb) or ulnar (toward the little finger). Whorls are oval formations, often making a spiral or circular pattern around a central point. If a pattern contains two or more deltas, it will probably be a whorl. There are plain whorls, central pocket loop whorls, double loop whorls, and accidental patterns (a pattern that does not conform to those already described).

Once the basic pattern is established, examiners can concentrate on the finer points. There are several basic ridge characteristics: the ending (a dead end with no connection), the bifurcation (forked ridge), and the island (enclosed ridge) or dot (isolated point); these may form composites such as double bifurcations, ridge crossings, or bridges. These are used as the basis for points of comparison, and some areas of the print may yield more points in a given space than others. An identification is made when the examiner decides that the degree of similarity between two prints is sufficient to conclude that both originated with the same person.

Currently in the United States there is no established minimum number of points of identification required to match a print of unknown origin to a reference or suspect print. The fingerprint examiner maps out the best comparison points, but might be faced with problems from latent print collection such as variations in pressure when prints were left, partial prints, or smudged prints. Figure 5.3 shows a comparison chart prepared for court purposes that maps out some of the best points in the evidence and reference sample. Best practice requires that a second examiner verify any identification.

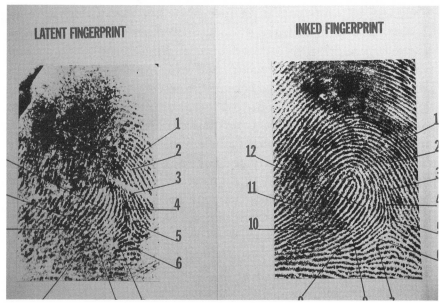

Fig. 5.3. A comparison chart prepared for court testimony showing corresponding individual characteristics on a latent fingerprint (*left*) and known fingerprint impression (*right*).

LATENT PRINT DEVELOPING METHODS

Latent prints on surfaces at a crime scene must be made visible, and the quality of the print recovered will depend on the type of surface material. When fingerprinting technology was in its infancy, prints were developed on nonporous surfaces using a soft brush with fine gray-black dusting powder; this method is still practiced today. It works best when used with fresh prints, before the oils dry. The excess powder is blown off, leaving a clear impression from the powder that adheres. The print can then be photographed, lifted with a tape, or placed onto a card. Colored powders were developed to contrast with surface colors, and some powders or dyes glow under alternative light sources. Fluorescent reagents, which react with amines from bodily secretions, yield fluorescent patterns, which can be useful on multicolored surfaces.

Chemical sprays have been developed that allow technicians to lift fingerprints from surfaces as rough as bricks and rocks or as slick as vinyl. Since traditional powder techniques may obliterate 10 percent of fingerprints, generally need a smooth surface, and don't always pick up older prints, this new technology could be a significant improvement. The spray contains iodine-benzoflavone or ruthenium tetroxide as an alternative to dry powders, and can treat large areas much faster than powders can. It does not replace the powder, but it expands the type and quantity of surface that can be analyzed.

Other methods have been developed for surfaces such as paper and cardboard. Prints can also be developed with chemicals such as iodine, ninhydrin, and silver nitrate. The superglue wand is a portable system used by investigators to fume at the scene inside cars and against immovable surfaces. Superglue fuming can provide a clearer image than dusting powder does, but it requires specific procedures be followed because the fumes are toxic. Lee can be seen using a superglue fuming system in figure 5.4.

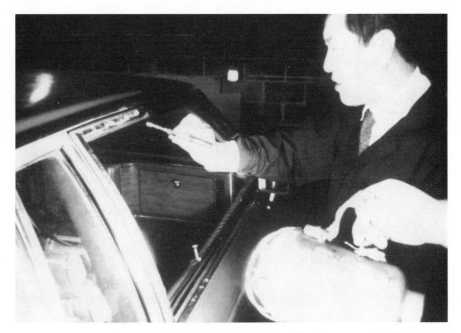

Fig. 5.4. Dr. Henry Lee fumes a car door frame with superglue during a homicide investigation.

Many items can be transported to a laboratory to be fumed under hoods, but care must be taken to prevent the area that has the fingerprint from touching anything. Those items that require observation using several different forensic techniques should also be taken to the laboratory.

Prints must also often be lifted from dead bodies for which there is no identification. Yet problems can arise. The epidermis of the skin, which is the exposed surface from which fingerprints are taken, may be missing, loose, mummified, or coarsened. If it's merely loose, as it will be during some stages of decomposition, the friction skin can be cut off and examined on slides. If the skin is badly wrinkled, either water or paraffin can be injected to make the surface firm, or a technician's finger can be inserted into it to provide a firm surface.

If it is mummified or decomposed into a dehydrated state, the skin may be too hard to work with. Some methods of hydrating the skin have been effective, including injection with water or glycerin, but the investigator may actually have to read the print directly from the finger rather than roll it onto a print card. In some cases, the print can be photographed or cast with dental casting material. It is also possible to cut the fingers off at one of the middle joints to immerse the digit in hand lotion or fabric softener to soften the skin.

If the body is in a state of rigor mortis, the joints may need to be massaged or bent back to loosen them. If the fingers are rigidly bent toward the palm, it may be necessary to cut some tendons to bend the hand backward as far as possible. Then the fingers can be braced together with a device called a spoon so that the tips can be inked and pressed against the fingerprint card.

DATABASES

Since 1972, fingerprint records have been retrievable via computer. For decades, latent print examiners had to make visual comparisons from a suspect print to cards kept in files, and the process could take weeks, even months. With the advent of the computer, the process was made considerably more efficient. Fingerprint files were stored in databases, which could be quickly accessed.

State and local agencies built up automated fingerprint identification systems, and in the 1980s the FBI opened the National Crime Information Center (NCIC), which expedited the exchange of information among law enforcement agencies. Each day this centralized agency receives more than thirty-four thousand fingerprint images to add to the database. The NCIC introduced a standard system of fingerprint classification (FPC), so the information could be uniformly transmitted from one AFIS to another. Each fingerprint image has demographic data associated with it within the NCIC database.

The computer scans and digitally encodes each fingerprint into a geometric pattern—a unique mathematical algorithm based on characteristics and relationships among print features and formations. Palm prints are divided into segments to allow for easier searching capability. In less than a second, the computer can compare a set of ten prints against a half million known prints (although getting actual matches can take longer). At the end of the process, the computer returns the set of prints that most closely matches the original, or no match may be found by the search. The scientists make the final determination, which involves a point-by-point visual comparison of the two sets of prints.

Types of AFIS include index systems, which store a lot of different types of information; ridge-angle systems, which store the angle of ridge flow at certain points on a ten-print card; and encoded minutiae systems, which store data about print minutiae in a convenient format. But AFIS results do not always come with the click of a computer key as one might see on television shows. Sometimes finding a match requires persistence.

NEW TECHNOLOGIES

Livescan is a computer technology used to take inkless prints. The finger is inserted into a machine that has a sensor pad that scans the print as a digital image, which can then be sent to an AFIS database to matching or storage.

A technique called vacuum metal deposition (VMD) uses an expensive high-tech instrument to lift fingerprints. An exhibit is placed inside the VMD chamber, and four to five milligrams of gold and several grams of zinc are loaded into evaporation containers beneath it. Pumps are activated that reduce pressure in the chamber, and a low-voltage current evaporates the gold, leaving a minute deposit on the exhibit. The gold absorbs into the fingerprint residue. In a separate container, the zinc is subjected to a similar method, in which it is heated and vaporized, and then deposited onto the exhibit. It adheres to but does not penetrate the gold to produce an image of the valleys that lie between the fingerprint's ridges. This enhancement makes the print visible in sharp relief when it is photographed.

Although this method has only recently been applied to latent fingerprint analysis, it has been in use since 1976 for other purposes. It is most effectively used for prints on plastic and glass, but it has also worked on cloth and currency. VMD develops more fingerprints than superglue fuming or other reagents, and it can develop prints on more types of articles than other methods, including leather surfaces, synthetic clothing, and polyethylene garbage bags. However, significant experience is required on the part of the examiner to get good results.

Another expensive technology is the argon laser. Under various wavelengths of light or when excited by a laser, certain body secretions fluoresce and can then be photographed. The argon laser produces a lot of heat and must be cooled, so it is not practical in instances where other methods will work just as well. Lower-power lasers have been made portable, and these, along with alternate light sources, have proven very useful in searching for latent fingerprints. A handheld alternate light system is employed for widespread fingerprint searches at crime scenes.

ISSUES IN THE COURTROOM

In *United States v. Llera Plaza* (2002), Judge Louis Pollak, a senior federal judge in the Eastern District Court of Pennsylvania, entertained a motion to evaluate fingerprint evidence against US Supreme Court standards set in 1993 in *Daubert v. Merrell Dow Pharmaceuticals, Inc.* These standards provided guidelines to aid the court in accepting novel science while barring junk science from the court-room. A long history of admissibility of expert testimony from fingerprint examiners did not impress Pollak as a way to legitimize this methodology as a science, nor did the fact that experts reportedly check one another's analyses. He found that the standard technique used for fingerprint examination failed *Daubert* on three points, notably, that the error rate has not been quantified, the "peers" are not scientists, and the millions of prints on record have never been properly analyzed for possible duplication. The only part of the standard it met was "general acceptance" by other examiners.

Pollak thus became one of more than three dozen judges since 1999 to question fingerprint analysis. His ruling focused on whether latent prints, which are generally partial, can be accurately matched to inked prints, which are complete. In a forty-nine-page opinion, he discussed the lack of scientific standards that controlled the technique. He would allow experts to show how comparisons are made, he said, and even to state that no two people have the same print, but he would not allow them to state that a specific latent print was made by a specific person.

Many were concerned about the impact Pollak's decision might have on both past convictions involving fingerprints and the future of such forensic testimony—even in technical areas such as ballistics and handwriting comparisons. Prosecutors worried about making stronger cases, especially when all they had were fingerprint comparisons.

Six weeks after his first ruling, Pollak reversed his decision and decided that fingerprint analysis passed the test. Apparently he realized his decision's far-ranging implications for all similar cases, as well as for other areas of forensic analysis. Yet, Pollak's reversal notwithstanding, the debates had begun, and other professionals began pointing out that fingerprint examiners lacked objective standards for evaluating whether two prints match, noting the fact that there was no fixed requirement as to how many points of comparison were sufficient. In short, it became an issue that there was no clear protocol for ensuring that different examiners would reach precisely the same conclusions about a fingerprint comparison and that the error rate had received no systematic attention. No one really knew how often examiners had been wrong, but in some cases they had, and those errors had victimized innocent people.

Stephan Cowans spent six years in prison after he was convicted of shooting a police officer in Boston in 1997. Fingerprint identification was crucial to his conviction, but after DNA analysis indicated he was not the shooter, the fingerprint was reexamined. It was not his, and in 2004 he was freed. (Tragically, three years later he was shot to death in his home.) In light of the misidentification, that police department's fingerprint unit was closed for evaluation.

A more famous case triggered another judicial review. Late in 2007, Baltimore County Circuit Court Judge Susan M. Souder ruled that fingerprint evidence was not sufficiently reliable to be used against a defendant in a capital case; thus it was excluded. During an attempted carjacking in January 2006, Warren Fleming was fatally shot in a Mercedes at Security Square Mall. Witnesses saw the shooter flee the scene in a stolen Dodge Intrepid. A tip led police almost two weeks later to twenty-three-year-old Brian Keith Rose, who was arrested. Partial fingerprints found inside both cars were matched to Rose.

Rose's defense attorneys challenged the admissibility of fingerprint evidence, stating that it had been admitted into the legal system prior to the date when standards were established for the admissibility of scientific evidence and that it had never been subjected to scientific scrutiny in the way other areas of forensic science and technology have. Just as Rose was scheduled to go to trial in October, Souder issued her ruling.

In a thirty-two-page decision, she acknowledged the long history of fingerprint evidence, but said that a history of use was insufficient reason for accepting that it was valid. Souder referred to an embarrassing case in which three latent print examiners from the FBI, along with a court-appointed fingerprint analyst, had misidentified an Oregon attorney as a suspect in a fatal 2004 train-bombing incident in Madrid, Spain. Two weeks after the attorney's arrest, the real perpetrator was identified and apologies were issued.

Souder criticized the common method of fingerprint analysis as overly subjective and lacking in clear standards, and did not agree that fingerprinting methodology was infallible with a skilled examiner. She thought it was precisely the kind of untested and unverifiable procedure the 1923 *Frye* ruling meant to banish. Since fingerprint evidence was central to the case against Rose, the prosecutor moved for a postponement, which was granted, but attorneys worried that the ruling could affect future cases in Maryland, as well as other areas of forensic methodology. Interestingly, the case was moved to federal court, where fingerprints had been accepted as reliable.

Some critics claim that fingerprinting came into the courtroom before there were any sophisticated means for evaluating it as a science. In the case of Thomas Jennings in 1910, the court failed to scrutinize the methods adequately, asking no real questions about the examiners' claims, and Jennings's appeal failed. But that did not necessarily mean fingerprinting was a science. Even so, fingerprint examiners claimed 100 percent certainty about their analysis. No one has yet established that all fingerprints are unique or that the technique of making comparisons is infallible. But only during the past decade has fingerprint analysis been challenged in the courtroom, and by then it had gained considerable cultural authority.

It seems likely that fingerprint analysis will sustain more scrutiny until it proves its fundamental assumptions through scientific procedures. Many studies are underway to show the statistical and scientific foundations of fingerprint analysis. Until then, analysts can at least show that no AFIS computer has come up with identical matches from two different people for a suspect print.

WHO ARE FINGERPRINT EXAMINERS?

Traditionally, fingerprint examiners often come from a law enforcement background. Police officers are taught as part of their training to collect fingerprints from suspects and to search for and process prints at crime scenes. When these examiners are part of a department's identification or crime scene unit, they often receive initial training in the classification of fingerprints for filing purposes. Since 2005 the IAI and other organizations have supported a Bachelor of Science degree, with a background in physical or forensic science, for all latent print examiners.

Latent print examiners must be able to recognize subtle differences in patterns and have keen powers of observation. As clearly demonstrated by the guidelines of the Scientific Working Group on Friction Ridge Analysis, Study and Technology (SWGFAST), the training of a latent fingerprint examiner is a long and extensive process. Individuals who choose to become latent print examiners often begin with an apprenticeship under a seasoned examiner. Latent print examiners must be trained in all areas of fingerprinting, including its history, the various ways to lift and preserve fingerprints at the scene or in the laboratory, the different surfaces on which prints are found and the advantages and disadvantages of each, the systems of classification, and the procedure for testifying in court. Formal study is part of the process, with many hours spent learning the importance of various characteristics at all levels of examination. An understanding of the individual friction ridge structure (e.g., continuity, texture, pore, and edge definition) for determining the existence of individualizing details is the focus of these years of study. In addition, the importance of the scientific method and quality assurance are stressed. Through hands-on training, student print examiners learn to identify patterns and compare latent fingerprints. Since print comparisons are a matter of interpretation, mistakes can be made if training is lacking, so experts work with many nonprobative cases to hone their abilities.

Despite the recent controversy, fingerprint analysis has proven itself over and over as effective in solving crimes, and given its solid record it will likely continue to be a reliable method in the future.

Chapter Six

FIREARMS EVIDENCE

The impact of firearms evidence on forensic investigation cannot be overrated. Dr. Henry Lee has lectured widely on the role firearms evidence has played in many famous—and infamous—cases.

In 1983, at the request of CBS and the Howard University School of Law, Lee set up a panel to reinvestigate the Sacco-Vanzetti case. Firearms experts reexamined each piece of evidence. At the time of the trial, some investigators used questionable techniques to show the involvement of the two accused in the crime. Ultimately, this modern-day panel agreed that one of the fatal bullets was fired from Sacco's Colt. However, other bullets and cartridge cases did not match the guns submitted as evidence during the trial, and no firearms evidence linked Vanzetti to the crime. The experts also found some evidence in the case that was highly questionable and other physical evidence that did not support witness statements. This case illustrates both the value of firearms evidence—when used properly—and some of the issues with nonscientific evidence.

On August 23, 1924, amid protests and furor from many prominent citizens, Nicola Sacco and Bartolomeo Vanzetti were executed for the murders of two men during an armed robbery. Frederick Parmenter and Alessandro Berardelli, employees of the Slater & Morrill Shoe Company, were transporting the company's $15,776.51 payroll when two armed men approached, shot them, and took the money. Witnesses saw the two robbers get into a car with several other men. They were described as looking Italian. Police questioned a number of immigrants, ultimately concentrating on several men who were active in radical politics. After the car used in the South Braintree robbery was found abandoned, the police questioned several known anarchists. In a planned trap, police were notified when the suspects, including Sacco and Vanzetti, arrived at a garage to pick up a car. Both men were armed when arrested. When questioned, Sacco and Vanzetti both lied to the police and the prosecutor about some of their activities, hoping to cover up their connection to several bombings and other terrorist activities. Figure 6.1 depicts the guns seized from Sacco and Vanzetti when they were arrested.

Fig. 6.1. The guns seized from Nicola Sacco and Bartolomeo Vanzetti. Ammunition fired from these weapons was compared to bullets from the robbery victims.

Vanzetti had shotgun shells in his possession when he was arrested. This was of great interest to the police. In December 1919 there had been an attempted robbery of a different shoe company in Bridgewater, Massachusetts. One of those robbers shot at the payroll truck as they were making their getaway. With little more than this to go on, Vanzetti was deemed the "shotgun bandit" and indicted for the Bridgewater attempted robbery within days of his arrest. He was quickly tried and convicted. He had no criminal record before his arrest.

On September 11, 1920, Sacco and Vanzetti were indicted for murder. Their trial began on the last day of May in 1921. At this time, right after World War I, many Americans resented "foreigners." It was also the period of the First Red Scare on the heels of the Bolshevik revolution in Russia. The case against Sacco and Vanzetti was highly publicized, both because of the political climate and because of their anarchist activities. It was, essentially, the "trial of the century"—for that decade, at least. More than seven hundred potential jurors were called to the courthouse in Dedham for the voir dire. After a week a jury was finally seated and the trial began. Several eyewitnesses were brought in to link Sacco to the South Braintree murders. One bookkeeper at the factory testified that she saw Sacco lean out of the window of a car. Other witnesses, however, could not or would not identify either Sacco or Vanzetti as the shooters. As is still common today, the eyewitnesses did not always agree with each other, and the stories of individual eyewitnesses changed.

The 1920s were a time of growth in the use of science in police investigations. Police were beginning to collect physical evidence from victims and crime scenes. Courts were beginning to accept expert testimony concerning tests conducted on this evidence. In addition to the eyewitness evidence in the case against Sacco and Vanzetti, two persons testified to "forensic ballistics" evidence. Four bullets were removed from the bodies of the two murder victims. These bullets were examined and compared with the guns the defendants had with them when they were arrested. Vanzetti was holding a .38-caliber Harrington & Richardson revolver. Sacco had a Colt automatic. One expert, Captain William Proctor, testified that one of the bullets was not fired from Sacco's Colt. Proctor did state that one bullet, called Bullet 3, was "consistent" with those fired by Sacco's pistol. This language implied that Sacco's weapon fired the bullet, but Proctor actually examined only some class characteristics of the bullet and could not identify the particular weapon that fired it. Charles van Amburgh, a second firearms expert, testified that he had taken extensive photographs of the bullets from the victims and compared these to photographs of bullets fired from Sacco's gun. After careful study, van Amburgh believed the "scratches" on Bullet 3 were caused by the barrel of Sacco's gun.

Firearms evidence against Vanzetti was limited to the weapon itself. None of the bullets taken from the victims was consistent with having been fired from his Harrington & Richardson gun. However, it was thought that one of the victims, Berardelli, had the same type of handgun on his person when he was killed. Testimony was given that the hammer on Berardelli's revolver was repaired; Vanzetti's handgun had a similar repair. The implication was clear.

Little other evidence was presented at the trial. That evidence included a hat left at the scene (no blood typing or DNA was possible at the time), a car suspected to be the getaway vehicle (with no prints linked to the defendants), and the false statements given by the two when arrested. On July 14, 1921, a jury found Sacco and Vanzetti guilty of both murders and sentenced them to death. Years of appeals followed. Because much of the evidence against these two was eyewitness testimony, some of which was recanted after the trial, there was a great deal of outrage about their convictions and sentence. Felix Frankfurter, who would go on to become a justice of the Supreme Court, wrote a lengthy article in 1926 in which he pointed out various errors the trial judge made, including some issues with the ballistics testimony. After this, the governor of Massachusetts formed what became known as the Lowell Commission to review the case and the evidence.

Dr. Calvin Goddard from the Bureau of Forensic Ballistics, which was established in New York in 1925 to provide firearms identification services throughout the country, agreed to reexamine the four bullets from the crime. To conduct his examination he used a newly developed tool—a specialized comparison microscope. This microscope allowed him to look at two bullets at the same time, determining directly whether significant markings were present on both bullets. He looked at the four scene bullets and test fires from Sacco's gun. In his opinion, Bullet 3 and the test bullet were fired from the same weapon. Some critics of Goddard's work insisted that he was biased in his examinations because he had previously studied the photographs and testimony of van Amburgh. However, the scientific approach used by Goddard impressed the governor, who refused to commute the sentences of Sacco and Vanzetti.

Even after their deaths, many have questioned the conviction of these two men. Because the bullets from the bodies and the handguns were the only physical evidence in the case, these items have been examined periodically by different firearms examiners during the past eight decades. Teams of firearms examiners have looked at the firearms evidence in the case, and their findings agreed with Goddard that Bullet 3 came from Sacco's gun.

THE HISTORY OF FIREARMS AND TOOL MARK EXAMINATION

Great strides in science and technology were taking place at the beginning of the twentieth century. The popular literature depicted the analytical, scientific detective, epitomized by Sherlock Holmes, as brilliantly adept at solving crimes. Science also was making an intrusion into courtrooms around the world. Police were able to use information gained through scientific methods of evaluation to include or exclude evidence or suspects. The science of forensic ballistics became one of the most useful methods to the police, especially after Colt and other firearms manufacturers perfected the mass manufacture of handguns and ammunition in the 1800s.

The first recorded case involving firearms comparison occurred in England in 1835. In that case a detective looked at the mold marks on a lead ball and compared those to markings on lead projectiles in the possession of a suspect. He also compared the paper that was used in firing the weapon with a newspaper in the suspect's room. In the 1860s, records indicate that when General Stonewall Jackson was mortally wounded during the Civil War, the bullet was removed and examined. The projectile was a .67-caliber shot. Looking at the caliber and shape of the bullet, the surgeon knew that Jackson had been shot by his own troops during the heat of the battle, because unlike the Confederate soldiers, Union troops used .58-caliber ammunition.

Soon courts began accepting testimony from gun manufacturers, sheriffs, detectives, and others familiar with firearms and ammunition on a regular basis. The next significant step for the field of firearms and tool mark examination came when experts began to publish their studies and findings, as is standard for scientists. For example, in 1900 Dr. Albert Llewellyn Hall wrote about the measurement of lands and grooves on bullets and the use of these data to distinguish ammunition fired from different weapons. Two years later, a Massachusetts court allowed expert testimony on rifling in gun barrels and the effects on the fired bullets. Victor Balthazard, a forensic expert in France, followed in 1909 with the publication of a method for comparing fired bullets, which he examined using detailed photographs (as van Amburgh had done in the Sacco-Vanzetti case). Various other publications in Europe and the United States dealt with forensic ballistics during this period.

Perhaps the most significant development of forensic ballistics during this time was the application by Charles Waite of modern scientific methods to firearms evidence testing in 1917. Waite, considered the father of modern firearms and tool mark identification, was hired in 1917 as an aide for a governor's commission that was reinvestigating a double murder. In 1915 a man named Charles Stielow left his home to find the bloody body of his neighbor's housekeeper on his doorstep. Stielow ran to his ninety-year-old neighbor's home, where he found him shot and unconscious. When that neighbor died a short time later, Stielow became a suspect. Although Stielow claimed that he did not own a gun, the investigation showed that he in fact possessed a .22-caliber revolver. Police called in a so-called ballistics expert named Albert Hamilton to examine Stielow's gun and the bullets from the victims' bodies. In spite of the fact that he did not test-fire the weapon, Hamilton declared that the bullets were indeed fired from Stielow's revolver. This testimony, along with Stielow's own lie, sealed his fate.

Before Stielow was executed, the governor of New York com-muted his sentence to life because he was not convinced Stielow was guilty. Then he created the commission that put Waite in charge of reinvestigating the firearms evidence. Waite brought the gun and the bullets to the New York Police Department, where several rounds of ammunition were fired. Waite could easily see that the markings on the bullets that came from Stielow's weapon did not resemble the bullets taken from the victims; the evidence bullets were smooth, while the test fires had numerous markings and gouges. To further illustrate that the evidence bullets were not similar to the test fires, Waite brought the two sets of bullets to a microscopist at Bausch and Lomb. Looking at the magnified bullets, the microscopist con-firmed Waite's findings.

Because of Waite's efforts, Stielow was freed. And if the story ended here, this alone would indeed be a remarkable achievement. But Waite was determined that frauds like Hamilton should be driven out of the courts. The Stielow case had stimulated in Waite two of the most important characteristics of all scientific pioneers: curiosity and determination. Waite was neither a scientist nor a gun expert, but he believed that if investigators, judges, and attorneys knew more about firearms and the individual markings on discharged bullets, justice would be better served. Unfortunately, the United States entered World War I shortly thereafter, and it was not until 1919 that Waite was able to begin collecting data about weapons made by twelve manufacturers of firearms in the United States. In doing this, Waite applied scientific principles and measurements to create an orga-nized, systematic study of modern firearms.

In 1925 Waite started the New York Bureau of Forensic Ballis-tics with John Fisher, a physicist, and Philip Gravelle, a chemist and photographer. These three men were soon joined by Goddard. Together they developed the comparison microscope, which is still used in firearms evidence examinations today, to assist in the com-parison of bullets, pellets, shotgun casings, and cartridge cases. They test-fired thousands of guns and compared the bullets and cartridge cases to each other. By the end of his firearms study, Waite was con-vinced that he had shown that each weapon, even one that is mass produced, possesses individual characteristics that are the result of the manufacturing process and that these unique flaws and imperfections in the weapon can be transferred to the softer metal of the ammunition. He further encouraged the use of a microscope to reveal the unique nature of these markings. Unfortunately, Waite died of a heart attack in 1926, leaving it to Goddard and others to continue applying his scientific approach to firearms analysis.

In addition to the Sacco-Vanzetti case, several other high-profile cases in the United States during the 1920s involved firearms evidence. The most notorious of these is probably what is called the St. Valentine's Day Massacre. On February 14, 1929, seven gangsters were executed by a rival gang in a garage in Chicago. This was a time of rampant crime and suspected police corruption in Chicago. It was the Roaring Twenties, when gangsters ran illegal alcohol and crime empires. Rumors of police involvement in the gangland execution were rampant. A grand jury was convened and Goddard was asked to examine the firearms evidence, which included bullets, shotgun casings, fired cartridge cases, and pellets. Employing the comparison scope, he was able to conclude that one shotgun and two submachine guns were used in the shootings. Because of the public outcry, he also examined the police department's submachine guns. None of the weapons he was given from the Chicago Police Department matched the firearms evidence.

In the 1930s, further advances were made in the field. In 1932 J. Edgar Hoover established the FBI Laboratory, which included a firearms lab among the latest in crime-fighting technology. Studies and publications continued during the decade, including several significant texts on the identification and comparison of firearms evidence. During the 1930s and the 1940s, many states and counties established their own crime or identification laboratories. Many of these included ballistics services. The first scientific meeting in 1948 of what was to become the American Academy of Forensic Sciences included two papers related to firearms comparison standards, cases, and controversies. Although the field continued to increase in knowledge and membership, it was not until 1969 that an organization was established dedicated to the development, study, and discussion of the firearms and tool mark specialty.

The Association of Firearm and Tool Mark Examiners was

formed in the decade that saw the assassinations of President John F. Kennedy, his brother Robert Kennedy, and Martin Luther King Jr. Firearms evidence was vital in those cases to answer questions such as how many shooters were involved, where they were located, and what were the trajectories of the bullets that caused the fatal wounds. As with many such cases, questions remain, and many people do not believe the conclusions drawn by the original firearms experts. Since 1970, AFTE members and many other forensic experts, including Henry Lee, have participated in the reinvestigation of these and many other shooting incidents.

The ability to link cases and weapons was enhanced with the computer age. In 1989 the FBI began an electronic network and database that captured images of cartridge cases in a digital format called DRUGFIRE. This database could then be searched using various algorithms that compared individual characteristics. Matches were confirmed by firearms examiners, in much the same way as AFIS hits are in fingerprint examinations. At the same time, the Bureau of Alcohol, Tobacco, and Firearms (ATF) developed IBIS, or Integrated Ballistics Identification System. This, too, provided the ability to digitize and compare firearms evidence. Unfortunately, the two systems were not compatible with each other. Ultimately, a new system—the National Integrated Ballistics Information Network— was developed. NIBIN, which will be discussed in greater detail later in this chapter, is currently in operation in various regions in the United States.

In 1993 the Supreme Court established a federal standard for the admissibility of scientific evidence. Many state courts have since adopted this *Daubert* standard. Firearms and tool mark analysis is among the forensic science disciplines that have been highly scrutinized as a result of this ruling. The thousands of members of AFTE and numerous governmental and academic institutions have sought to show the continued value and validity of this specialty in today's investigations and legal proceedings.

FIREARMS EVIDENCE EXAMINATION

Whenever a tool (including a firearm) is used, the force of the tool creates marks on the softer surfaces it contacts. The tool surface has certain general manufacturing characteristics (e.g., width, edge shape, surface pattern) as well as visible and microscopic flaws in its surface that are unique to that specific tool. Those flaws are transferred to the surface of the softer material as individual scratches and striations, or tool marks. Firearms and tool mark examiners use these facts to compare spent bullets and cartridge cases that have been fired from a gun to each other and to the weapon. Other tools, such as wire cutters, pliers, screwdrivers, and the like, may also create individual marks.

To assist in their examinations, firearms examiners use a modern comparison microscope, similar to the one designed by Waite, Gravelle, and their colleagues. Examinations of evidence begin with proper notation and documentation of the general or class characteristics of the item. Some of these can be seen without magnification, called macroscopic examination. Class characteristics help the examiner categorize the tool or gun that made the marking. Individual characteristics, the unique scratches (striae) that result from flaws, usage, and imperfections of the tool, can be linked to a particular weapon or tool.

Matching a specific firearm to ammunition components, such as bullets and cartridge cases fired from that weapon, is possible because of the way in which handguns and rifles are made. When gun barrels are manufactured, grooves are cut in a spiral down the inner surface of the barrel. This process is called rifling. Rifling puts a spin on the projectile as it passes through and out of the gun barrel, making the shot more stable and accurate. The lands and grooves are transferred to the projectile, which has a slightly larger diameter as it passes down the barrel.

Modern ammunition is often in cartridge form. A cartridge typically contains a case, primer, propellant, and a projectile. When a gun is discharged, the firing pin hits the primer and initiates a chemical reaction in the ammunition cartridge. This explosion creates heat, gases, and a great deal of pressure. As the force of the discharge sends the projectile through the barrel, an equal and opposite force slams the cartridge case against the breech face (the back of the barrel). The forceful contact of both the cartridge case and the projectile against the surfaces of the gun causes the transfer of the class characteristics (manufacturing) as well as the individual characteristics (flaws and imperfections) to the surface of the projectile.

When a fired bullet is recovered at the scene of a crime or from a victim's body, the examiner must first note the class characteristics of that projectile. These are primarily the bullet caliber and rifling characteristics. In the United States, caliber refers to the diameter of the bullet and is designated as hundredths of an inch (e.g., .38); Europeans use millimeters to measure ammunition (e.g., 9mm). An examination of the diameter, weight, and other physical characteristics of a bullet help the expert identify the type of ammunition used. Manufacturers vary the shape and composition of bullets to alter their penetration and aerodynamic properties. Penetration, for example, is affected by the design, hardness, weight, and speed of the bullet. Bullets are usually made of an alloy of lead, which may also be covered in another metal—for example, copper or steel—or a material such as nylon. Bullet shape may also differ; the most common shape is round-nosed. Knowing the manufacturer of ammunition that was used in a crime may provide important investigative leads when searching a suspect's home or locating a possible source of the ammunition.

If the bullet is sufficiently intact, the firearms examiner can determine the rifling pattern on the bullet. The number, direction, pitch, and width of the grooves and lands on the bullet provide class characteristics that can be used for preliminary comparison of various bullets. These characteristics may also provide the identification of possible types of weapons that may have fired the bullet. The General Rifling Characteristics (GRC) index is a database that provides the rifling characteristics of common weapons. To find a match, examiners search the tables for the measured number and width of the individual lands and grooves within the measurement error rate. The table provides some common manufacturers of weapons that produce similar rifling patterns. These data can provide investigative leads to the police or eliminate weapons of record without a search.

It is the comparison of a fired bullet with a test fire from a weapon that constitutes the individualizing process in firearms examinations. When a weapon is submitted for analysis, the firearms expert first records all information about the weapon and checks the weapon and barrel for trace materials (e.g., blood, tissue, hair, DNA evidence, and fingerprints). Then the gun is checked to determine if it is operable, how much force is necessary to pull the trigger, and whether the safety lock functions properly. After all this, the examiner fires the weapon using the same or similar ammunition under controlled circumstances. The bullets are fired into a testing tank or trap that will not affect the markings on the bullet as it passes though the tank medium. (This often is water, but may be a different material.) The test bullets and the bullets recovered from the scene are then mounted on a comparison microscope. The examiner rotates the bullets to become familiar with their unique markings. Then the bullets are compared in a side-by-side examination of the unique and consistent markings created by the weapon. This can be a time-consuming and painstaking process. Modern comparison microscopes have digital imaging capabilities and enhanced lighting and other features. These allow for the storage of information and of the photographs that demonstrate the match. The skill and experience of the examiner, however, are the most important factors in a firearms examination. It takes a skilled and experienced analyst to conduct these comparisons so no errors are made.

Fired cartridge cases are also valuable for examination. When a semiautomatic or automatic weapon is used to fire a projectile, the ammunition cartridge case is ejected from the gun. A revolver retains cartridge cases, but these may be found on a suspect, in his home, or at a scene. As described above, class and individual markings transferred to this cartridge case can be used for identification and comparison. It should be noted that ammunition does not have to be fired for the transfer of tool marks to the cartridge to occur. The markings on cartridge cases can be striations that result from a scraping action in the weapon or they can be impression marks, which are caused when the cartridge case and the weapon impact each other because of the high-pressure force of discharge. Class and individual characteristics may be found on firing pin impressions, breech face marks, chamber marks, ejector marks, and extractor marks. The extent and usefulness of these marks is determined by the type of weapon, the type of ammunition, and whether the cartridge has been fired.

Striated action marks are produced when a cartridge has been loaded into and ejected from an automatic or repeating weapon. Chamber marks occur when a loaded or unloaded cartridge comes in contact with the flaws in the inner chamber surface. These marks are most prominent if the cartridge has been fired. Extractor marks are usually striations made when the hooklike extractor pulls the cartridge along until it is ejected. The ejector then expels the cartridge out of the chamber. Impact of the ejector with the cartridge case causes additional marks that can be striae or impressions and can be used for comparison purposes.

When the cartridge is fired, the impact of various parts of the weapon on the cartridge case causes impression marks. The most common of these are firing pin marks and breech face marks. When the firing pin strikes the primer of the cartridge case, it makes an impression, and the unique characteristics of the firing pin nose may be transferred to the primer area of the bullet. Sometimes the cartridge will not fire if there is a problem with the primer or if the firing pin does not strike with sufficient force to initiate the primer. In such cases, the firing pin impression may still be useful for comparison. The most common impression marks used in individualization are breech face marks on the base of the cartridge. When the cartridge case is slammed into the breech face because of the recoil force when a shot is fired, a negative impression is made of the breech face and its manufacturing flaws. As with individual rifling characteristics, the markings formed on the cartridge case may provide the basis for classification of a firearm or individualization of the evidence.

Macroscopic and microscopic comparison of bullets and cartridge cases can yield three possible results: an identification, an exclusion, or no conclusion. An identification, which is really an individualization, is a positive match between two ammunition components or between a component and a particular firearm. An exclusion definitively shows that the two items compared do not match.

If no conclusion can be reached, it means the firearms examiner has noted insufficient characteristics (either the quality or the quantity are lacking) for a match. While the expert may note similar class characteristics, it would be inappropriate to imply a stronger association than that the components are in the same class. Firearms examiners may also conduct testing to determine operability, gunshot residue, shot shell components, and trajectories.

NIBIN

The National Integrated Bullet Information Network is a program of the ATF. Through this program firearms laboratories are provided with equipment that allows them to view and store bullet and cartridge case markings as digital images. A firearms examiner is shown using the NIBIN system in figure 6.2. These images are automatically compared to determine possible association among evidence from different cases and jurisdictions. If similar bullets or cartridge cases are located in the database, the likely match candidates that

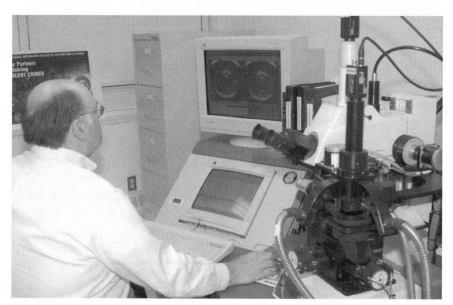

Fig. 6.2. A firearms examiner compares cartridge case markings using the NIBIN workstation.

possess similar markings are shown to the firearms expert. The examiner then conducts an examination of the actual evidence if a specific candidate appears to be a match based on the digital images.

As of summer 2008, more than 200 sites of 174 agencies have received NIBIN equipment. Because these organizations all provide data to the NIBIN system, it is possible to link cases that occur in various parts of the country. In many cases, law enforcement is provided with investigative information that would not be available any other way. For example, the snipers who operated near Washington, DC, in October 2002 were linked through this system to shootings elsewhere in the nation. Often, the only evidence at a shooting scene is a cartridge case that has been ejected from a gun. These shootings can now be associated through NIBIN, providing evidence of gang activities or serial assailants. Since the implementation of this program, more than 1.2 million pieces of firearms evidence have been entered into NIBIN and there have been nearly twenty-five thousand "hits" against the database.

TOOL MARK EVIDENCE

Firearms examiners also conduct other tool mark analysis. A tool mark is a cut, scrape, impression, or scratch caused by one surface coming in contact with another. The characteristics of the harder material are transferred to the softer surface. As with firearms, examination is based on the identification and comparison of class and individual characteristics of the tool. Characteristics such as the size, the shape of the working surface of the tool, and the distance between teeth of serrated tools are class characteristics that can be used to identify the type of tool used. For example, if the tool mark has a width of approximately one-quarter inch and the edge appears flat and even, pliers or a saw can be eliminated as having made that mark. Also as with firearms, the individual characteristics of a tool are created during the manufacturing process. Flaws and defects in the working surface of the tool will be unique to that object. In addition, use of the tool can alter its appearance, as with the chipped edge of a screwdriver.

One of the difficulties involved in matching a tool mark to a specific tool that is not a firearm is the variation of markings that are possible depending on how the tool is used. Factors such as the force applied and the angle at which the tool is used can affect which individual characteristics are present in the marking. The examiner, then, must experiment with various positions of the tool in order to obtain the proper patterns. Opponents of tool mark comparisons argue that this means different but similar tools could be used to produce the same markings, making a match useless. Experts respond by noting that if individual characteristics are examined, mistakes will not be made with individualization. Results may be inconclusive, but this will not falsely identify a tool and implicate the owner if tests are conducted properly.

The tool mark examiner can arrive at conclusions similar to those for firearms: A particular tool made the tool mark that was observed, the tool did not make the mark, or the test is inconclusive.

SHOOTING RECONSTRUCTION

When a shooting occurs, it is often necessary to determine who fired the shot and where the shooter was located relative to the victim when the shot was fired, or the distance of the weapon from the target. These determinations may help to prove or disprove a suspect's, victim's, or witness's account of a shooting or provide other important information to the investigation. Shooting reconstruction is another example of the teamwork that is vital to forensic investigation. Information from the investigators, the crime scene, the medical reports, the medical examiner, the laboratory examination of physical evidence, and the pattern documentation must all be considered in order to properly interpret the incident.

One consideration is the presence or absence of gunshot residue (GSR) on a shooter's hands or clothing. GSR is composed of minute quantities of materials from the primer and gunpowder that escape through openings in the weapon and from the muzzle. The vapor that contains these materials is deposited on nearby surfaces, usually including the hands, sleeves, and target surface. Typically, major components of gunshot residue that are used for identification are lead, antimony, and barium. Other components that are released upon firing a weapon—such as nitrates or nitrites, soot, and partially burned gunpowder—are useful for testing target surfaces for muzzle-to-target distance determination; however, these chemicals are too common to be of value as a screening test to indicate whether a particular individual fired a gun. (The old "paraffin test" that is sometimes described in detective stories was a screening test for nitrates/nitrites. The paraffin supposedly lifted the gunshot materials from the hands of the shooter and was then tested with a chemical that turned blue. Unfortunately, other materials also cause this change, so the test was abandoned in this form.)

The ASTM International guidelines indicate that the samples taken from the hands of a suspect should be subject to scanning electron microscope (SEM) examination and elemental analysis. The SEM will reveal the shape of minute particles that contain lead, barium, and antimony. The distinctive shape of these particles and the identification of the three elements provide evidence consistent with gunshot residue. It should be noted that a person can also have GSR on his hands from handling a recently fired gun or from being near a discharged weapon. The absence of gunshot residue is not definitive, either. Factors that affect the presence of gunshot residue on the hands include the amount of time between the shooting of a weapon and the taking of the samples and whether the person washed his hands or perspired a great deal. In one case, a woman was reportedly found by her husband with a gunshot wound. She was on the bed and the handgun was next to her. When he was tested for gunshot residue, his swabs were positive. This led to much speculation about whether his report of the incident was accurate. It was learned, however, that when the husband called 911, the dispatcher told him to move the gun. This action could have resulted in the GSR detected on his hands.

When GSR, soot, and unburned or partially burned gunpowder are deposited on a target surface, it may be possible to estimate the distance from which the shot was fired. Each weapon produces a somewhat consistent pattern of deposit of these materials depending on the type of weapon, barrel length, the type of ammunition, the type of target material, the angle of the shot, and several other factors. When the actual weapon is available, the examiner will conduct test fires from various distances into material similar to the target material of the crime. Those test fires are then examined for the distribution of GSR, both with and without chemical and alternate light enhancement. The GSR may be transferred to photographic paper or another surface for ease of examination and testing. The target material is also examined by the same methods.

The approximate distance of the end of the gun muzzle to the target may be determined by comparing the patterns of GSR distribution. The general patterns of gunshot residue may be described as follows:

1. *Contact, or "point blank."* If the gun is held against the target, soot will be visible around the bullet entrance hole. Few or no unburned or partially burned powder particles will be found on the surface of the target. The force of the gunshot will carry these materials into or through the target, creating tears and damage to the target.

2. *Close range.* If the gun is less than six inches from the target surface, residues will be deposited around the bullet hole. A dense soot pattern will be visible in this area. Other components will also be deposited in a tight pattern. The target surface will have little or no damage other than the bullet hole.

3. *Medium range.* As the distance from the target increases, so does the size of the gunshot pattern. If the gun is fired between one and three feet away from the target, visible deposits of partially burned or burned gunpowder, nitrates, and soot will be scattered around the entry hole. In general, as the distance increases, the pattern spreads out, and fewer particles are deposited on the target surface. The angle of the shot will have an effect on the distribution of these materials.

4. *Long range, or "distance shot."* If the gun is discharged more than five feet from the target, there usually are no detectable residues on the target surface. The GSR particles will fall off because of the force of gravity before they reach the target.

Even if no weapon is recovered, the approximations described above may be valuable to the investigation. In one case, a suspect in a shooting claimed that he was struggling with the victim, who pulled out a revolver, and the gun went off. Witnesses said the suspect was across the room when he shot the victim. An examination of the victim's jacket showed dense soot and particles in a small area around the bullet hole. The fibers around the hole were torn and burned. These facts clearly indicated that the witnesses were mistaken in their account of the incident.

The trajectory of the projectile from the time it leaves the weapon to when it hits the target can be crucial to some investigations. Trajectory determines the angle and direction of the projectile and the possible position of the shooter based on the examination of the bullet holes in a target. The angle of trajectory may be determined using rods or strings (the physical projection method) or through the use of lasers (the optical projection method). These methods are based on the fact that over short distances, the pathway of a projectile is a straight line. Whichever method is used, careful observation and documentation is necessary. Once the trajectory line has been established for a particular shot, the shooter theoretically could have been anywhere along this line. It is then that other information, such as observed GSR patterns, the height of the shooter, structures or topography in the area along the trajectory, and possible ways in which the weapon was held must be considered. For example, if there is no building or structure from which to fire, a shot that angles downward could be fired only from a location along the trajectory line that corresponds to the physical limitations of the human form. Figure 6.3 shows Lee and his team as they reconstruct the trajectory of a gunshot fired through a car window.

Sometimes, determining the bullet trajectory in a shooting case can assist in the identification of other important physical evidence. A victim was reported in an alley in a city that was plagued with shooting violence. The wounded boy died before he got to the hospital. No bullet was recovered from his wound during the autopsy. Describing the scene, witnesses indicated that the boy was running away when he was shot. Several guns were recovered from suspects, but they were of little use with no bullet for comparison. Henry Lee

Fig. 6.3. Dr. Henry Lee and the forensic team determine
the trajectory of a bullet fired into a moving vehicle.

returned with detectives to the scene and used a mannequin wearing
the victim's clothing and the entrance and exit wound information
from the medical examiner's report to mark the trajectory of the
bullet as it entered, passed through, and then exited the body.
Extending this trajectory by laser, the likely path of the bullet after
it left the victim's body was established. The area along this path
was searched, and a spent bullet was found near a brick building.
Although the bullet was slightly deformed, clear rifling characteristics were present. Arguments were made that the bullet could have
come from any number of shootings that had occurred recently or
from some unreported incident. At the laboratory, firearms examiners worked with criminalists to remove the trace materials caught
in the bullet. Several layers of fabric were noted and subsequently
shown to be similar to the layers of clothing the shooting victim was
wearing, in the correct sequence by type of fabric. By determining
the trajectory of the fatal bullet, valuable evidence was found that
could be conclusively linked to one of the guns.

One of the more controversial cases is the shooting of President
John F. Kennedy. Kennedy was assassinated in November 1963

while riding in a motorcade in Dallas. After more than forty years, there is still disagreement concerning the trajectory of the bullets fired and whether a single gunman, Lee Harvey Oswald, could have fired a shot from the book depository building that had sufficient power and trajectory to shoot both the president and Governor John Connally, who was injured in the incident. Both camps have used the Zapruder film, photographs of the assassination, and experiments to support their positions.

Immediately after the assassination, the Warren Commission determined that Oswald had acted alone. He fired three shots at the president in a downward direction: One shot missed and hit a curb, which was verified by damage to the area and injury to a nearby spectator; one shot, the most controversial, was fired at Kennedy's back and also wounded Connally; a third shot entered Kennedy's right temple and exited through his skull. One group of scientists has examined film and documentation of the shooting and has conducted numerous experiments that they state show the single-shooter theory is likely. Scientists reconstructed the bullet trajectories based on the injuries of the victims and the forensic findings. This reconstruction also supports the determination that the same bullet injured both Kennedy and Connally, which is also a point of controversy. More recent studies by the single-bullet theorists point out that Connally was in a position slightly lower and to the right of Kennedy, arguing that with his body in the particular position shown in the film, one bullet could have followed the pathway from the shot through the president into the governor's arm and through to his leg. Proponents of this reconstruction also rely on test results that demonstrate the effects such a trajectory would have on the condition and appearance of the type of ammunition.

The opposing theory states that it is physically impossible for one bullet to have traveled through Kennedy's upper back, travel upward and through his neck, deviate downward to the right, hit Connally in the back over his right armpit, tumble through his chest, exit at the right nipple, change course again into his right wrist, shatter the bone, exit, and enter his left thigh. After this extraordinary trajectory, that bullet then fell out of the thigh wound onto the gurney, where it was retrieved in "pristine condition." Figure 6.4 is

Fig. 6.4. Exhibit 399 of the Warren Commission, the so-called magic bullet that struck both President John F. Kennedy and Governor John Connally on November 22, 1963.

a close-up photograph from the Warren report of this bullet. This so-called magic bullet has been the basis of the multiple-shooter theory. Proponents of this theory also point to the Zapruder film, which appears to show the president moving against the direction of applied force as if the shot came from above and behind him. In a later reexamination of the evidence, most experts agreed that the shots that killed the president all came from a rear trajectory.

One noted exception was pathologist Cyril Wecht, who claimed the autopsy record and wounds received by Kenendy make this medically impossible. Wecht reported that, in his opinion, at least one bullet must have been fired from the right front (such as from the grassy knoll near Dealey Plaza) to cause the entrance and exit wounds to the skull. Recently, however, modeling techniques and 3-D computer animation were used to show the trajectories of the shots as proposed by the Warren Commission and how the single bullet did not have to be "magic" if the relative body positions and activities of the passengers in the car were taken into account during the trajectory determination.

It is unlikely that there will ever be a complete resolution of this case and it will continue to be revisited by forensic experts. If the bullet (Commission Exhibit 399) had been preserved in its original condition, modern DNA technology may have been able to provide a more conclusive answer to the dispute. If both Kennedy's and Connally's DNA were on the bullet, this would show that this bullet did in fact hit both men. If the DNA of only one of them was present on the bullet, this would prove otherwise. Unfortunately, there is no blood or tissue from the bullet that can be analyzed, and the dispute will continue unresolved.

As this example illustrates, the facts of a case can sometimes be interpreted in more than one way. There are often additional, unknown facts or factors, such as the movement or exact body position of a person at the time of a shooting, that cannot be determined in retrospect. When forensic examiners disagree in their interpretations of the facts, as in the Kennedy assassination, it is up to a jury or other appropriate panel to decide which is the most reasonable and likely scenario.

TWENTY-FIRST-CENTURY LEGAL CHALLENGES TO FIREARMS EXAMINATION

As discussed previously, firearms and tool mark evidence has been accepted in courts for almost a century. In previous decades, results and conclusions of this long-standing and widespread discipline were easily admitted during a trial. However, several significant challenges to traditional forensic evidence have put firearms and tool mark examiners on the defensive. Critics have closely evaluated the *Daubert* factors (scientific testing of the underlying theory, peer review, general acceptance, and potential or actual error rate) for tool mark identification and found it lacking. The responses of experts in the face of these challenges reveal to some critics the shaky foundation of firearms and tool mark testing methods.

Opponents of tool mark analysis include this discipline among the junk sciences of forensics. In contrast, many lawyers and judges, rightly or wrongly, use DNA analysis as the gold standard against which other forensic procedures are measured. They look at the application of the scientific method in forensic DNA analysis, how DNA procedures were developed and validated, and the statistical basis of the interpretation of results. Then they seek similar information from firearms experts. Articles in law journals and briefs written in support of motions to exclude forensic firearms evidence in courts have repeatedly pointed to several problems. The major issues fall into a few categories: whether tool mark examination is really scientific, the "absolute" identification of one tool to the exclusion of all others in the world, the failure to use statistics in tool mark comparisons, and the reliance on subjective visual examinations as the primary method to evaluate tool marks.

The most significant issue is the fact that a result depends on the experience and training of the firearms expert to identify class and individual characteristics. The AFTE Theory of Identification, also recently adopted as part of the Scientific and Technical Working Group for Firearms and Tool Marks (SWGGUN), states that each examiner must decide when there is sufficient agreement of tool marks "to constitute an identification." The theory goes on to state that identification is made when the agreement between two items "exceeds the best agreement demonstrated between tool marks known to have been produced by different tools and is consistent with agreement demonstrated by tool marks known to have been produced by the same tool." The theory continues: "That 'sufficient agreement' exists between two tool marks means that the agreement is of a quantity and quality that the likelihood another tool could have made the mark is so remote as to be considered a practical impossibility." It is clear that under this policy, visual examination of the tool and the tool marks is the primary method of analysis.

Critics claim that visual examination means the process is totally subjective, and that courts should bar its use. They point out that tool mark comparisons have no basis in statistics and there is no database that can be used to determine the occurrence of those characteristics among the tool marks (as there is for DNA). So how can the relevance of a match be determined? Firearms experts point out that individual characteristics of tool marks are unique, so their occurrence is just that—unique! In addition, the examinations are not totally "subjective" because measurable objective characteristics are looked at, and those marks are evaluated by a trained specialist. While it is true that every firearm or tool ever made has not been tested and compared to others of the same type, the unique nature of the markings makes the comparison a "practical identity." Some examiners testify that this means a certain tool made the markings "to the exclusion of all other such tools in the world," but clearly this statement is a stretch of the Identification Theory, and the difference between practical and absolute identity should be pointed out to a jury.

Nevertheless, the firearm and tool mark examiner cannot escape the fact that her training and experience are the authority behind the conclusions reached. Throughout the history of forensic science, experts in each discipline, including firearms and tool marks, have conducted improper examinations and reached erroneous conclusions. Look at the case that brought Waite to the study of firearms! However, when a *competent* firearms examiner completes an examination, isn't that result reliable and valuable? Should the test results be excluded simply because attorneys are not comfortable with relying on the subjective evaluation of objective characteristics? Ultimately, the issue lies in the court's ability to distinguish between well-trained analysts who use appropriate procedures and draw well-founded, unbiased conclusions from those who don't use acceptable methods and are not objective in their approach to their work. This means that judges and attorneys must ask about the training, experience, and proficiency testing of experts before they testify. Officers of the court must themselves work with AFTE members and other tool mark examiners to learn about the training and experience each competent examiner should have.

FIREARMS AND TOOL MARK EXAMINER TRAINING

It is apparent that the accuracy of a tool mark comparison ultimately depends on the examiner's ability to determine class, subclass, and individual characteristics. This requires extensive training in the examination of firearms, ammunition, and ammunition components. As with any scientific training, theory and background information must also be studied. Thorough knowledge of the workings of firearms is essential. Hands-on evaluation of numerous types of spent bullets and cartridge cases from known guns is necessary before any comparison of evidence can be attempted. Some of this information can be gained from careful study in college courses, workshops, or tutorials. Online or computer-assisted training modules are also available from several sources. The majority of the experience must be gained from actual examination of the guns, tools, and markings in a laboratory. This also must be done under the tutelage of a recognized, experienced firearms and tool mark expert. The AFTE has an extensive training manual that outlines the recommended course of study for becoming a firearms examiner. No minimum training time is required, but a two-year apprenticeship is typical. This training must include written and oral examinations and competency/proficiency testing.

In the past, most firearms examiners were police officers or government agents who had a working knowledge of weapons. Some were gunsmiths, armorers, and manufacturers. At present, firearms and tool mark examiners are not required to hold a college degree, although it is highly encouraged, and experience with firearms can substitute for academic training. Today, many students who major in forensic science in college have an interest in becoming firearms and tool mark examiners. Their background in the scientific method, quality assurance, and other general aspects of the field are valuable. Many of these students do not have the essential knowledge of weapons and ammunition, however, and require more extensive training in that area before they can do casework. Because of the lack of trained firearms and tool mark examiners to fill current open positions, the ATF, local forensic organizations, and laboratories have developed various accelerated training programs to fill this critical need.

Both the AFTE and SWGGUN recognize the need for the continued education and proficiency testing of qualified examiners. Recommendations for continuing education and training include both classroom and meeting experiences. The AFTE has a comprehensive scientific program at each annual meeting and a peer-reviewed journal that has a long history of publishing the latest in research and case studies. Curiosity and discipline are necessary to achieve a basic level of training and to remain current in this discipline.

Chapter Seven

TRACE EVIDENCE AND CHEMICAL ANALYSIS

I n more and more cases, trace and transfer evidence have proved to be the linchpin that convinced a jury. These types of evidence have been particularly important when no valuable DNA evidence has been found. Dr. Henry Lee and Elaine Pagliaro can recall many cases in which the trace and transfer evidence were crucial to cracking the case. One case especially comes to mind.

On a cool spring morning in 1985, a jogger was running through the local baseball park in West Haven, Connecticut. He saw a person lying on the grass and went over to see if he could help. What he found was the body of a woman, face down and cold. When police arrived, they noted little disturbance in the area. The woman, who was wearing a jogging outfit, was not known to the police. Lee and the medical examiner were called to the scene. When Lee arrived he noted a large stain on the woman's pants. He also warned detectives about disturbing the trace evidence on the body. A large number of fibers and some other debris were on the rear of the pants, fibers that could not have come from the grassy area where the body was found.

There were no signs of injury—no stab wounds, bullet holes, or strangulation marks on her neck. The detectives suggested that perhaps she had collapsed while jogging earlier in the morning. Lee thought foul play was likely for two reasons: First, the condition and location of her body suggested that she was placed in the spot where she was found; and second, her clothing was damp and the outline of her body was clearly visible in the early morning frost when her arm was lifted. She had been in this field for many hours. After thorough documentation, some of the fibers on her clothes were collected and brought to the forensic laboratory so they could be analyzed. Meanwhile, police began searching for witnesses and inquiring whether any missing-persons reports were filed or if any suspicious activity was noted in the area.

Later that day, the police heard of reports about Connie Bova, a young woman from another town who had not reported for work. Her husband, Mark, stated that Connie left for the store and he hadn't seen her since. Her car was not at home; police subsequently found it in the parking lot of a store in West Haven. Had Connie been abducted from the store lot? Police were puzzled. Family insisted that Connie, who was meticulous about her appearance, would never have left home to go shopping in a jogging outfit. Mark's story did not add up, and police began to suspect he had killed his wife and dumped her body in the field. But what evidence would be available to link him to the crime? Only Mark's and Connie's fingerprints were in the car, but the lack of other evidence was not probable cause.

At the laboratory Lee, Pagliaro, and their coworkers examined the victim's clothing and autopsy samples for clues. Biological stains were found on her shirt. The stains were identified as human saliva, but the genetic markers matched Connie's. No tissue or identifiable material was found under her fingernails. Numerous fibers were still on the pants; hundreds of gold-colored fibers were found, mostly on the back of her pants. Hundreds more were on her sweatshirt. Pagliaro put the fibers under a polarizing light microscope and found they all were nylon, with similar structure and color. To verify that the nylons were chemically the same, infrared analysis was conducted on representative fibers. When the testing was completed, it was clear that the police should seek out a possible source for almost one thousand gold-colored carpet fibers. Lee hypothesized that the transfer of such a large number of fibers could indicate a struggle on that gold carpet. Lab scientists also found a large number of small wood particles. Microscopic examination showed that these wood particles were not bits of twigs from the ground, but were consistent with chips and fragments of wood.

Police obtained a search warrant for the Bova home, where there were no evident signs of a struggle. No damage to any of the furniture or walls was observed. What detectives did notice was the gold carpet in the master bedroom. Samples of this carpet were collected as comparison standards for the laboratory. Wood and sawdust were noted in the garage, so detectives also collected some of these materials. When the car was searched, additional wood fragments were found on the driver's-side seat and carpet areas.

The carpet fibers from the Bova home were microscopically and instrumentally similar to the fibers on Connie's clothing, providing another link to the home. Mark Bova explained away the fibers by telling police that Connie often did her exercises on the carpet. The wood chips from the clothes, car, and garage were sent to Dr. Bruce Hoadley, a wood expert who had worked with the forensic lab on several other cases, including the reexamination of the Lindbergh baby case. Hoadley was asked to compare the types of wood in the evidence with the known sample collected from the Bova garage. During microscopic study of the wood, Hoadley found that several pieces had greenish-colored deposits, which looked to him like the stamp that is placed on wood when it is pressure treated. The criminalists at the laboratory compared the colored material on the three samples using a visible spectrophotometer and found that the instrumental color characteristics were identical. At some point in time, Connie Bova's back and buttocks had come in contact with the wood debris that was on the floor in her garage. Those same wood fragments had transferred to the driver's side of her car. Lee proposed that this occurred when Connie's body was transported to the secondary crime scene in West Haven.

With physical evidence showing that the house was the primary crime scene, investigators continued to build the case against Mark Bova. Some time later, Mark's ex-girlfriend went to the police and told them that she had witnessed Mark killing his wife. In fact, she said, they took turns holding a pillow over Connie's face until she stopped breathing. Mark then moved the body into the garage, where he put Connie into her car, brought her body to West Haven, and then left her car in the parking lot. The ex-girlfriend said she had also helped to clean up and get rid of some evidence. At the time, she and Bova were having a romantic relationship, but now he had another girlfriend and his ex wanted to tell all.

Mark Bova was indicted for the murder of his wife, and he was later convicted. His ex-girlfriend pled guilty to conspiracy to commit murder and tampering with evidence. Without the trace evidence to link the victim to the primary crime scene, this case would probably have remained unsolved.

CHEMICAL AND MATERIAL ANALYSIS METHODS

Microscopy

A large number of chemicals and materials are encountered by each of us every day. At one time, most materials were natural substances or relatively simple derivatives of natural materials. As science began to develop synthetics, the nature and appearance of objects, clothing, transportation, and many other things became increasingly varied. Modern manufacturing techniques have allowed the creation of many items in large numbers and for uses that previously were unimaginable. At the same time, scientists have been developing analytical methods beyond the wet-chemistry bench methods that were used in most labs at the end of the nineteenth and the beginning of the twentieth century.

The microscope was the first tool widely utilized in forensic science. This instrument was used to magnify and examine physical characteristics of objects, such as spent bullets (see chapter 6). Lower-magnification scopes, sometimes called stereoscopes, let the scientist examine hair roots, fabric, surfaces of materials, and other objects at five to two hundred times their actual size. This level of magnification is sufficient to provide a clear view of characteristic edges, surface composition, and some detail for the classification of materials. The higher magnifications—40× to 1000×—of the compound microscope allow for the examination in greater detail or the identification of minute components and materials. Tissues may be examined for type and damage, as in histology and pathology. The absolute identification of semen, for example, is easily accomplished through the microscopic identification of spermatozoa.

The microscope also allows the observation of chemical reactions on a small scale, limiting the amount of evidence that must be consumed by a test. In the forensic lab, microchemical testing has been applied in the analysis of drugs, blood, body fluids, soils, paint, and any number of other substances. A small particle of an unknown substance can be classified or identified by placing it on a glass slide and adding a drop of chemical reagent to it; the observed reaction will tell the scientists something about the chemical nature of the substance on the slide. Characteristic crystals that form as a result of mixing known reagents with the evidence, for example, are still used as a test for some drugs or explosives. The polarized light microscope (PLM) is especially useful in identifying fibers, plastics, crystals, minerals, drugs, chemicals, and other substances based on their optical and microscopic properties. A skilled microscopist can often reliably identify a substance using PLM in a very short period of time.

The scanning electron microscope is a very powerful microscope that uses an electron beam instead of light to visualize samples. Materials can be magnified thousands of times to reveal particles that are not visible with the unaided eye and even details of the structure of the material. This type of microscope is also used in industry, by museum conservationists, and by many other types of scientists. In one homicide case, an SEM was used to reveal the microscopic structures of algae on a suspect's T-shirt, which was washed out in a pond near the victim's home. When the SEM also has elemental analysis capabilities, the elemental composition of individual particles may be determined. While it is often used for the analysis of gunshot residues, scientists can also use this method to analyze paints, metals, and many other materials. The ability to "map" the presence of particular elements in the layers of a paint chip or a fragment of metal, for example, is useful for classification and comparison of these materials. Other adaptations of the microscope in its various forms are used for multiple purposes in the modern forensic laboratory.

Undoubtedly one of the most influential forensic scientists of the past fifty years was Dr. Walter McCrone, the "father of modern microscopy." At the time of his death at age eighty-six, McCrone had instructed more than twenty thousand students in the art of microscopy. Those students are now leaders in the application of microscopy in the fields of environmental analysis, forensic trace evidence analysis, art conservation, museum conservatorship, pharmaceuticals, engineering, as well as anywhere that material particle testing is necessary. McCrone did not start out using a microscope, but had a rather traditional background in chemistry as an undergraduate student. During his doctoral studies at Cornell University, McCrone was inspired by another great microscopist, Émile Chamot, and became fascinated with the value of microscopy in the analysis of organic materials. After receiving his doctorate in organic chemistry in 1942, he accepted a position as a microscopist and materials scientist at Armour Research Foundation.

It was the creation of the McCrone Institute in 1956, however, that really brought McCrone's enthusiasm and knowledge to the forensic community. The institute conducted microscopical analysis for businesses, museums, art collectors, and law enforcement agencies. In addition, McCrone traveled the country teaching forensic scientists and others the proper use and value of the microscope in chemical analysis. His enthusiasm extended to the microscopic slides containing the many collections of reference materials that he himself compiled. He relished telling students in his classes of the samples he retrieved from the air conditioner filters of hotels he stayed in across the country! McCrone applied his skills as a microscopist to a number of famous forensic cases, including the Shroud of Turin (McCrone insisted his findings showed the shroud was a painting and not blood), the Vinland map (a forgery), Beethoven's hair (McCrone discovered lead poisoning), and numerous paintings by great masters (some authentic, some forgeries).

As instrumental analysis became more affordable and accessible to crime labs, McCrone touted the value of microscopic examinations and urged its use by scientists. As stressed by his admirers and colleagues after his death, McCrone devoted his professional life to the use of the microscope in modern analysis and teaching chemical microscopy, even as others dismissed it. During his more than sixty years as a chemical microscopist, McCrone published more than six hundred technical papers and sixteen books and chapters. Every forensic microscopist has the particle atlas or another McCrone work at her desk. His forensic legacy is still carried on by many of his students, including Dr. John Reffner, Dr. David Stoney, Dr. Thom Kubic, Skip Palenik, and Dr. Thom Hopen, and by the three separate McCrone organizations, one of which still provides teaching, training, and research in applied microscopy.

Chromatography

Chromatography is a process that separates mixtures into their separate components. In general, this separation involves a "moving" phase, which carries and separates the molecules, and a "stationary" phase. For example, in paper chromatography, the paper is the stationary phase. The sample, such as ink, is spotted on the paper. The solvent liquid moves up the paper, carrying the soluble ink components with it. The relative distance a sample component travels or the time it takes to separate and be detected by an instrument is a useful chromatographic characteristic. Thin-layer, gas, and liquid chromatography are commonly used in forensics. Because chromatography separates components of mixtures, instrumental chromatography is often linked to other instruments for identification of the separated component molecules.

Chromatography may also be used as a preliminary identification or comparison tool. For many years drug laboratories ran samples of known drugs spotted on a thin layer of silica gel on a glass plate. An unknown evidence sample from a drug case was also put on the plate. After a solvent moved up the plate, the distance the evidence sample traveled was compared to the travel of the known drugs. This resulted in a tentative identification of the evidence. (Thin-layer chromatography is seldom used for drug analysis in forensic labs at the present time and has been replaced by instru-

Fig. 7.1. The car fire shown was set using snack food as ignition material. As seen in the last panel, these fatty chips will sustain a fire without additional accelerant.

mental or chemical assay techniques.) Similarly, when a gas chromatograph (GC) is used under specific laboratory conditions, a known hydrocarbon takes a certain amount of time to leave the column and be detected by the instrument (retention time). If a seized-evidence sample is run in the GC and takes the same amount of time, this is a preliminary identification of the chemical in the evidence. Because other substances may leave the GC after the same amount of time, however, this preliminary identification must be confirmed using a more specific method, such as mass spectrometry. Samples from a fire scene, such as that depicted in figure 7.1, are commonly analyzed by gas chromatography.

SPECTROSCOPY

When a chemical substance is exposed to energy, that energy affects the molecules in various ways, depending on the wavelength or type of electromagnetic radiation used. This interaction results in a characteristic pattern for a specific compound. Spectroscopy is the study of these patterns. When infrared radiation is absorbed by a polyester sample, for example, the specific pattern in what is called the "fingerprint region" of that spectrum tells the analyst that the sample is polyester. In addition, other peaks on the spectrograph correspond to different types of chemical bonds in the molecules. This also helps the scientist classify the substance and figure out what material is present. The identification process works best if the sample is relatively pure.

In the 1980s, spectrometers were micronized, meaning a sensitive instrument was hooked up to a microscope, allowing minute particles of material to be examined. Previously, larger and more pure samples had been necessary, and these were often not available as forensic evidence. And testing had required time-consuming preparation. The appearance of microspectrophotometers meant that the small amounts of materials—trace evidence—that are often encountered in forensic cases could easily be analyzed. Computerized libraries containing thousands of reference samples can now be purchased, providing a fast way to identify an unknown material.

Spectroscopy can also be applied as a tool for comparison if the sample is a mixture, such as paint. With these types of complex materials, a microscopic Fourier transform infrared spectrometer (FTIR) can be used to obtain a spectrum of an unknown sample such as a paint chip taken from the clothing of a hit-and-run victim. A known sample of paint collected from the suspected vehicle is then tested and the two spectra compared. If the samples have the same layer and color structure but do not have the same infrared spectra, the forensic examiner can conclude that the car tested was not the source of the hit-and-run sample. If the two spectra are very similar, however, the scientist can conclude that the car tested is a *possible* source of the questioned evidence. FTIR is such a valuable tool for paint comparison that a national automobile paint database has been established. Scientists can search the database for similar paints when there is a victim and no known vehicle. In one case, a young boy was hit by a car while riding his bicycle. A large paint smear was found on the bike and an FTIR spectrum obtained. When the database was searched, the paint was similar to a 1988 Jeep product. This provided an investigative lead to the police, who then questioned owners of red 1988 Jeeps who lived in the area. One of the red Jeep owners questioned confessed to the hit-and-run.

Another microscopic adaptation of a spectrometer is the ultraviolet-visible microspectrophotometer. As with the FTIR, the microscopic sample is irradiated with energy, in this case light across the spectrum, from the infrared through visible to ultraviolet light. Micro UV-VIS analysis has proven to be particularly useful in the comparison of colored materials. If two dyed-red nylon fibers are from the same source, the absorbance (or transmittance) spectra of these two red dyes should be similar. Even subtle differences can be detected by this instrument; if the spectra are not similar, the examiner can state the two samples are mutually exclusive.

Mass spectrometry is an instrumental technique that fragments gaseous molecules into ions by bombarding them with high energy. The mass of each ion is determined as they are separated. Knowing the mass of the ions, the scientist can identify the original molecule that was present. This is a highly valuable tool in the analysis of chemical mixtures. The mass spec is usually linked to another instrument such as a gas or liquid chromatograph that will separate the mixture, allowing each component to be analyzed and identified individually by the mass spec.

TRACE AND TRANSFER EVIDENCE

Forensic scientists encounter a large number of materials in casework. These materials are often unknown and must be identified through a series of steps, depending on the nature of the material. Evidentiary materials are often transferred from one source to another (hence the term "transfer evidence") or they are present in small size or quantity ("trace evidence"). Through the use of the tools described above, the forensic chemist or trace evidence analyst is able to compare characteristics of evidence and reference samples.

The most common types of trace or transfer evidence encountered in the forensic lab are hairs and fibers. These may be found at the scene, on the victim, on the suspect, or at another significant location. While seldom individualizing, such analyses often provide valuable circumstantial evidence to support an investigative hypothesis or eliminate possible associations in a case.

Hairs

Mammals have hair. Hair is a structure that grows out of the dermis in the hair follicle. Only the root of a hair, which is in the follicle, is living tissue. If an actively growing hair (anagen phase) is removed from the skin, a large amount of tissue from the follicle will adhere to the hair. Hairs that have stopped growing (catagen phase) have irregular roots. Hairs that are ready to fall out naturally (telogen phase) usually have a bulb-shaped root with little cellular material. If a hair root with sufficient cells is tested, nuclear DNA analysis can associate that hair with an individual. If insufficient cells are present or there is no root, the hair shaft must be examined.

The remainder of the hair, the hair shaft, consists primarily of the protein keratin, which is organized in three major areas, as shown in figure 7.2:

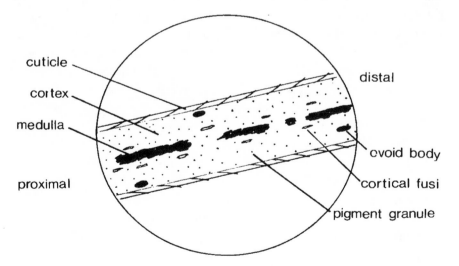

Fig. 7.2. A cross-sectional representation of a hair.
Major portions of the hair and inclusions are highlighted.

1. *Cuticle (outer layer)*. The cuticle of the hair consists of over-lapping scales that point toward the tip of the hair. Cuticle scales may be irregular (imbricate), as in humans, or they may have characteristic patterns (petal, coronal, etc.). Scale patterns may be useful in identifying the type of animal from which the hair originated.
2. *Cortex (middle layer)*. The cortex is composed of elongated cells. This portion of the hair may contain several types of inclusions, such as pigment granules, cortical fusi (air spaces), and ovoid bodies (oval pigmented structures).
3. *Medulla (innermost layer)*. The medulla may or may not be present in a hair. When present, it may have no definite form (amorphous) or be very structured, as in many animal hairs. It may be opaque or translucent. The medulla may also be continuous, discontinuous, or fragmented. These characteristics vary both from species to species and from individual to individual. In animal hairs, the medulla generally is a much greater ratio of the hair diameter than human hairs and may be useful for species identification.

The microscopic examination of a hair may yield information as to the type and arrangement of these components along the hair shaft. Animal hairs can be identified and may be useful for linking the evidence to a location. Human hair characteristics can be examined for an indication of the location on the body from which the hair originated (somatic) and possible ethnic (biogeographical) origin of the hair donor. Because hairs are individual structures produced by a living organism, no two hairs will be identical. In fact, because hairs grow over time, different portions of the same hair may appear markedly different. In addition, physical condition, diet, chemical treatment, and environment may also affect the formation of hair characteristics. This means it is not possible to absolutely identify the individual source of a hair through microscopic examination; a hair can be excluded as coming from a particular source by this method, however.

Microscopic hair examination and comparison to known samples is conducted using a comparison microscope, typically at magnifications of 40× to 400×. Hairs of the same somatic origin are compared side by side. If no significant differences are noted between the known and the questioned hair, the examiner can conclude that the known person is included in the possible sources of the questioned hair. If significant differences are noted, that person may be excluded as a source of the hair. Hair comparison can be a time-consuming process when done correctly by a trained examiner, but the quality of the analysis depends on the training and experience of the trace analyst.

Microscopical hair comparisons have come under legal attack as subjective analysis that is highly suspect, for many of the same reasons as firearms evidence (discussed in chapter 6). Some infamous cases of poorly trained individuals drawing improper conclusions have brought these challenges to the forefront. However, a well-trained forensic hair expert can provide valuable circumstantial evidence, particularly when it comes to excluding potential sources.

If a hair is not excluded by microscopic examination and there is no root tissue for nuclear DNA testing, mitochondrial DNA (mtDNA) analysis can be carried out on the hair shaft. In cases where the hair evidence is critical, mtDNA should be conducted whenever possible. It should be noted that mtDNA testing is not individualizing. (For more about DNA, see chapter 8.)

Fiber Evidence

Sometimes portions of fabric are collected as evidence. When this is the case, in addition to the fiber content, the weave pattern of the fabric, the cut or torn edges, and the overall composition are examined. It may be possible to physically match a piece of fabric with the original source. If threads are located, the number of strands composing the thread and the direction of twist are important characteristics. Evidence fibers are usually found as individual fragments among the materials collected at a scene or from clothing. The amount of fiber present varies depending on the nature of the fiber, the material from which it is originated, whether the fibers were released as a result of damage to fabric, and the nature of the contact causing the transfer. The examination of these fibers includes determining the class of fiber, its structural and optical characteristics, its chemical composition, and the nature of its dyes or inclusions.

Fibers fall into three general categories: natural, regenerated, or synthetic.

1. *Natural fibers.* These may be of plant, animal, or mineral origin. Asbestos is a natural mineral fiber that once was used as insulation in furnaces and safes, and around pipes, as well as in other building materials. While it is an important fiber for environmental protection and worker compensation investigations, most crime laboratories seldom encounter this fiber. Numerous plants are used for their strong fibers that are woven into clothing and used for materials such as ropes, carpets, padding, twine, and other materials. The most common fiber encountered in the forensic laboratory is white cotton. In recent years, natural plant fibers have become more common, and many more exotic materials, such as bamboo, are being used for clothing. Animal wools have been used for centuries. Hair from sheep, goats, alpacas, and other long-haired animals can be found in natural form or dyed in clothing, blankets, upholstery, and carpets. While not as common as in the past, fur coats, hats, rugs, furniture, and other items may also be sources of natural fibers in evidence.

2. *Regenerated fibers.* The first manufactured fibers were regenerated fibers such as rayon and acetate. These fibers are formed when dissolved plant materials are reformed into fibers with slightly different physical properties than their natural counterpart. For many years rayon was used primarily in manufacturing other products, but it has again become popular for clothing in recent years.

3. *Synthetic fibers.* The creation of synthetic fibers in the 1930s brought versatility and affordability to manufacturers. Nylon, the first commercial synthetic material, was useful as a substitute for silk. Numerous forms of nylon have since been developed, as have many other different synthetic fibers. Because synthetic fibers are often extruded through a die, the fiber can have any cross-sectional shape that adds to its sta-

bility, strength, or appearance. Two types of synthetic or two colors of the same material can be extruded together to produce compound fibers. There literally are thousands of synthetic fibers used for myriad purposes. Common evidence fibers include nylon (carpets), polyester (clothing, bedding), polypropylene (indoor-outdoor carpet), olefin (mats, carpets), and fiberglass (insulation).

As with hair analysis, fiber analysis begins with an examination of the visible characteristics of the fiber. The color, length, diameter, twist, and other characteristics are noted. Then a microscope is used to classify the fiber. If the fiber is natural, microscopic examination is the only classification method that is of any real use. (Chemically, all common animal fibers, except for silk, are keratin; all plant fibers are cellulose.) Microscopic examination of synthetic fibers, especially when a polarized light microscope is used, can help to identify the type of fiber. Nylon, orlon, polyester, and the like all have characteristic optical properties. The color, cross-sectional appearance, and variation are all also noted.

The type of synthetic fiber can be identified by the FTIR spectrum since the synthetic fibers are made of chains of repeating chemical units that are cross-linked together. Those chemicals and the way they are linked produce an individual spectrum. If the spectrum is not readily identified, the library of possible sources can be searched. If a fiber is dyed, the dye can be analyzed using the microspectrophotometer. Other instrumental techniques may be useful for identification and comparison of fibers, depending on their structure and composition.

When crime scene investigators collect a set of known standard fibers, this sample is subjected to the same analysis as the unknown evidence sample. As with all microscopic examinations of multiple specimens, the use of a comparison microscope is recommended.

Fire Debris

Each year billions of dollars worth of property is destroyed by fire and explosion. Some of these are naturally occurring; in many cases, they are not. Fires are set for profit, personal motive, or emotional trigger. Fire investigators in those cases attempt to determine the cause of a fire through the examination of burn patterns and the analysis of materials found at the point of origin. Samples of the fire debris are collected from burned areas that look suspicious to the investigator based on their location or appearance. In some cases, dogs trained to detect flammable liquids may be brought to the scene. These dogs are trained to "alert" investigators when they smell an odor of an accelerant. Samples collected from the fire scene are placed in airtight containers (such as paint cans) to prevent any ignitable liquid that may be present from evaporating further.

At the laboratory, the scientist opens the can quickly to check the contents and attempts to detect an accelerant odor. An accelerant is a flammable/ignitable liquid or solid used to start or extend a fire. If an odor is strong, the examiner may heat the container to vaporize the flammable substance. A portion of the vapor from the can is then extracted with a syringe and injected into a gas chromatograph. The components of the vapor mixture will be separated in the column of the GC, exiting at different retention times. The resulting gas chromatogram may be compared to standard patterns of commonly used ignitable substances, such as gasoline or kerosene, or compared to possibilities stored in a library in the instrument.

In most instances, the forensic chemist extracts the residues of flammable liquids from the fire debris. This may be done directly by using a solvent or activated charcoal. If charcoal is used, a strip or tube of this material is suspended over the debris as it is heated to vaporize volatile materials. The charcoal absorbs the hydrocarbons in the vapors. The charcoal is later removed from the container and washed with a solvent to remove the vapor residues. After the solvent is evaporated, the liquid is injected into the GC for analysis.

The method of choice for most fire debris samples is the use of a GC attached to the mass spectrometer. As noted earlier, after each component of the sample mixture is separated, it is energized in the mass spec and forms characteristic ions. The scientist evaluates the data and determines if the chemical that is identified is flammable and if it is a characteristic component of a common accelerant, such as gasoline. It should be noted that the forensic chemist cannot ultimately state whether the ignitable liquid detected was, in fact, used as an accelerant. Flammable materials may have been present at the scene for other reasons. For example, if the fire was in a garage, gasoline may have been present in storage containers, in equipment, or from a previous spill. Scientists often work with investigators to collect flammable materials that were routinely stored at the site of a fire and samples of building materials from the scene that may break down during combustion.

Many laboratories use other instruments in the course of chemical and trace evidence analysis. X-ray diffraction, pyrolysis GC, and Raman spectroscopy are just a few of the applications of analytical chemistry that have proved useful in this forensic discipline. Many other materials may be analyzed in these units, including paints, glass, soil, explosives, and unknown substances.

TRAINING TO BE A FORENSIC TRACE ANALYST OR CHEMIST

Those interested in becoming forensic chemists must have an extensive background in chemistry and instrumental analysis. A degree in a subdiscipline of chemistry, chromatography, or forensic science provides a proper foundation for the routine chemical and instrumental tests these examiners conduct. For example, trainees in forensic chemistry typically spend months analyzing samples of known flammable liquids of different types that have been burned under conditions simulating a building fire.

Similar academic preparation is necessary to analyze trace evidence. Specific applications—such as SEM, PLM, and others—may be learned at the laboratory or through specialized forensic classes or workshops. However, proficiency when microscopic comparisons are the basis of conclusion, as with hairs and fibers, requires extensive training; for example, in a recent development program, an examiner spent eight months training daily on the microscopic characteristics and comparison of human hairs. Often trace analysts begin with one or two areas of specialization before gaining competency in additional subdisciplines.

Theoretical knowledge and practical application of the various instruments used must be second nature. Continuing education keeps analysts abreast of new instruments, techniques, and applications. As with all forensic disciplines, forensic chemists and trace analysts must conduct hands-on testing of mock case samples and demonstrate competency before assuming casework. Career-long continued proficiency testing in each of the subdisciplines in which casework is performed is standard.

Chapter Eight

DNA EVIDENCE

Dr. Henry Lee has asserted confidently that the greatest development of the past fifty years, which dramatically changed the face of forensic science, was the creation of "DNA fingerprinting." He has wondered if Sir Alec Jeffreys had any idea in 1984 of the impact he would have on forensics when he first applied his DNA techniques to criminal investigation in Leicestershire, England.

After Jeffreys's first use of DNA procedures, scientists modified and adapted other DNA technologies, and many cases have been solved using DNA typing in its various forms since 1983. Lee served on several DNA advisory boards as DNA-testing procedures were developed and applied in forensic cases in the United States. He also has overseen efforts in his own laboratory to retest evidence in unsolved homicides and sexual assaults using these new methods.

Lee has seen the concept of DNA seep into the fabric of everyday life and the awareness of every citizen. He even has a collection of "DNA" advertisements and materials to show this, including DNA perfume and beer! Lee also understands that this knowledge has brought a great responsibility on the part of the scientist to explain, in legal proceedings and other venues, the significance of DNA findings so that justice may be achieved for victims and suspects alike.

On the cold morning of November 22, 1983, the body of fifteen-year-old schoolgirl Lynda Mann, who had been reported missing the night before, was found in the village of Narborough in Leicestershire, England. The child had been raped and murdered. Her body was found at an area of the shire called the Black Pad, and the murderer soon was called the Black Pad Killer by the media. A semen sample taken from Lynda's body was analyzed using standard biological procedures available the time. These test results indicated that the semen came from a person with type-A blood. Additional markers called isoenzymes were also developed; these eliminated 90 percent of the adult male population as the source of the semen. Unfortunately, at that time there were no additional markers that could be used to identify a perpetrator. Police carried out an intense investigation, conducting thousands of interviews and following up hundreds of leads. Their investigation failed to provide additional leads in the case. Eventually, police checked the records of every person in the area who had ever been arrested for rape or an indecency charge and interviewed likely candidates. After months of extensive work, police had exhausted all leads. By April 1984 the case was officially cold.

Three years after Lynda's death, Dawn Ashworth, also fifteen, was found strangled and sexually assaulted in the same town. Her body was discovered on a path within sight of the previous crime scene. Semen samples recovered from Dawn's body revealed her attacker had the same blood type as Lynda's murderer. From the similar modus operandi and the genetic marker testing, it was likely that the same person committed both murders. Investigators developed a lead that brought a local man, Richard Buckland, to the attention of the police. Buckland was a seventeen-year-old porter at a local psychiatric hospital. When questioned, Buckland confessed and gave a graphic description of the crime, including details that had not been released to the public. He confessed to the murder of Dawn Ashworth, but insisted that he had not harmed Lynda Mann. He had blood type A, but police needed a stronger link for the trial.

A short time earlier, forensic scientists Dr. Peter Gill and Dr.

Dave Werrett had published an article with Jeffreys describing a possible method to use for DNA testing of forensic evidence. DNA had never been used for forensic casework, but the work of these scientists and the application of DNA fingerprinting in immigration cases showed that it had great potential for forensic casework. The police contacted Jeffreys and requested his assistance in proving Buckland was the Black Pad Killer. Jeffreys's tests proved that the two murders were indeed committed by the same man—but, to the dismay of the police, that man was not Buckland! This was the first time an innocent person was exonerated using DNA profiling.

Back at square one, the police decided to take an unprecedented step. The hunt was on to find the man whose DNA matched the semen found on the victims. In what is now called an intelligence-led or dragnet screening, police asked five thousand males between the ages of thirteen and thirty-four in three area towns in Leicestershire to cooperate with the investigation by providing blood or saliva samples for comparison to the evidence. Biological samples from those men who were the same blood type as the killers would be subjected to the new DNA fingerprinting. No matches were made. Police were perplexed—that is, until someone reported a suspicious conversation in a pub. It seems a man named Ian Kelly was overheard talking about posing as a friend, Colin Pitchfork, and giving a blood sample in his place while using a fake identity card. Reportedly, Pitchfork had also approached several men and offered to pay them to take his place during sample collection.

Police quickly located Pitchfork, who had actually been on the original list of arrestees police reviewed after Mann's murder, but he had been eliminated as a suspect because he had been caring for his baby the night of Mann's death. When questioned by the investigators, Pitchfork quickly confessed. The new blood sample police took from Pitchfork was tested. His DNA matched the semen profiles from both victims. In 1988 Colin Pitchfork was sentenced to life imprisonment for the murders of Dawn Ashworth and Lynn Mann.

FORENSIC BIOLOGY: HISTORICAL PERSPECTIVE

In 1901 Karl Landsteiner observed that when blood from some people was mixed with another person's blood, clumping of the blood occurred; however, when the same blood was mixed with samples from some other people, this did not cause the same reaction. What Landsteiner had discovered were the ABO blood groups: People were found to belong to one of four different groups (A, B, both A and B, or O) based on the reactions of their blood when mixed with known samples. This important discovery allowed medical personnel to transfuse blood into people who were wounded or undergoing surgery, which saved millions of lives. For his great discovery Landsteiner was awarded the Nobel Prize in Medicine in 1930. During the years that followed, scientists discovered that red blood cells contain many other molecular substances called antigens, such as Rhesus (Rh), that determine other blood groups. (Most adults know their ABO blood type and whether they are Rh positive or negative because it is important for medical purposes.) Because liquid blood is seldom found on significant evidence in criminal cases, Leone Lattes's 1913 discovery of a way to test the ABO blood type of a bloodstain was important. Lattes had discovered a valuable tool for investigators that could provide reliable results when the bloodstain was relatively fresh. Soon other tests for the detection of A, B, and H (present on type-O blood cells) antigens were developed. Most people were found to have soluble blood group antigens in their body fluids as well, so tests were developed in forensic labs to detect antigens in semen, saliva, and urine. These blood and body fluid tests were used routinely in forensic serology labs until the early 1990s.

During the 1940s and 1950s, scientists discovered numerous proteins and enzymes in blood cells and blood serum. Similar proteins were studied in other body fluids. Among these proteins were polymorphic enzymes (those that exist in various forms but carry out the same function). These are called isoenzymes. It was later discovered that the form(s) of an isoenzyme that a person has is inherited—different genes result in the production of different enzyme forms. In the 1960s, scientists in England developed tests that could distinguish these different isoenzymes in a blood or body fluid stain. The test, called electrophoresis, was based on the way the different protein forms move in an electric field. This test was also useful for separating serum proteins and the different forms of hemoglobin, such as fetal hemoglobin and the form that causes sickle cell disease. Because studies were done of various populations, forensic scientists could provide statistical estimates of how frequent a particular isoenzyme or other protein was in a chosen population.

The amount of stain available for testing may be very small in a forensic case, so criminalists next developed "multi" systems, in which two or three isoenzymes could be tested on the same sample. These procedures were somewhat controversial at the time, and many discussions and court arguments were held concerning the proper medium in which to conduct the separations. Isoenzyme and protein analysis allowed scientists to provide statistics that limited the population of possible sources to one in thousands or hundreds of thousands, depending on the number of enzymes tested and the types that were detected.

As discussed earlier, the world of forensic science was revolutionized in the 1980s with the discovery of DNA fingerprinting by Alec Jeffreys. Figure 8.1 shows the state of forensic biological analysis before and after the introduction of DNA testing. Jeffreys was a biochemist at the University of Leicester in England. On September 11, 1984, Jeffreys was reviewing some test results in a study on the protein myoglobin. The samples were a random grouping that was derived from animals, plants, and one of the technicians and her parents. In what he likes to call a "Eureka moment," Jeffreys noted that each sample on the X-ray had a unique banding pattern, and he realized he was looking at a DNA-based identification for each specimen. He called this pattern the "DNA fingerprint." The implications of this discovery were obvious to the research team—it could provide irrefutable evidence in paternity testing and criminal cases.

Jeffreys has said that many discoveries lend themselves to various applications, but scientific curiosity must be the basis behind the process. Soon the value of his discovery would be shown. Early the following year, a lawyer who had read about Jeffreys's findings

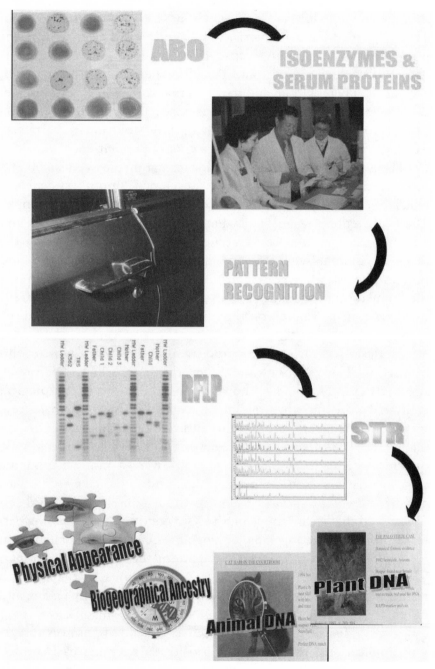

Fig. 8.1. The analysis of biological evidence before DNA (*top*) and subsequent to the introduction of RFLP DNA analysis.

called him concerning an immigration case. A boy who was a British subject, but had left the country for Ghana at an early age, was stopped by immigration officials when he tried to reenter England. His passport had been tampered with, and officials assumed he was a substitute for the actual holder of the passport. Traditional serology included the boy as a member of the family, but his actual relationship (for example, son, nephew) could not be positively determined. Jeffreys took blood from the boy's mother and three undisputed children (the father was not available) and compared their DNA with the boy's. His work showed that the boy was the child of the mother and father of her three other children with 99.9 percent certainty. The public loved the fact that this new DNA procedure saved a young boy from the injustice of deportation, and other immigration and paternity cases quickly followed.

In 1985 the German government asked Jeffreys to perform his test on the remains of a man from South America who had been identified as Dr. Josef Mengele, a notorious Nazi who conducted experiments on human subjects in Auschwitz during World War II. While forensic anthropologists and odontologists had determined that the man was indeed Mengele, these conclusions were disputed by some. The German government hoped this new test could satisfy the critics and close this chapter in the country's history. Jeffreys and a colleague extracted DNA from a femur. Blood from Mengele's son and his son's mother were compared to the bone DNA patterns. The conclusion was that it was a 99.94 percent certainty that the skeleton was Mengele's.

That same year, Jeffreys realized that modifications were necessary to enable the use of his DNA-testing procedure in forensic casework. Soon genetic profiling was developed, and it was quickly put to the test in the Narborough cases. Within a short time, the success of DNA profiling revolutionized the way biological samples were analyzed.

The first use of DNA fingerprinting in a criminal case in the United States was in Florida in 1987. The FBI Laboratory adapted the DNA procedures under the direction of Dr. Bruce Budowle and began taking DNA cases in 1989. In addition, the FBI started classes to teach the theory and DNA techniques to scientists from forensic laboratories across the country. Soon DNA profiling was conducted on many major cases, identifying suspects and exonerating those who were wrongly accused.

At about this same time, scientist Kary Mullis conceived the idea of copying DNA molecules in a mixture that mimicked the activity in the cell. This process, known as the polymerase chain reaction (PCR), allowed scientists to start with very small amounts of DNA and make exact copies, which could then be used to carry out various studies and diagnostic tests. Dr. Henry Erlich led the scientists at Cetus Corporation in developing Mullis's idea into the first commercial test for DNA based on the PCR process. This HLA-DQalpha test (now designated DQA1) was used in a 1986 civil paternity case, *State of Pennsylvania v. Pestinikas*, which was the first DNA case in the United States. Mullis was awarded a Nobel Prize for his discovery. PCR DNA testing has become a primary method employed in the fields of forensic science and medicine, medical research and diagnostics, anthropology, botany, and paternity testing, to name a few.

FORENSIC SEROLOGY

With the advent of DNA testing, some basic serological techniques (such as ABO blood typing) were discarded by forensic biologists. Today, serological analysis is generally limited to identifying the type of biological evidence present in a sample. This testing, however, is often necessary to prove the elements of crimes, such as sexual assault, and provides key information for the DNA analyst. Knowing the source of the DNA provides valuable information for a complete and proper interpretation of the DNA results. For example, if a body fluid is identified on the skin of a victim, whether that sample is human and, if so, whether it is saliva or semen will determine how it is extracted and its potential significance. After the type of biological material is identified, the evidence is individualized, or linked to (or excluded from) a particular person by DNA typing.

The process of analysis begins with recognizing and identifying the presence of biological evidence for further testing. A critical step in this process occurs even before the evidence is submitted to a laboratory, because the evidence can be contaminated and the DNA results affected if the evidence is not collected and stored properly. At the laboratory, various screening tests tell the scientist if a stain is blood, saliva, semen, and so on. Screening stains saves sample, time, and money. Stains that are negative for a body fluid are not usually tested for DNA. These screening tests are simple to use and very quick, but they are only preliminary tests. A confirmatory test must be performed to state conclusively that a particular body fluid is present. In most cases, confirmatory tests should be conducted by trained laboratory personnel. A body fluid stain should be individualized by DNA only after this conclusive identification, unless confirmatory testing will consume the specimen.

Reddish-brown stains that may be blood must be screened prior to DNA typing. Most screening tests for blood are color tests based on the ability of the heme portion of hemoglobin in the red blood cells to increase the rate of the release of oxygen from hydrogen peroxide. Various chemicals, such as o-tolidine, phenolphthalein (Kastle-Meyer), tetramethylbenzidine, and luminol have been used for this test. When these chemicals are applied to the test sample, they will change color if oxygen is released from the peroxide. (In the case of luminol, a pale bluish-green visible light results.) These tests are extremely sensitive. However, color changes may also occur with other substances besides blood; thus, a positive reaction indicates that the sample *could* be blood. A positive screening test should never be considered conclusive for the presence of blood. A confirmatory test is required to show that blood is present. At one time, microcrystal tests were used to confirm the presence of blood, but microcrystal tests do not indicate what kind of blood is present.

Today, the confirmatory test of choice in most forensic cases also determines if the blood is human. This can be done by testing for human hemoglobin. Manufactured test strips are used in most labs for this process. The stain is soaked in saline or a special solution supplied with the strips, after which a few drops are added to the strip. Within ten minutes, a human bloodstain will give a positive result. Scientists also like this test because it uses very little sample and is extremely sensitive. Sometimes a bloodlike stain is too small to do both this test and DNA analysis. At the present time, if no identification of the source of the stain is conducted, the DNA analyst can state that the DNA is human, since DNA profiles can be developed only from human DNA, but cannot state conclusively that the blood itself is human, as any source of human DNA may produce a profile.

Of all the body fluids, forensic serologists most frequently look for semen. Statistics show that the greatest number of crimes against persons in which evidence is subjected DNA testing are sexual assaults. Among the tests available for semen is color screening. The most common screening method for semen is the acid phosphatase (AP) test. Acid phosphatase is usually present in high levels in semen, but can also be found in other substances, such as plant matter, so the presence of semen in a stain must be confirmed. This is easily done by identifying spermatozoa using a microscope or by using test strips to detect the human seminal protein p30, also called prostate-specific antigen (PSA). This is very similar to the screening test done to determine the level of PSA in the serum of men to check for prostate cancer. Some laboratories skip the test for spermatozoa in stains before conducting DNA testing, believing that Y-chromosome DNA (discussed below) is all that is needed. The presence of the Y chromosome means the DNA is from a male, but does not show that semen is present. Since all cells from a male will have this chromosome, the limiting of testing to DNA alone may affect the charges in some sexual assault cases.

Tests may also be conducted to identify other biological substances, such as saliva, urine, gastric fluid, and fecal matter. After biological evidence has been characterized, DNA analysis may be conducted on that sample. Not every sample is subjected to DNA testing, however; for example, if a trail of bloodstains is found at a crime scene, the laboratory may test only a few of those stains, considering that the pattern indicates a single blood source. It should be noted that this practice also maintains the remainder of the samples for the opposition to test if they so desire. If the incident involves crimes against or injury to persons, the laboratory may require a known sample from those person(s), if they are known, for comparison to any DNA profiles developed from the evidence specimen.

The strength of DNA as evidence is based on its stability combined with the sensitivity and discriminating power of DNA analytical techniques. Only about 40 percent of forensic cases contain biological materials that may be suitable for DNA analysis, and not all DNA test results provide information that aids a case investigation. In those cases that have informative DNA results, however, the possibility of solving a case greatly increases.

FORENSIC DNA TYPING

DNA Typing Methods

DNA typing may be based on detecting differences in the DNA base sequence between two samples or on differences in length of portions of the DNA that result from the number of repeated units that appear in a row (tandem repeats). The number of repeated units at some specific region (locus) of the DNA can vary from person to person. DNA tests that detect such differences in length are currently the most common type of forensic DNA analysis.

Current DNA methods use PCR techniques. After the chosen portions of DNA are copied in a process called amplification, large amounts of DNA identical to the original are made, typically more than 1 million times the amount of DNA that was in the sample at the beginning. The original PCR tests, such as DQA1, were highly sensitive, but they did not have the discriminating power of the more involved DNA fingerprinting method, DNA restriction fragment length polymorphism (RFLP) analysis. The typical PCR method employed by the forensic community today amplifies and detects short tandem repeats (STRs). STRs at many loci (more than sixteen) can all be amplified in one tube at the same time, producing this powerful information using a minimal amount of sample and time. Because differences at many loci are tested for in each sample, STRs have great discriminating power. Most labs currently test at least the thirteen "core" loci, the STR loci that are included in CODIS. Figure 8.2 outlines the steps in a typical STR DNA analsyis. Modifications of STR techniques allow for the detection of minute quantities of

DNA from contact (sometimes referred to as "touch DNA" or "low copy number DNA" testing). These procedures often change the testing conditions so that more copies of the DNA are made. Such testing was conducted in 2008 in the JonBenét Ramsey case to confirm the presence of foreign male DNA that was not from Ramsey family members. The DNA profile from the same person was found in several locations on the victim's clothing using this technique.

STR typing can also be focused on the Y chromosome. This is an important forensic development because it makes it possible to obtain a DNA profile in samples that have a low concentration of male versus female cells. If there are many more female than male cells, the DNA profile from the female may be detected using standard STR testing. This may happen, for example, if a male touched the jacket of a female victim in an area that also contained her blood. By targeting only the Y chromosome during the amplification process, the female cells are ignored because they only contain X chromosomes. Y chromosomes are inherited from the father, and all males within a family blood line will have identical Y-STR profiles.

Forensic DNA Analysis

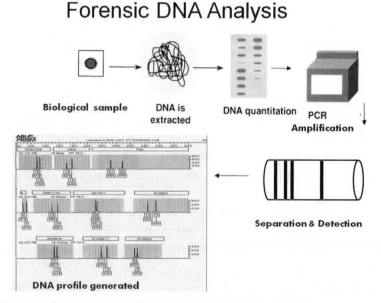

Fig. 8.2. The steps in the forensic DNA analysis of biological evidence.

This type of testing has been used to trace lineage in some famous cases, such as proving the descendants of Thomas Jefferson and Sally Hemings. Because the Y chromosome is passed down from the father, Y-STR DNA testing is not as discriminating as standard STR analysis; it is, however, becoming more common, and a reference database of Y-STR profiles from all over the United States is available online as a searchable listing for use by forensic DNA analysts.

Single base sequence differences called single-nucleotide polymorphisms (SNPs) have also been developed for use in forensic samples, but these tests are currently not part of the routine forensic testing conducted in most crime labs. SNPs are now a commonly used research tool for determining the genetic basis of disease and physiology.

While most of the DNA of forensic interest is in the nucleus of the cell, DNA is also found in the mitochondria (the source of energy production), which are plentiful in the cell. Mitochondrial DNA analysis has recently been added to the battery of forensic tests employed in the analysis of biological specimens. Mitochondria are inherited from the mother, so all offspring in a maternal line will have the same mtDNA. For example, your mother and your mother's sister have the same mtDNA, as do you and that aunt's children. Forensic scientists can test mtDNA in many types of samples that are not suitable for standard nuclear DNA analysis. These samples include hair shafts, old bones, and degraded DNA.

Typically, mtDNA typing involves PCR amplification followed by determination of the actual base sequence of the DNA. Mitochondrial DNA analysis of hair shafts has provided an additional objective test that can be applied to human hairs that could previously only be compared microscopically. Mitochondrial DNA analysis was first introduced in a US criminal trial in the summer of 1996 in *State of Tennessee v. Ware*, in which the FBI laboratory analyzed a hair found in the victim's throat and compared the results to those from the suspect's blood. Since then, more and more laboratories have started conducting mtDNA tests. In 2003 the FBI, in association with four states, established regional mtDNA laboratories, which made mitochondrial DNA testing more readily available across the country. One area in which mtDNA testing has been very useful is in the identification of unknown skeletal remains. The

Armed Forces Laboratory has used this technique to identify many previously unidentified remains of military personnel. The association of remains with missing persons through mtDNA testing is now a major focus of the FBI and the NIJ. Mitochondrial DNA sequences have been combined to establish the Missing Persons mtDNA Database. The sequences obtained from unidentified remains can be compared to a corresponding database of samples from family of missing persons or other sources to effect an identification.

Steps in DNA

No matter which of the DNA methods is used, certain steps must be followed for the proper isolation and typing of DNA. The following is a brief outline of those procedures.

1. *Documentation.* Before any sample is analyzed for a DNA profile, the nature of the evidence, its size, and other characteristics should be noted. This is particularly important with DNA and serological testing, because the evidence will be altered or consumed by the process. At times, the stain pattern may end up being more important than the actual DNA result.

2. *DNA extraction.* Most DNA analysis methods require the DNA to be isolated from the biological sample and then purified. Various procedures may be followed, all of which must protect against the contamination of the sample by other DNA that may be in the area or by other samples. Automated systems are employed in some labs for this step.

3. *DNA quantification.* In DNA casework, the forensic analyst must determine the quantity of human DNA in an unknown sample. This ensures that the proper amount of human DNA is used in subsequent steps and that the DNA that is being tested is, in fact, human.

4. *DNA amplification.* The DNA is amplified using PCR, which makes copies of the DNA in specific known regions. This process occurs in an instrument called a thermal cycler, which controls the heat and the environment of the test materials.

5. *Separation of amplified product.* Once the DNA is amplified, various techniques are used to separate the amplified products. Many of the current procedures use capillary electrophoresis to separate the products by size; others use mass spectrometry or microarrays to complete this process.

6. *Interpretation of results.* Depending on the method used, results may provide the sequence of the DNA segment amplified or the STR alleles present in that sample. Alleles are the different forms of the DNA that are present in the population.

INTERPRETATION OF DNA RESULTS

When DNA analysis is conducted in a forensic setting, the goal is usually to compare DNA profiles obtained from evidence to DNA profiles developed from known samples—the victim's, the suspect's, or that of another named source—and to determine if that individual could be the source of the evidence DNA. An example of a comparison of DNA profiles is shown in figure 8.3. Ultimately, when these comparisons are conducted, the DNA examiner can provide three basic interpretations:

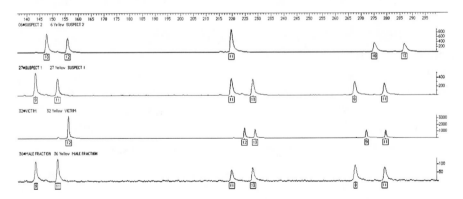

Fig. 8.3. An example of results obtained from PCR DNA analysis in a sexual assault case. Allele peaks were detected in samples from (*top to bottom*): Suspect #1, Suspect #2, Victim, and the evidence sample sperm portion.

1. *Inclusion.* DNA markers from the known source "K" are present in the evidence sample "Q." The conclusion is that person "K" could be the source of the DNA evidence. A statistic, based on the occurrence of each STR marker detected in the sample when compared to a database of known persons, is given that represents this probability.
2. *Exclusion.* DNA markers from the known source "K" are not present in the evidence or questioned sample. Therefore, person "K" could not be the source of the DNA from the evidence.
3. *Inconclusive.* No conclusion can be made as to a possible source of the DNA evidence. The results, if any are obtained, cannot be interpreted.

When the comparison results in an inclusion, or DNA match, the scientist must report a related statistic—how common or rare the evidence profile is. This statistic, called the random match probability, is based on the number of times a particular allele has been demonstrated in a tested population. Depending on the type and number of loci tested, this can be an extremely small number, for example, one in several million. Because of the publicity DNA testing has received, some people may think that if a DNA result is reported, this is conclusive proof that an individual commited a crime. However, the DNA result cannot in itself state anything about the importance of the result in a criminal case. For example, if a suspect's DNA is found at a crime scene, there is no way to determine when the biological sample was deposited. This evidence must be considered by the jury along with other important facts of the case relating to how the DNA evidence may have been produced. As the sensitivity of DNA testing increases and techniques to detect DNA present in extremely small quantities, such as touch DNA techniques, are applied to evidence, the interpretation of this data becomes more critical.

OFFENDER DATABASES

In 1990 the FBI Laboratory began a program called the Combined DNA Index System. This program provided software that enabled federal, state, and local laboratories to exchange and compare DNA profiles electronically. Within a very short time, most states passed laws that required certain convicted offenders to provide biological samples for DNA analysis and called for the creation of DNA databases against which profiles from cases with no suspect could be compared. The formation of the CODIS network represented a revolution in forensic science.

CODIS uses two main indices: the Forensic Index and the Offender Index. The Forensic Index contains DNA profiles from crime scene evidence. The Offender Index contains DNA profiles of individuals convicted of or arrested for various offenses defined by state and/or federal law. CODIS software enables local laboratories (LDIS) to feed DNA data electronically to a designated state laboratory (SDIS). Each state has an administrator who is responsible for maintaining the quality of the data in SDIS and sending the data into the national database (NDIS), which also receives DNA profiles analyzed by the FBI Laboratory. NDIS became fully operational in October 1998. As of October 2007, NDIS contained more than 5 million DNA offender profiles and two hundred thousand sample profiles in the Forensic Index. Federal law requires that the FBI ensure the quality of the DNA profiles included in NDIS and the privacy and security of the system.

When a DNA profile from an evidence sample is submitted to the Forensic Index, the evidence profile is compared to all the other profiles within the Forensic Index and also searched against the Offender Index. If CODIS software finds the same DNA profile in either index, it identifies the two profiles as a match, commonly called a "hit." After an offender hit, qualified laboratory personnel analyze the known DNA samples again to either confirm or refute the match. This confirmation is done to ensure that no problems or errors occurred that could have resulted in an incorrect DNA match. The verified DNA hit provides sufficient evidence to law enforcement to focus on a suspect in a previously unsolved case. Usually, law enforcement then obtains a second sample from the offender by search warrant; this sample is also tested to compare with the evidentiary samples. As the number of samples in the Offender Index increases, the number of hits against previously unsolved cases increases dramatically. If the hit is with another profile in the Forensic Index, this may provide valuable information to investigators by linking cases (even those in different states) that previously were not known to be associated and identifying serial cases. By comparing these cases and combining information, additional investigative leads may be developed that could solve these cases, even if the perpetrator is not initially identified.

As the offender/arrestee databases increase in size, new evidence-based issues arise. For example, should familial searches be allowed? In some cases, a search of the offender database does not result in an exact match, but the presence of an individual with many matching alleles may indicate that a close relative of the offender likely deposited the unknown sample. Familial leads could provide an important investigative tool for law enforcement. Detractors have questioned the value of this practice in light of the possible violations of the constitutional rights of family members.

CURRENT TRENDS IN DNA ANALYSIS

Recently, ethnic- or race-specific DNA markers have been used to provide investigative leads in several cases. By studying a set of DNA SNPs, the DNAPrint Genomics laboratory was able to assess the biogeographical ancestry of a suspect* in a ten-year-old sexual assault/murder case. Since the first widely publicized case of this kind in 2003, there has been much interest in biogeographical DNA testing by citizens and law enforcement alike. (In fact, any individual can contact DNAPrint Genomics or a similar company and have the laboratory provide an ethnic ancestry assessment.) This type of application of DNA typing clearly has its detractors among some scientists, privacy advocates, civil libertarians, and other individuals, who argue that there is great potential for abuse of this technology in the form of racial profiling. Other scientists have been concentrating their efforts on pigmentation and eye color genes as sources for investigative leads, believing that such a focus will provide less divisive and more practical information for investigators.

NONHUMAN DNA ANALYSIS

The DNA of dogs and cats has been characterized for breeding purposes and classification. Zoos and animal protection organizations use animal DNA profiling to limit harmful genes when mating endangered species. DNA typing has also been used to determine whether animals are new species or are members of a known, existing species.

Nonhuman DNA has also played a significant role in several criminal cases. Cases have been reported in which DNA profiling of animal hairs were used to link the suspect with the crime. Plant material profiles have been compared to link a suspect to the location where a body was found. Studies have also been conducted to link large caches of illegal plants, such as marijuana, with each other, resulting in more severe charges against drug dealers. While nonhuman DNA seems like a good tool to provide valuable circumstantial evidence in difficult cases, some courts have rejected the use of this testing during trial because of the lack of appropriate databases or the inability to determine the significance of a match. Even in jurisdictions where animal or plant data are not admitted in court, these nonhuman DNA tests may still provide valuable information to investigators.

THE INNOCENCE PROJECT

The power of DNA profiling to identify the perpetrator in a case was clear from the first time the technique was used. Of equal importance is the ability of DNA to exclude individuals who did not contribute the biological sample found in the evidence. Before the Narborough case, conventional serological testing was used to provide some level of individualization of biological samples. Those results may have eliminated some persons, but large percentages of the population were often left as possible candidates. Traditional serological techniques were also unable to separate potential sources of the genetic markers in body fluid mixtures, because those markers were found in the liquid portions of the sample. A procedure called differential extraction, developed at the time of the Black Pad case, now allows scientists to separate sperm DNA and epithelial cell DNA, in effect isolating the male perpetrator's sample.

Studies conducted when DNA testing was being incorporated into forensic casework showed that 25 percent of persons included by traditional serology were later eliminated as suspects when DNA profiles were analyzed. Recognizing the power of DNA to exclude those who are falsely accused in criminal cases, attorneys sought to provide for DNA testing in postconviction appeals.

Attorneys Barry Scheck and Peter Neufeld founded the Innocence Project at Yeshiva University's Benjamin Cardozo School of Law in New York. They used DNA profiling in 1989 to exclude a convicted felon as the source of DNA in evidence that had not been analyzed before his trial, resulting in the first exoneration by DNA. Since that time, they have been responsible for 218 postconviction exonerations. These exonerations have been achieved primarily through DNA analysis in cases where that testing was not available or had not been done at the time of trial. The original convictions were often based primarily on eyewitness misidentifications, false statements, suspected coerced confessions, and faulty or intentionally fraudulent forensic testing. Statistics maintained by the Innocence Project indicate that sixteen people were sitting on death row at the time they were exonerated by DNA.

As new and more sensitive DNA methodologies are developed, it is expected that exonerations will continue. It is also hoped that such injustices will occur far less frequently in the future, as DNA testing is conducted by qualified scientists in most cases prior to trial. Because of the clear impact the Innocence Project has had on achieving justice, many states have now passed postconviction testing statutes that allow convicted offenders to file a motion for DNA analysis on samples that were not tested before trial. (Some states have passed laws that limit the time in which these motions

Dr. Lee in 1959 was the captain in charge of criminal investigation for the Taiwan police department.

Dr. Lee in 1975, when he received his doctoral degree in biochemistry.

In over 40 years, Dr. Lee has received numerous honorary degrees from universities in the United States and abroad.

Dr. Lee received an award for solving his first homicide while on the Taiwan police force (upper left). The awards honoring his work in forensic science continue to this day.

A photograph from the early days of the forensic science program at the University of New Haven.

Some of the many publications of Dr. Lee.

Dr. Lee has been involved in some of the most famous forensic investigations, from
O. J. Simpson to Caylee Anthony.

CourtTV filmed Dr. Lee at various locations for his television show, *Trace Evidence*.

Mercy Hospital in Ohio, where Sister Margaret Ann Pahl was strangled and stabbed in the hospital chapel in 1980.

In 2005, Dr. Lee and the investigative team reexamined evidence in the Sister Margaret Ann cold case.

Numerous news articles, magazine stories, and books discussed the so-called Wood-chipper Murder Case for months after the remains of Helle Crafts were located along the Housatonic River in Connecticut.

The investigative and prosecutorial team for the first trial of Richard Crafts.

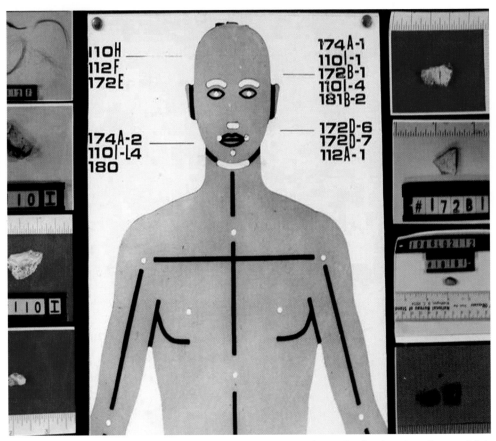
A portion of the court display prepared by Dr. Lee to show the body areas from which the fragments of bone and the dental crowns originated.

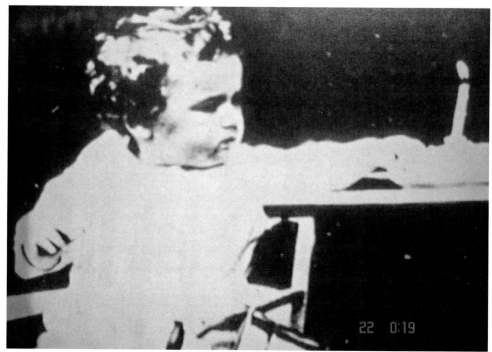

A photograph of Baby Lindbergh, taken at his first birthday. (Courtesy of the New Jersey State Police.)

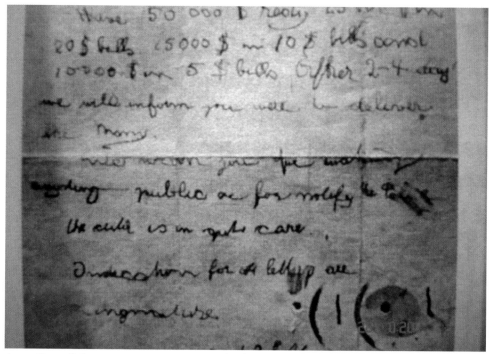

A portion of the ransom note sent to Charles Lindbergh after his son was kidnapped. (Courtesy of the New Jersey State Police.)

The ladder used to enter the baby's room was found leaning against the side of Lindbergh's house. (Courtesy of the New Jersey State Police.)

The attic from which boards were taken to construct the ladder used during the Lindbergh kidnapping. (Courtesy of the New Jersey State Police.)

THE WEAPONS

Mannlicher-Carcano carbine

Iver-Johnson Cadet .22

Remington Model 760 .30-06 Caliber

Weapons used in three assassinations: President John F. Kennedy (top); Senator Robert Kennedy (middle); and Martin Luther King Jr. (bottom).

Nov 22, 1963 JFK

Wecht urges truth, justice

Controversy still exists about the assassination of President Kennedy in 1963 as reported by the Warren Commission. Dr. Michael Baden (bottom left) and Dr. Cyril Wecht (bottom right) have presented different interpretations of the evidence in that case.

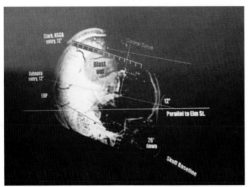

Lee on JFK assassination:

Dr. Lee and other forensic scientists reexamined the evidence in the Kennedy assassination. The trajectories of the bullets that impacted the president's skull (upper left) and the "magic bullet" trajectory (upper right) are shown.

During the investigation of the Elizabeth Smart kidnapping case, Dr. Lee demonstrated that a chair could be used to access the window and gain entry into the house (left). A detective tests Dr. Lee's theory and easily reaches the damaged window (right).

Henry Lee among experts poised to join Levy family investigation

Washington (AP) — Three forensics experts, including Connecticut's Henry Lee, have joined the investigation into the death of Chandra Levy, a Levy family lawyer announced Friday.

"The family has a right to either know what was done, was done properly, or to confirm what was done," said lawyer Billy Martin. "We're asking for a second opinion."

The three experts are: Lee, a former commissioner of public safety in Connecticut, who has investigated 4,000 homicides; Dr. Michael Baden, a former New York City medical examiner; and Dr. Cyril Wecht, the Pittsburgh coroner who was an expert witness in actor John Belushi's death.

The three examined Levy's remains at the District of Columbia

medical examiner's office, went to Rock Creek Park, where the remains were found more than a year after the federal intern vanished.

"We would hope that the forts of this team will in way be able to assist the effi D.C. police and the FBI in mining the cause of Cha death, and hopefully the who killed her," Martin sai

Chandra Levy's family asked Dr. Lee to investigate the death of their daughter after her remains were located in a park in Washington, DC.

The many faces of Dr. Lee during his more than 50 years of public service.

may be made.) Other laws require authorities to retain critical evidence for the length of a sentence in case new DNA procedures are developed.

EDUCATIONAL REQUIREMENTS FOR DNA ANALYSTS

Those who want to be DNA scientists should obtain formal education in molecular biology, biochemistry, forensic science, chemistry, or a related field. DNA laboratories that are accredited or participate in the CODIS network must follow the DNA Advisory Board guidelines formulated and issued by the FBI Laboratory director. In addition to technical and quality assurance procedures, the guidelines include specific coursework requirements for DNA analysts. Scientists conducting DNA testing and interpretation of results must complete courses in genetics, biochemistry, and molecular biology. They must also have training in statistics and population genetics as it applies to forensic DNA analysis. Analysts must complete a training program with written and/or oral testing and show competency in every procedure they perform. Many laboratories have highly formalized training programs DNA analysts must undergo once they are hired and before they can start casework. Individuals who conduct only database sample testing may be subject to less intense training than individuals who handle various types of evidentiary samples. Many laboratories hire persons to work at various levels in the DNA lab. Some DNA units hire technicians to assist with the hands-on steps in the analysis of DNA. The educational and work experience requirements may be reduced for these positions.

DNA analysts must receive continuing education each year, which can be in the form of classes, workshops, specialized training at the laboratory, or online courses. In addition, each person in the DNA unit must be proficiency tested twice a year in each step and in the type of testing he performs. These requirements have been established to help the labs maintain high-quality testing by DNA examiners who understand both the theory behind and the implications of this discipline.

Chapter Nine

FORENSIC DRUG ANALYSIS AND TOXICOLOGY

T he use of poison as a weapon dates back to the earliest days of recorded history, but even today, homicide by poisoning is not unknown. In conjunction with Dr. Michael Baden and Dr. Brian Donnelly, Dr. Henry Lee gave a seminar in 2005 on medical personnel who killed their patients. This presentation showed how the medical examiner, the toxicologist, and the criminalist are all crucial in solving those difficult cases. While the team approach was critical in those cases, it often fell to the toxicologist to confirm the presence of a deadly poison or drug.

On September 6, 2000, Dr. Michael Swango signed a plea agreement with the Office of the United States Attorney for the Eastern District of New York and admitted that he had intentionally murdered Aldo Serini in September 1993 at the Veterans Affairs Medical Center in Northport, New York, by injecting one or more toxic substances that caused respiratory failure. This event ended one of the most notorious killing sprees in medical history. In 1984, as a young doctor but serving as an EMS technician, Swango tried to poison coworkers with arsenic-laced doughnuts. He was convicted of aggravated battery and served five years in prison. After his release, Swango applied for a position as a resident physician in South Dakota. When asked why he was incarcerated, Swango admitted the basic facts of his conviction, but claimed that the evidence was from a discredited crime lab.

Impressed by Swango's manner, the head of residents, Dr. Anthony Salem, invited Swango to be part of the resident program in South Dakota. Because of concerns that Swango's felony conviction might prevent him from being certified by the medical board, Salem wrote to Ohio State University to verify Swango's records. Eventually, Salem learned that Swango had not been invited back after his internship ended in 1984, because he was suspected of tampering with a patient's IV. (The patient did not die, but was paralyzed for some time with symptoms that were similar to those of a curare injection.) Salem decided to discharge Swango after learning the details of the incident in Ohio.

In 1993 Swango applied to the residency program at the Northport VA hospital and began a four-year residency in psychiatry there in July. During the next three and a half months three patients under Swango's care died: George Siano, Aldo Serini, and Thomas Sammarco. Swango was terminated on October 22, 1993. Suspicions were raised, but while federal investigations were being conducted and fraud charges were compiled, Swango fled the United States and was hired as a physician at the Zimbabwe Association of Church Hospital (ZACH). Two patients at ZACH also demonstrated respiratory and neurological paralysis while under Swango's care, and his employment in Zimbabwe was terminated in 1995. Swango continued to seek medical appointments, and in 1997 he received a job offer in Saudi Arabia. While in Chicago en route from Africa to the Middle East, Swango was arrested by federal agents on false-statement and controlled-substance charges that had been filed in the Eastern Judicial District of New York as a result of his activities at the VA hospital in Northport. Swango was imprisoned for these crimes, which gave investigators time to obtain additional evidence and finalize charges related to the suspicious deaths.

Investigators believed Swango had injected substances into his patients in New York and elsewhere, causing their deaths. In 2000 the Inspector General's Office of the Department of Veteran Affairs, hoping to solve the series of suspected murders that had occurred among Swango's patients, asked Dr. Fredric Rieders, founder of National Medical Services, to help identify the toxic agents. The team needed to find and analyze the toxic chemicals involved in the deaths before Swango was released from prison. Rieders was no stranger to high-profile forensic cases with unique toxicology questions. Several years earlier it was Rieders's lab that identified traces of the preservative EDTA in blood samples on a pair of socks in the O. J. Simpson trial, indicating that blood from a vacuum tube containing that preservative and not from a wound had made those stains. It was suspected that Swango used two chemicals to poison his victims: succinylcholine (a muscle relaxant) and epinephrine (a stimulant). Both compounds are difficult to pin down as causes of death because their chemical properties make them tough to isolate. In addition, these chemicals are naturally occurring and exist in the living body.

To make the task even more difficult, there were differences in the types of tissue examined by the NMS team, and some samples came from embalmed bodies while others had not been preserved. All of the bodies, however, had been buried for many years, so the scientists had to develop new methods to detect the compounds in dead and decaying tissue. Toxicologists used liquid chromatography and time-of-flight mass spectrometry, two of the most sensitive methods used for analytical forensic testing, with modified procedures to isolate and identify the toxic materials. Testing proved that Swango killed all three patients by administering injections of toxic substances: George Siano died after an injection of epinephrine caused cardiac arrest, while Aldo Serini and Thomas Sammarco had been given fatal doses of succinylcholine. Facing the death penalty, Swango pled guilty to the murder of the three veterans.

THE HISTORY OF TOXICOLOGY

As Rieders did in the Swango case, the job of a forensic toxicologist is to apply the techniques of analytical chemistry and combine these with an understanding of the adverse effects of chemicals on humans. The knowledge of toxins, materials that exert a life-threatening effect upon living organisms, predates written history. Toxic materials exist in many forms (gaseous, liquid, and solid; animal, mineral, and vegetable) and may be ingested, inhaled, or absorbed through the skin. Poisons are a subgroup of toxins. When ancient people encountered harmful plants, moldy grains, and venom from animals, the effects of those encounters were noted and passed along to other members of the family or tribe. Food that did not kill or make you sick was okay to eat. Later, hunters learned to use toxins to catch prey and dispose of enemies.

One of the earliest-known writings on animal venom and plant extracts for hunting, warfare, and assassination comes from ancient Egypt. The Ebers Papyrus (c. 1550 BCE) contains information on many poisons, including hemlock, aconite, opium, and metals such as lead, copper, and antimony. It includes more than eight hundred recipes for poisons and seven hundred drugs with specific indications and dosages. Of particular interest are the case histories contained in the papyrus, including discussions of modes of application of toxins and drugs. Egyptians also used chemicals in their justice system. Trial for serious crimes was by "penalty of the peach," in which the accused was made to ingest distilled peach pits, which are high in hydrocyanic acid. If the accused died, he was guilty.

Other ancient writings reflect careful study of and knowledge about toxic materials, especially poisons. Legend holds that Shen Nung, the father of Chinese medicine and agriculture, compiled a forty-volume work titled *Pen Ts'ao* (*The Great Herbal*) around 1735 BCE. These volumes contained lists of poisons, medicines, and drugs, most of them originating from plants. Between 1500 and 1200 BCE, a Sanskrit document called the Rig Veda was written as an account of Hindu medicine. The Veda discusses many diseases, conditions, and ailments, and includes medicinal and poisonous plants and antidotes. In ancient Greece, Hippocrates wrote of poisons, adding the clinical toxicological principles of chemical therapy and dosage to his instructions. In Rome, Sulla issued the first law against poisoning; this later became a regulatory statute directed at careless dispensing of drugs in 82 BCE. By this time extensive knowledge of the poisonous effects of various metals and other chemical substances was commonplace.

The knowledge of poisons and chemicals grew throughout the centuries. Medieval treatises were written in every country. Poison was used as a way to advance and eliminate enemies. Lucrezia and Cesare Borgia are perhaps the most notorious poisoners of that time. As knowledge of biology and organic chemistry grew, so did the emerging field of toxicology. The father of modern toxicology was Mathieu Orfila, who laid the groundwork for pharmacology, experimental therapeutics, and occupational toxicology. Orfila was a Spanish doctor and chemist who worked in the French court. In 1813 Orfila published a two-volume work on the characteristics of poisons, their effects on the body, the pathology involved, and legal medicine implications. This was the first time forensic and clinical toxicology were combined with analytical chemistry. Orfila developed methods to use autopsy material and chemical analysis in a systematic way that provided legal proof of poisoning. In 1819 he developed tests for the presence of various poisons in blood and used a microscope to identify and evaluate blood and semen stains. As his fame grew, Orfila consulted on many criminal cases. One of the more famous—and perhaps the first recorded use of forensic toxicology in a court case—involved a French woman named Madame Lafarge, who was accused of poisoning her husband with arsenic. Tests conducted by another chemist before the trial were inconclusive. During the trial Orfila had the body exhumed and used his own tests to find traces of arsenic in the man's organs. Madame Lafarge was found guilty and sentenced to life in prison. Orfila made many contributions to toxicology, including developing chemical tests to detect poisons in tissues and fluids, relating symptoms to specific damage to body tissues, and conducting experiments to determine the response of various organs to different doses of many chemicals.

The twentieth century brought great advancements in chemistry and technology, and forensic toxicology expanded accordingly. Much of the work done in forensics during the first half of the century was related to industrial and consumer toxicology. The first journals devoted to experimental toxicology were published in Europe during the 1930s. That decade also brought legislation that created legal standards and government powers to regulate the sale and distribution of food, drugs, and cosmetics. One of the more tragic incidents leading to such legislation was the Lash Lure case. Lash Lure was a mascara containing a chemical, p-phenylenedi-amine, that caused blisters and ulcers on the eyes, eyelids, and faces of women who used the product. One Lash Lure customer had ulcers that were so severe an infection set in, leading to her death; other women were blinded by the chemical. The cosmetic industry denied that the mascara was the cause of these injuries, but the public was outraged and Congress acted. Lash Lure became the first cosmetic banned from sale in the United States. The legislation that was passed at this time mandated quality and identity standards for foods, prohibited false therapeutic claims for drugs, included cosmetics and medical devices under the authority of the Food and Drug Administration (FDA), and specified the FDA's right to inspect factories and control of product advertising.

In the 1950s the FDA expanded its interest in toxicology and its focus on the harmful effects of various carcinogens. The Society of Toxicology was founded in 1961 to enable scientists to exchange ideas and present research findings. Today, every country has its own toxicology organization. In the 1960s the journal *Toxicology and Applied Pharmacology* began publication as a forum for publication of peer-reviewed research and case reports. Board certification began in the early 1980s as a way of ensuring a minimal level of competency among persons conducting toxicological analysis. There are currently more than 120 journals dedicated to toxicology and dozens of professional scientific organizations with thousands of members.

A field related to forensic toxicology is forensic drug analysis. When Congress began regulating the sale of various chemical substances and prosecuting those who violated that law, it was necessary to provide appropriate proof of the nature of these materials in a court of law. This is where the drug chemist comes in. The drug chemist applies the procedures of analytical chemistry to test the actual materials that are controlled substances. These may be street drugs, plants, prescription medicines, and sometimes over-the-counter medications. The scientist who conducts drug analysis must understand the nature and appearance of the chemicals used to make the drugs. Specialized training in the recognition, documentation, and collection of the chemicals used to make these controlled substances may also be required.

FORENSIC/ANALYTIC TOXICOLOGY

Forensic toxicologists may test samples from living or dead individuals. When a toxicologist receives blood, body fluids, or tissue samples to analyze, the task may appear quite daunting. There are thousands of chemicals, plants, and biological substances that can be introduced into the body in a variety of ways. Once the toxin or drug is absorbed, it often is changed or broken down into different chemicals during the process of metabolism. So the toxicologist must be able to identify both the original substance and any metabolic products. Compounding the difficulty, different toxins may be found in various amounts in different organs, depending on the nature and the form of the material. For example, the liver is often adversely affected by the introduction of drugs or toxins since it functions to maintain the chemical balance of the body. Blood from the stomach and intestines flows into the liver before entering general systemic circulation. If the blood contains large or consistent amounts of toxins, the liver attempts to filter these out, resulting in damage of several kinds to the liver, with notable effects on the individual's physical and physiological condition.

HUMAN PERFORMANCE FORENSIC TOXICOLOGY

According to the Society of Forensic Toxicologists (SOFT), the human performance forensic toxicologist determines the absence or presence of ethanol and other drugs and chemicals in blood, breath, or other appropriate specimen(s), and evaluates their role in modifying human performance or behavior. Samples from living persons are usually submitted in the form of blood or urine. The forensic toxicologist must extract from these fluids the chemicals and other toxins of interest.

Concern about the effects of substance abuse on individuals and in the workplace have significantly increased the number of samples collected and analyzed for both illicit and prescription drugs. Employees in certain professions—such as police, firefighters, emergency medical personnel, and others—are required to be free of illicit drug use. Random drug testing is performed to ensure that these professionals are drug free. In the workplace setting, urine or hair is usually the sample submitted. In recent years, most agencies have begun testing hair samples instead of urine. These samples are more easily collected, and the unadulterated state and integrity of the sample are more easily ensured. In addition, since the substances of interest are deposited over time, if an individual temporarily refrains from drug use to produce a clean urine sample, substances from use in previous months can still be deteced in the hair.

Laboratories that are specially certified for drugs of abuse (chemicals that are used in excess or illicitly because of the effects felt by the user) test the urine or hair for a specific set of substances that are commonly abused. Instrumental analysis, typically gas chromatography–mass spectrometry, is used to isolate the chemicals in the samples and identify each component of the mixture.

The most common application of human performance testing is in determining whether a person is driving under the influence of alcohol or drugs. Because a person must typically take in substantial amounts of alcohol to feel its effects, the quantities ingested are often relatively easy for scientists to detect in blood. For example, two beers (4 percent alcohol each) contain approximately 30 grams of alcohol. These two beers can easily lead to diminished driving performance in many individuals. While alcohol is metabolized relatively quickly by the liver, in individuals who are actively drinking, it takes hours for their blood alcohol level to fall below the point of impairment.

Extensive studies have been carried out relating the alcohol concentration in the blood to performance capacity. In general, individuals with a blood alcohol level of approximately 0.05–0.15 percent (50–150 mg/dL)—which can result from consuming several beers— demonstrate decreased inhibition, poor coordination, blurred vision, and slowed reaction time. Increasing blood levels to 0.15–0.3 percent results in slurred speech, visual impairment, hypoglycemia, and staggering. Severe intoxication symptoms include poor muscular coordination, hypothermia, vomiting and nausea, and convulsions. In adults, coma and death are typical with alcohol levels above 0.5 percent. Tragically, the incidence of binge drinking and resulting death has increased in recent years on college campuses in the United States.

A blood alcohol concentration of .08 or .10 g/dL is the defined limit for DUI in most states. The testing of blood alcohol is usually a relatively straightforward process. Because alcohol is volatile, heating a blood or other tissue sample vaporizes any alcohol that is present. The vapor is then injected into a gas chromatograph, which separates the volatile substances based on the amount of time it takes for each component to pass by the detector (retention time). By running certain standards at the same time, the toxicologist can determine the presence and the amount of alcohol in the sample. The percentage of alcohol (weight to volume) in the sample is easily determined from this information. During testimony forensic toxicologists are often asked about the effects of alcohol at the blood levels detected. Because there may have been a delay in obtaining a blood sample from a suspect in a DUI case, the toxicologist may have to back calculate to determine the blood alcohol level at the time the individual was operating the vehicle.

Other drugs may also affect driving performance; reports indicate that both illicit drugs and controlled substances such as cocaine, marijuana, and barbiturates are a growing concern. Most states have passed laws that include penalties for driving under the influence of drugs that affect the nervous system, brain, or muscles of a person so as to impair, to an appreciable degree, the ability to drive a vehicle.

DRUG-FACILITATED SEXUAL ASSAULT

According to the national statistics, more than 270,000 sexual assaults occurred in 2008, which is one sexual assault every two minutes. The use of drugs, with or without alcohol, significantly increases an individual's risk for sexual assault. In some cases, the drugs are taken voluntarily by the victims; in other cases the victims are given substances without their knowledge. Some victims voluntarily drink sufficient alcohol or drugs to reduce or eliminate their ability to consent to sexual activity. Others may have had one or more alcoholic drinks, but left a drink unattended; they describe losing track of events after consuming a small amount of the drink, and then waking in an unfamiliar environment, inappropriately clothed, or with a sensation of having had sexual intercourse. In some reported cases, the victims were not even aware they had been assaulted until videotapes or photographs were seized that showed the perpetrator committing the rape while the victim was sedated. Victims often are confused and sleepy for some time following the event. Researchers have reported that almost 62 percent of sexual assault cases involved the use—voluntarily or involuntarily—of drugs; these situations are classified as drug-facilitated sexual assault (DFSA).

Although the media has labeled drugs such as Rohypnol and gamma hydroxybutyrate (GHB) as "date-rape drugs," these drugs are used in only a small percentage of cases. In fact, ethanol is the most commonly identified substance in investigations of DFSA. Although no other single drug is as common as alcohol, benzodiazepines (antianxiety drugs and sleeping agents) are present in a significant number of drug-facilitated sexual assault cases. Because of the vast number of potential substances that may be used in DFSA, the analysis of evidence in these crimes is a huge challenge for the forensic toxicologist. Many of the drugs used for DFSA are low-dose chemicals whose effects are enhanced by the presence of alcohol. Because very small amounts of these drugs can sedate a person, it is difficult to detect the presence of the drug in a biological specimen unless sensitive methods are used in a forensic toxicology laboratory; hospital and clinical labs seldom have procedures suitable for these tests. Another problem is that the drug has often been eliminated from the body by the time the victim is examined. The effects of the drugs used often result in a substantial delay between the drugging and the reporting of the crime, making blood unsuitable as a sample to identify the drug or its metabolites (the products to which the drug is converted by the activities of the body). In DFSA cases, urine should be collected and tested to maximize the possibility of detecting the drugs commonly used to facilitate the sexual assaults.

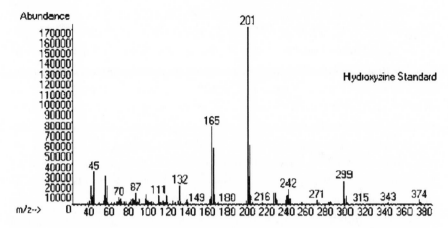

Fig. 9.1. The mass spectrum of hydroxyzine, a common antihistamine.

Guidelines for the analysis of forensic samples suggest the use of both screening and confirmatory tests to identify the chemicals present in the specimens. Screening tests may be classic microcrystal tests, color tests, or other available procedures, often depending on the type of drug suspected. Confirmatory tests in modern toxicology laboratories are instrumental tests, usually separation techniques coupled with the mass spectrometer. When results are obtained, the toxicologist must determine the significance of finding a particular drug in the forensic samples. Making this determination often requires more information than just the analytical findings. Questions concerning activities of the victim, medications, and voluntary use of recreational drugs provide the background from which the data may be interpreted. Figure 9.1 shows the mass spectrum of a common antihistamine that may be found during toxicological screening.

POISONS

A poison is any agent capable of producing a harmful response in an organism. Toxicologists may help diagnose poisoning in a living patient or analyze the postmortem samples of a suspected victim of poisoning. Both situations require a vast knowledge of potential poisons and a comparison of the symptoms of the patient to the physiological effects of various toxic substances. Much of the analysis for poisoning is based on a comprehensive case history, patient symptoms, and a systematic approach to the analysis. Availability of possible poisons is also considered when the toxicologist attempts to identify the harmful susbstance. As with most analytic toxicology, the possibilities are so numerous that some materials may go undetected and the actual poison may not be identified.

One of the situations in which forensic toxicologists encounter poisoning is as a form of child abuse. Children may be given potentially harmful substances for punishment or to stop them from crying. In one recent 2007 case, a six-month-old baby was brought to the hospital unresponsive with shallow breathing. Toxicological analysis revealed high levels of the active ingredient in an over-the-counter cold medicine; the father had given the child a large dose of this medicine to make him sleep. Other common agents used intentionally to poison children include laxatives, salt, narcotics, cleaning fluids, and diuretics.

One of the less common—but remarkable—examples of poisoning as child abuse occurs in cases of Munchausen by proxy syndrome. One of the most harmful forms of child abuse, Munchausen syndrome by proxy was named after Baron von Munchausen, an eighteenth-century German dignitary known for telling outlandish stories. This psychological condition involves the creation or aggravation of physical symptoms in a child by a primary caretaker, who attempts to gain attention and recognition by publicly appearing as a dedicated and loving parent—but who, when alone with the child, deliberately makes him sick. A caregiver may induce symptoms by injecting children with various drugs or adding poisonous substances to the child's food. In these cases, the medical symptoms inevitably lead to multiple diagnostic tests, and the toxicologist is often not consulted until some time after the initial symptoms appear. In addition to medical specimens, in these cases the toxicologist also tests foods and other materials that came in contact with the child, if they are available.

The toxicological analysis in a poisoning death involves the four basic steps of all analytic toxicology: (1) obtaining a detailed case history, (2) collecting appropriate specimens, (3) analyzing samples, and (4) interpreting the findings. When poisoning is suspected, the toxicologist attempts to determine what poison was administered, how the poison was delivered, what dose was administered over what period of time, and whether the dosage was sufficient to cause significant harm or death.

The actual testing conducted depends on the nature and form of the suspected poison. Arsenic, for example, has been the method of choice of some infamous real and fictional murderers. As early as the 1830s, chemists used tests for the presence of arsenic to analyze tissues, food, soil, and other materials. The poison was detected by depositing it on a specific surface that contained mercury This test was refined and used through the early part of the twentieth century. As analytical methods for other substances were developed and technology advanced, so did the tests for arsenic. Instrumental analysis for metals, including arsenic, became the method of choice with the adoption of atomic absorption spectroscopy. The current state-of-the-art test for arsenic and other metals is inductively coupled plasma mass spectrometry (ICP-MS).

POSTMORTEM TOXICOLOGY

When most autopsies are carried out, the pathologist removes samples of various tissues from the decedent for toxicological analysis. Postmortem forensic toxicology determines the absence or presence in human fluids and tissues of drugs and their metabolites, chemicals such as ethanol and other volatile substances, carbon monoxide and other gases, metals, and other toxic chemicals. The toxicologist then evaluates the role of these substances as a determinant or contributory factor in the cause and manner of death. While the cause of death may appear straightforward, most pathologists will not provide a final report on the cause and manner of death without first obtaining a complete toxicological report from the laboratory. Many factors can make the identification of toxins in cadavers a difficult process. Often, small amounts of drugs or toxins are found in the tissues. Some chemicals may preferentially deposit in certain organs or redistribute from one site to another in the body after death. The tissues may have begun to decay, further complicating the detection and analysis process. In addition, as with the Swango case, chemicals used as poisons may naturally occur in the body, so the toxicologist must determine if the quantity of substance detected is significant.

There are hundreds of thousands of potential chemical substances, foreign to the human body, that a forensic toxicologist might identify. In addition, many of the chemicals present in the body, such as the succinlycholine and epinephrine in the Swango case, can have deleterious effects if administered inappropriately or in improper dosage. Because of the number of overdose cases involving street drugs or prescription medications, forensic toxicologists often analyze pathology samples for the most common basic and acidic drugs. This may limit the possibilities to hundreds or thousands of chemicals. Scientists may seek the assistance of investigators if prescription medications are a suspected cause of death, requesting a complete listing of the medications found at an incident scene. Because of the large number of possible agents, the forensic toxicologist often needs to conduct several types of tests on the same sample to remove several classes of chemicals. These extracts of the various specimens are then tested for metabolites, the intact drug (which is often not found), and other agents that may have acted to enhance or block the effects of the drugs or chemicals.

FORENSIC DRUG TESTING

Like toxicologists, forensic drug chemists conduct screening and confirmatory tests to identify drugs submitted to the laboratory. Unlike toxicology, the substances analyzed in the drug lab are in their original states or have been altered with other chemicals that can be separated or identified along with the drugs. Common screening tests conducted on drug evidence are listed in table 9.1. The majority of the materials identified in a drug lab include common street drugs, prescription medications, and over-the-counter medications. Identification and analysis may be based on both an observation of the appearance of the material and the chemical and instrumental data. If the evidence submitted is a pill, for example, the scientist will search a database such as the *Physician's Desk Reference* (PDR) to match the color, size, shape, and nature of the pill to those listed in the PDR.

Drugs can be classified according to several schemes. One way to classify drugs is on the basis of their effects on the body.

- *Narcotics*. Narcotic drugs have a recognized use in medicine and are most often taken for pain relief. Morphine and its derivatives are in this group of painkillers. Opium is the source of morphine and many other compounds such as codeine and oxycodone. Oxycodone (sold as Oxycontin) is an addictive painkiller that has recently been the target of robberies of pharmacies and doctors' offices.
- *Stimulants*. Stimulants increase physical energy level and heighten mental state. Amphetamines and methamphetamines are common types of stimulants. The growing use of crystalline methamphetamine has become the focus of law

Common color/presumptive tests for drugs

Name of Test	Positive Result
Marquis	*Heroin, morphine, and opium-based drugs* turn the solution purple.
Cobalt thiocyanate	*Cocaine* turns the liquid blue.
Dillie-Koppanyi	*Barbiturates* turn the solution violet-blue.
VanUrk	*LSD* turns the solution blue-purple.

Table 9.1. Some common color tests for drug analysis.

enforcement initiatives. Cocaine is a powerful stimulant that can be purchased in powder, which is snorted or injected, or in "crack" form, which is usually vaporized and then inhaled.

- *Hallucinogens.* Hallucinogens produce an altered mental state. These drugs exist in chemical and plant forms, affecting perception of oneself or one's environment. Some hallucinogens have been part of religious and cultural practices in various parts of the world. The most common plant containing hallucinogenic properties is marijuana and its many forms. Lysergic acid diethylamide (LSD) is probably the most well-known and most potent hallucinogen. This drug was used during psychiatric treatment until some of the harmful consequences of using it became apparent. Phenylcyclidine (PCP) is a street drug that is relatively inexpensive to produce. PCP often causes violent responses, with temporary great strength and resistance when others try to restrain the user.

- *Depressants.* Depressants dull the senses, reduce respiration, and lower energy levels. Alcohol is a commonly used depressant; sleeping pills and tranquilizers are also included in this category. Rohypnol is a common tranquilizing drug used widely at raves and clubs.

- *Performance-enhancing drugs.* Performance-enhancing drugs are taken primarily by athletes and bodybuilders to enhance performance or build muscles. Anabolic steroids and some stimulants are used by athletes to gain an advantage over their opponents or to increase strength. The effects of steroids on mental and emotional state and the damage they can cause to various organs, especially in adolescents, has led to strict controls on these chemicals.

Examples of some of the street drugs from these categories are depicted in figure 9.2.

Drug testing involves the identification of the material, and, in some cases, the quantity of the drug that is present. The Scientific Working Group for the Analysis of Seized Drugs (SWGDRUG) has formulated guidelines for testing illicit substances (see table 9.2.). Identification is carried out by first performing screening or pre-

Table 9.2. Analytical Techniques in Drug Analysis
(from SWGDRUG Guidelines) Decreasing discriminating power from A to C.

Category A	Category B	Category C
Infrared Spectroscopy	Capillary Electrophoresis	Color Tests
Mass Spectrometry	Gas Chromatography	Fluorescence Spectroscopy
Nuclear Magnetic Resonance Spectroscopy	Ion Mobility Spectrometry	Immunoassay
Raman Spectroscopy	Liquid Chromatography	Melting Point
	Microcrystalline Tests	Ultraviolet Spectroscopy
	Pharmaceutical Identifiers	
	Thin Layer Chromatography	
	Cannabis only: Macroscopic Examination Microscopic Examination	

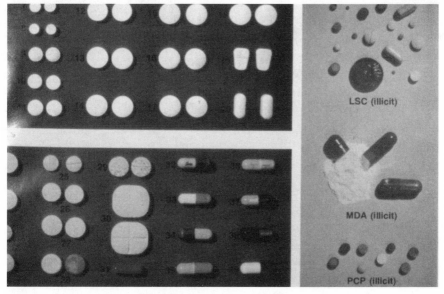

Fig. 9.2. Some manufactured and illicit controlled substances.

sumptive tests and then a confirmatory test. Color or other screening tests are used in the lab to help identify the class of drug being analyzed. This knowledge provides information so that the proper extraction and testing procedures can be performed for drug confirmation. Screening tests may also be conducted by law enforcement officers when seizing suspected drugs. These color tests can be purchased as kits, making the tests safe and easy to perform. While these are presumptive tests, they do provide sufficient probable cause for arrest or further investigation. SWGDRUG recommends at least two techniques be carried out so that the test combination identifies the specific drug present and precludes a false positive identification.

When the scientist analyzes a drug sample, the results are used to identify the presence of the illicit drug. Other materials, called cutting agents, are often also present; they are used to dilute the drug concentration, to provide the means of delivery, or for transport. Usually it is not important for the drug chemist to know what percentage of an evidence item is actually the drug. Some laws, however, base the penalty for possession on the actual amount of the

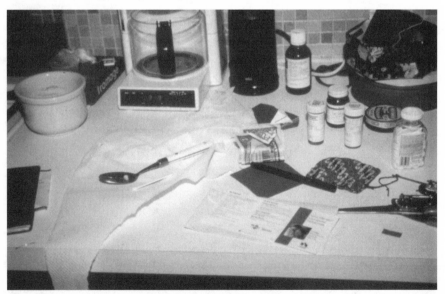

Fig. 9.3. Materials used to produce street drugs on the counter at a clandestine lab.

controlled substance present. When this is the case, the forensic chemist must conduct a quantitative analysis to determine the actual quantity of the target drug. Additional steps must be taken to conduct quantitative analysis and ensure its accuracy.

Some drug chemists are specially trained to assist investigators in searching clandestine laboratories that make illicit drugs and seizing chemicals and other materials used to produce these drugs. This is potentially a dangerous assignment, since many of the chemicals used can be explosive, and because some drug dealers set up booby traps to harm anyone entering their clandestine labs. A clandestine lab discovered by a drug task force is shown in figure 9.3.

EDUCATION AND TRAINING

Toxicologists must have an extensive background in the physical sciences, usually including an undergraduate degree in chemistry or biology. Some portion of the forensic toxicologist's graduate training must be in analytical chemistry and toxicology. Board certification programs for individual practitioners require a doctorate in the natural sciences from a recognized, accredited educational institution. Before becoming certified, toxicologists must have three years of full-time professional experience in forensic toxicology. Additional training in a postdoctoral program, practice, research, education, or administration is required, with other appropriate professional activities. Once these minimum criteria are met, a certification examination is required. Certification generally demonstrates that the individual possesses appropriate knowledge and skills to conduct analysis and interpretation of findings as a forensic toxicologist.

Technicians who work in a toxicology laboratory under a scientist with a doctorate are not required to have a doctorate themselves, but must have a degree in physical science or a related subject that includes sufficient coursework in analytical chemistry techniques. Continuing education is important to remain current in methodologies and areas of controversy. All toxicologists should participate in proficiency testing specifically geared to their areas of testing, such as blood alcohol, urine drug testing, and postmortem type samples.

At a minimum, drug chemists should have a bachelor's degree in a physical or forensic science. Coursework should include both organic and analytical chemistry. Intensive training in the techniques and theory applied to the testing of seized drugs is given to all scientists prior to their analysis of casework. In addition, drug chemists must demonstrate competency in the testing procedures and continued proficiency in the laboratory. Once trained, analysts should receive additional training each year that is appropriate for the types of testing the laboratory conducts. It is the responsibility of all scientists to remain current in their field.

Because individuals working in these laboratories have access to controlled substances, extensive background checks and polygraph tests are usually required. Persons working in drug laboratories are expected to have no history of illicit drug use or abuse of controlled substances. An examination of forensic misconduct Web sites reveals several individuals who succumbed to the temptation to use samples of the drugs submitted for evidence. Strict guidelines for accurate record keeping for drug evidence quickly revealed the illegal activity. Nevertheless, persons working in a drug analysis laboratory must not only be able to work in close proximity of these controlled substances, but under the pressure of large casework backlogs.

Chapter Ten

FORENSIC ODONTOLOGY

D r. Gus Karazulas is a skilled forensic odontologist, a forensic dentist who assists to identify unknown victims by their teeth and to match teeth impressions from suspected perpetrators who may leave bite marks. He has identified human remains and worked on several significant homicide cases with Dr. Henry Lee, including the Woodchipper Murder. In a recent case, Karazulas has been asked to look at some bite mark evidence and wanted Lee to review the case with him. In one case, he explained that the bite marks were on the back of a child who was the victim of abuse. The hospital personnel who treated the child had washed the bite wounds without first taking a sample for DNA analysis, so Karazulas had been asked to compare the bite marks to teeth impressions from several individuals who lived with the child in an effort to identify the abuser.

Karazulas had no DNA to work with and no photograph of the bite marks until twenty-four hours after the child was first examined. He and Lee concentrated on the computer images in the case file. Because of the angle, location, and time involved, they realized that individualization would likely be impossible. But Lee confirmed the conclusions as Karazulas was able to exclude some of the suspects in the case. The remaining suspects were interrogated by the police, and the live-in boyfriend of the mother eventually confessed to the abuse.

The work of Lee and Karazulas has always proved fruitful, including the case described below.

Carla Terry went out on the evening of January 12, 1991, in Hartford, Connecticut, but never came back. A man walking his dog the next day found the body of the twenty-eight-year-old in a plastic bag on a snowbank; she had been beaten and strangled. She also had bruises on and around both breasts that were later identified as human bite marks, and her lack of defensive wounds indicated she might have been acquainted with her killer. Investigators received a phone call from a woman who said she had seen Terry in a bar, teasing Al, a man in his forties. It did not take long to identify this person as Al Swinton, since his business card was in Terry's pocket and they frequented the same bars. In Swinton's Chevy Chevette detectives found a plastic bag the same color, size, and manufacturer as the one used to wrap Terry's body, and in Swinton's basement they found a distinctive black bra that Terry's family identified as hers.

Because of the bite marks on Terry's breasts, a warrant was issued to obtain Swinton's teeth impressions. Since Swinton's left and right bicuspids were turned inward rather than being flush with the other teeth, his bite was unique. The upper left central and lateral bicuspids were also tipped forward, and on the lower jaw there were spaces between several teeth. Swinton submitted to having his teeth cast, and Karazulas compared the plaster mold and impressions to the bruises found on Terry. He believed they were a match; however, a judge ruled that the state must prove the marks were made at the time of Terry's death. Since this was beyond the state of the art for forensic odontology, Swinton was freed and the investigation went cold.

Cold-case detectives reexamined the bite mark photos from the Terry homicide in 1998 with newly available technology: Lucis, an image-processing software developed by Barbara Williams that can differentiate much finer contrast variations than is possible with the human eye and enables users to see detail that would be either difficult or impossible to see otherwise. Karazulas and Major Timothy Palmbach of the Division of Scientific Services in the Connecticut

Department of Public Safety scanned the bite mark photograph into a computer at Image Content Technologies, the manufacturer of Lucis, in New Britain, Connecticut, and adjusted the contrast levels to obtain the best reading. These images are shown in figure 10.1. Karazulas also made a transparent copy of Swinton's teeth from the plaster molds made in 1991 and used Adobe Photoshop to superimpose them over the enhanced picture. It was a perfect match, but this had already been established. They were still faced with the issue of when the bite mark had been made.

When an individual's heart stops, the healing process stops, and from the color of Terry's skin, investigators could tell that between the time she died and the time she was found, no changes had taken place on her body. The bruise represented a fixed point in time—the approximate time of her death. Starting with this premise, Karazulas attempted to replicate the bruise color by clamping the upper and lower plaster cast of Swinton's teeth onto his own arm. Taking a constant stream of pictures to verify his work, he timed how long it took for the color in his arm to return to normal. He observed that between fifteen and twenty minutes after it was made, the bite mark disappeared. Comparing the color of the strangulation marks on the victim, the color of the bite marks on her breasts, and the color of

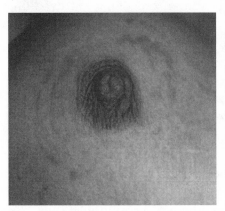
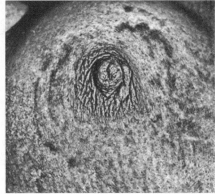

Unenhanced bite mark   LUCIS – Enhanced bite mark

Fig. 10.1. The bite mark on victim Carla Terry in the *State of Connecticut v. Swinton* case. The left photograph is unenhanced; the right was produced using Lucis computer software. (Courtesy of Dr. Gus Karazulas.)

the bite mark on his arm, Karazulas determined that Terry had been bitten about ten to fifteen minutes before she was strangled. He repeated this test more than fifty times, getting the same results each time. This finding effectively put Swinton with Terry at the approximate time she was strangled. Swinton was arrested again, and this time the case went to trial.

The state presented several computer-enhanced images of the bite marks found on Terry, and Palmbach explained how Lucis worked to bring out more image detail than the unaided human eye could see; the bite mark photograph had 255 layers of contrast, whereas the eye perceives only 32 layers. The program allowed investigators to select a particular range of contrast to focus on the details. Palmbach demonstrated how the photo looked before and after the enhancement, stating that nothing had been added to or removed from the image.

Karazulas described how bite mark comparisons are done and demonstrated how different types of teeth leave distinct marks on the skin. He described how he had examined the molds made from the defendant's teeth, which showed several unique characteristics. He had also looked at the original bite mark photos from the autopsy, and he could tell that the bruises had been made by the offender standing in front of the victim, approaching her head-on. Karazulas showed the jury which teeth had made which marks. He used models made from the molds to show how Swinton's bite matched the bruise, noting that there was nothing in the bruise that was not associated with something in Swinton's teeth: Every unique characteristic of the defendant's dentition had a corresponding mark in the bruise. The final step was to use Photoshop for the superimposition. For this he made a wax impression from the molds and placed this on a copy machine to create a paper copy of the image. He then traced the image and copied it onto a clear piece of acetate to produce the transparent overlay. He testified that these were fair and accurate renditions of the original photos and molds; thus, the component parts of the superimposed overlays were authenticated.

The defense team hired a forensic odontologist to create similar overlays with Photoshop to demonstrate that, in his opinion, the bite mark in question was not Swinton's. Nevertheless, Swinton was convicted and sentenced to a term of sixty years. He appealed to the state supreme court, claiming the trial court had improperly admitted the computer-enhanced bite mark photographs and Photoshop exhibits without providing a proper foundation. Because the court had not utilized expert testimony as to the adequacy of the computer programs used to ensure accuracy, Swinton wanted this evidence thrown out. The forensic experts admittedly did not understand precisely how these programs actually worked, and thus the defendant's constitutional right to confront such experts had effectively been denied.

The state claimed that the exhibits were illustrative evidence, not scientific, and so did not require the testimony of a computer expert. The Supreme Court decided that the enhancement did reveal parts of an image not otherwise available, and therefore it was not merely simulation evidence. Based on precedent set by cases that used videotape enhancements, the court concluded that the trial court had properly admitted the computer-enhanced photographs, since Palmbach had conducted the tests himself and was able to explain the steps he used to produce the enhancement. Karazulas had a colleague produce the bite mark images he used for comparison, however, and the court decided that those images should not have been admitted. However, Karazulas's testimony regarding exhibits other than those created by Photoshop rendered harmless the improperly admitted images. In addition, the defense had undermined its argument by having its own expert use Photoshop in a similar manner. The conviction stood.

HISTORY

Forensically, teeth are valuable for identification of the dead and of perpetrators who leave impressions of their bite marks on victims or at crime scenes. The history of forensic odontology includes both types of cases.

Silversmith and dentist Paul Revere has been called the father of American odontology because in 1776, he identified General Joseph Warren, killed at the Battle of Bunker Hill, from a false tooth he had made for the man. Other dentists since then have made similar identifications, often in a forensic context. As discussed in chapter 2, in a Boston courtroom George Parkman was identified via his jawbone and three teeth in 1849, allowing the prosecution of his murder to proceed.

A dramatic case of dental identification occurred in Paris in 1897. Under France's Third Republic, charity sales lured crowds of aristocrats. During one such bazaar on May 4, in front of the wooden building where more than one hundred charities were represented, a gas lamp exploded. The fire spread quickly, collapsing the building. One hundred forty people were killed, leaving officials with a massive number of identifications to make. The charred bodies were taken to the nearby Palace of Industry and laid out in rows. While surviving relatives identified most of them, thirty bodies were too badly burned for anyone to identify. Among those who came to find a loved one was the Paraguayan Consul, looking for the body of Duchesse d'Alençon, sister to Empress Elizabeth of Austria. Observing that the teeth of these victims remained intact, he asked dentists who may have treated the victims to consult their records, and with this approach most of the remaining victims were returned to their families.

In terms of identifying offenders from unique dentition, five bite mark bruises on the corpse of an Ohio woman in 1870 inspired a dentist to actually bite the victim's arm himself to demonstrate what a bite mark bruise looked like. He then offered his arm to the chief suspect to bite, while a second dentist made a dental cast to show how the suspect's missing tooth made his bite mark both unique and a match to the victim's bruises. However, the defense attorney insisted that teeth were too similar to make such distinctions, so the suspect was acquitted.

A landmark criminal case was *Doyle v. State of Texas* in 1954. A bite mark was found on a piece of cheese at the scene of a burglary. The suspect was asked to bite a similar piece of cheese, and both a firearms examiner and a dentist independently came to the same conclusion—it was a match to the cheese from the scene. This testimony helped to secure a conviction.

Noted British pathologist Cedric Keith Simpson used bite mark evidence in several prosecutions during the 1960s. Among the most prominent was the 1967 murder of Linda Peacock, a fifteen-year-old schoolgirl from Biggar, Scotland. Officials discovered her body in the local cemetery, strangled and beaten. On her right breast was an odd bruise, apparently made during a struggle. Dr. Warren Harvey examined it, concluded that the bruise was a bite mark, and declared that the killer's teeth were somewhat jagged.

A systematic search was undertaken that included a local detention center for young males. The inmates were asked to provide impressions of their teeth to compare to the bruise, and Harvey narrowed the suspect pool to five. Each was asked for another impression, and Harvey and Simpson assisted and they identified seventeen-year-old Gordon Hay as the likeliest suspect. One of Hay's teeth was pitted in two places by a disorder known as hypocalcination, and the pits matched the impressions made on the victim's breast. As part of his presentation, Harvey made an examination of the teeth of 342 soldiers. Only two had pits of any kind, and none had the two pits that shaped Hay's teeth. Harvey concluded that Hay's teeth were so unique that it would be virtually impossible to find another set of teeth like his that came as close as Hay's to matching the bruise impression.

Hay's defense attorney asked that this evidence be ruled inadmissible, but the judge allowed it, so a dental expert for the defense attempted to refute it. Hay was nevertheless convicted of murder, and an appeals court upheld the conviction.

Since 1970, forensic odontology has been a recognized division of the American Academy of the Forensic Sciences. While still a source of controversy and challenged for its lack of standards, forensic odontology has been accepted in many courts and has been a valuable tool in the identification of the dead. Among the most prominent odontologists is Dr. Lowell Levine, a codirector of Forensic Science Services of the New York State Police and a consultant to New York City's medical examiner. He has been involved with the identification of members of Russia's Romanov family and Nazi war criminal Josef Mengele, as well as identifying victims in numerous mass disasters. But Levine is perhaps most renowned for his role in the conviction in Florida of serial killer Ted Bundy.

Bundy's first trial in Florida, which began in 1979, centered on two murders that had occurred on January 15, 1978. Lisa Levy, age twenty, and Martha Bowman, age twenty-one, were in bed in the Chi Omega sorority house at Florida State University in Tallahassee. A man wearing a blue knit cap crept in and struck them with a wooden log until they were dead. A sorority sister, Nita Neary, saw the man run from the house and she called the police. It turned out that the killer had left bite marks on Levy's buttocks.

Bundy's six-year crime spree had spread across the country from Washington State to Florida, claiming the lives of at least thirty young women. After Bundy's arrest for the Chi Omega attack, investigators requested that he provide a dental impression, but Bundy refused. The investigators then got a search warrant that authorized them to get the impression, which they did in a surprise trip so as to prevent Bundy from grinding his teeth down to disguise his bite. In addition to the impression, odontolgist Dr. Richard Souviron took photographs of Bundy's front upper and lower teeth and gums.

At the trial, Souviron described the bite mark on Levy as the jury examined the photographs. He pointed out how unique the bite mark was and showed how it matched the dental impressions of Bundy's teeth. He demonstrated the structure of alignment, the chips, the size of the teeth, and the sharpness factors of the bicuspids, lateral, and incisor teeth. Then he put an enlarged photo of the bite mark from Levy on a board and laid over it a transparent sheet with an enlarged picture of Bundy's teeth.

Souviron explained that the mark was a double bite: The attacker bit once, then turned sideways and bit again. The top teeth remained in the same position, but the lower teeth left two rings. That gave Souviron twice as much to work with to prove his case. When questioned by the defense about the subjective nature of odontology interpretation, Souviron explained that he had done several experiments with model teeth to be assured of the reproducibility of his analysis.

Then the state called Levine, who testified that for the marks to have been left on the skin in the manner evident, the victim had to be lying passive, probably knocked out or killed. He also explained to the jury the history and practice of forensic odontology.

Fig. 10.2. Comparing a bite mark on the skin of a sexual
assault victim with the plaster model of the suspect's teeth.

Along with the eyewitness testimony of Neary, the bite mark evidence helped to convict Bundy. This was the first case in Florida's legal history to rely on bite mark testimony. Ten years later, after another trial and conviction, Bundy was executed. Figure 10.2 shows the method of comparison of a bite mark to a plaster model.

IDENTIFICATION OF HUMAN REMAINS

The identification of the dead is usually a straightforward process. Most people die surrounded by family and friends, in medical care, or in other circumstances where there is no question of who the decedent is. However, situations in which a person dies while away from home, during a natural disaster, as the result of a mass accident, or as a result of human-made destruction can present a challenge to investigators. When circumstances occur that are not within the norm, other methods must be used to identify the individual. These methods include fingerprints, DNA analysis, and dental identification. Because dental material is relatively stable, investigators often rely on identification using dental information. In these instances, the forensic odontologist is called upon to assist in the identification of a decedent by examining the remains and comparing remaining dentition with dental records. If dental records are not available, the odontologist may use information from photographs or other records to make an identification.

If a body is found in the United States with no indication of the individual's identity, dental information can be entered into missing-persons database stored in the National Crime Information Center or compared to data that is part of the National Institute of Justice initiative on missing persons. This database contains mitochondrial DNA information in addition to physical characteristics of missing persons for use in confirming identity. If there is no initial indication of the identity of the decedent, dental information, along with other anthropological data, can provide an indication of the age, gender, habits, and sometimes the occupation of the victim. This information can then be used to narrow the possibilities.

This type of dental characterization is particularly useful in cases such as airplane crashes. When ValuJet Flight 592 went down in a swamp in Florida, the authorities spent many days recovering a few remains of victims. Because there was a flight roster, the investigators had a clue to the identity of those victims, but they needed to assign an identity to each specimen that was collected. DNA analysis was necessary in some cases. In other instances, the dental and medical records of the passengers and crew were obtained, and painstaking documentation of the dentition of samples collected from the swamp was carried out. Most of the 110 passengers were never located, and a marker was placed to honor the deceased victims of that crash.

Isolating and identifying human remains when there is no formal list of victims is a much more difficult task. In 1995 Henry Lee and several other forensic scientists and pathologists flew to Croatia under the support of AmeriCares to help search for and identify the victims of the recent conflict in that country. Officials had discovered mass graves from 1991 and 1992 that contained multiple victims of the war. Local records were incomplete—the records either never existed or were destroyed during the fighting and destruction. Because there were no burial preparations, many of the bodies were in various stages of decay, changing facial features and other individualizing marks. For many hours each day, the scientists removed bodies, one by one, from the grave and examined them for any possible indicators of their identities. Dentition and facial characteristics were used to estimate the age and general appearance of the victims. Lee and Baden are shown in figure 10.3 examining some of the exhumed remains. Many family members looking for loved ones had photographs that scientists compared to the decedents. These families had been searching for years for persons they thought had been taken prisoner or were displaced. These pictures were also used to confirm the identity of the dead based on the teeth and facial structure. This humanitarian work of Lee and other team members allowed closure for many family members and a proper burial of each decedent according to family religious and social customs.

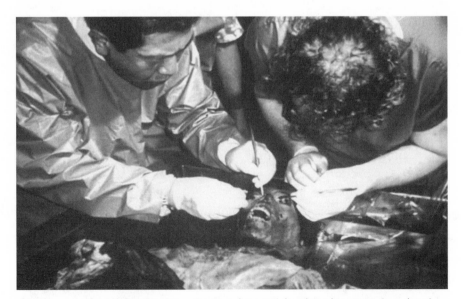

Fig. 10.3. Dr. Henry Lee and Dr. Michael Baden examine dentition in an effort to identify a casualty of the conflict in Bosnia.

BITE MARK EXAMINATION

Forensic dentistry relies on pattern recognition, documentation, collection, and comparison. A forensic odontologist has two primary roles: identification and comparison analysis. In the former, deceased individuals can be identified by dental work they had done while alive, as well as by the wear characteristics their teeth have acquired. In the latter, teeth are viewed as tools that leave a characteristic mark. Experts identify patterns by examining either a whole or partial set of teeth. They first determine whether a mark is a bite mark and then whether the bite is human or animal. They then record every detail about size, appearance, color, and location of the bite on the body or substance, as well as the presence of other bites. Generally, the teeth that leave the strongest impressions in human bites are in the front, both top and bottom. Once a mark is identified as human, investigators look for a suspect to make a comparison against the evidence.

The physical characteristics that will appear in both a bite mark and the suspect's teeth include:

- distance from cuspid to cuspid
- shape of the mouth arch
- evidence of one or more teeth out of alignment
- teeth width and thickness
- spacing between teeth
- missing teeth
- curves of biting edges
- unique dental procedures
- wear patterns, such as chips or grinding

All parts are examined in detail and compared, preferably in a "blind test" in which the odontologist has no information about the suspect. The various characteristics of the mark are noted, taking into account the various factors that may affect the appearance of the bite mark. For example, biting into fatty areas leaves a less-defined impression than biting into skin over muscle. Bite marks made before death have a different appearance than postmortem impressions, which have no associated bruising. Bite marks on living victims require special care. Because of the differences in the mark that may result from the portion of the body injured and time that has passed, photos should be taken over several stages, as healing will change the color and shape of the mark, which eventually will disappear.

Markings on the skin from a bite may indicate such things as the biter's jaw musculature and tongue-lip coordination. Bite marks inflicted slowly show a "suck mark," with an abrasion pattern that resembles a sunburst. Bites made during a struggle often fail to leave a clear pattern, and thus can be difficult to identify.

The American approach to charting teeth, which is one among more than two hundred methods used around the world, is called the universal system. A number is assigned to each of the thirty-two adult teeth, beginning with the upper right third molar and ending with the lower right third molar. Each tooth has five visible surfaces, and the composite information about each surface makes it possible to create a grid, or odontogram, that is believed to be unique to each individual. This means that people who have dental disorders, gum problems, or poorly formed teeth are easier to identify.

There are between thirty and seventy-six factors to consider, including matching for striations, whorls, indentations, pitting, and abrasions, and often this is done using computer-enhanced photography. Teeth can chip, wear down, or be reshaped in various ways. After baby teeth, the teeth that we have will not necessarily remain the teeth we live with. There are restorations, fillings, rotations, tooth loss, breakage, implants, and injuries that can make one person's teeth unlike anyone else's. Odontologists seek a sufficient number of points of similarity between the evidence and the suspect to be able to say with a reasonable degree of medical certainty that this bite mark was made by this suspect.

PROCEDURES

During an investigation, the area around the bite mark is wiped with sterile cotton swabs moistened in distilled water to collect any saliva left behind, and the cotton is then air-dried and placed in a sterile tube. The preserved saliva can later be used to create a DNA profile and used for comparison.

Collection of bite mark impressions on human skin requires a specific, stepwise procedure: A ring is formed around the bite area with a mix of powder and liquid acrylic that extends beyond the bite. After this hardens, a high-resolution casting material is applied and allowed to set. Another vinyl substance is applied, and then an acrylic layer. Then this material is removed and dental stone is poured onto the impression and allowed to harden. If the bite has left a deep enough impression, the shape of the teeth will be captured.

Photographs for use in court involve using a specialized photographic rule, which is essentially two rulers, one laid against the length and one against the width of the subject area. As with all evidence, photographs are also taken without the scale to show a complete and accurate picture of the bite mark area. Care is taken with the camera angle to make sure it is perpendicular to the bite mark, but other angles and light settings may be utilized as well. Photographs can then be enhanced with computer technology. Older techniques involved tracing by hand on clear acetate, and some methods depend on infrared or filter procedures.

Properly scaled photographs are important to the legal process, as is the type of equipment used. Manually operated cameras with close focusing capability and an external flash are best. The camera must be rigidly supported, as with a tripod, because the details must be precise. Using both color and black-and-white film is preferable to using only one or the other. Sometimes the bite mark area has to be shaved to get a proper photo; this should be done with extreme care. When the wound is on a curved surface, photographs are made from several angles to capture the arch in the images.

Digital cameras can be especially useful, given the computer software available for enhancements. A poorly lighted photo, for example, can be brightened, and particular spots on a photo can be highlighted and enlarged for better examination. Digital photos can also be corrected for angular distortions, and digital software allows for electronic transmission to other specialists and for easy storage of image data.

Once a suspect is identified, dental impressions or molds are made of his upper and lower set of teeth (always observing constitutional rights by first obtaining written consent or a search warrant). From these impressions, the odontologist creates a transparency or computer image. Photographs are made of the maximum opening of the mouth and the way the suspect bites. The bone structure of the jaw is examined, along with the biting dynamics of the muscles and tongue. Sample bites are taken and master casts made. A mouth swab or blood is also taken for DNA testing. If any of the teeth appear to be recently chipped, ground, or broken, the relative age of the condition is estimated. A continued dental history of the suspect should be charted, especially after the incident, given the possibility that he may attempt to change his bite profile. (Several murderers have done this; one went so far as to have all his teeth pulled!)

In addition to bite marks left in an attack, there may be defensive bite marks left on an offender when a victim fights back. Thus, it is often a good idea to get dental impressions of victims, just in case this link is made later in a case.

Forensic odontologists can also analyze bite marks on food in cases where a perpetrator might have taken a bite out of something in the victim's home and left it behind. Bite marks left on food, such as cheese, fruit, or a sandwich, offer a three-dimensional impression, which is superior to the two-dimensional impression often left on skin. A bite might penetrate the skin, but often leaves only bruising, and sometimes the blood marks of a bruise are mistaken for the impression of a tooth. Skin can be distorted when bitten, or the teeth can slide during the act of biting. Some bites are forceful enough to leave a good impression; others are not. However, certain firm but soft foods, soft wax, and chewing gum can record a clean impression.

During the spring of 1996, thirteen-year-old Richezza Williams ran away from her home on Long Island. She got involved with a gang of drug suppliers and ended up in Easton, Pennsylvania, calling herself Materon Buffy Smith and claiming she was nineteen. Then she disappeared from Easton.

On August 11 an eyewitness came forward to tell police that she had seen three men drag Smith into the basement at her house. She saw the men gather what appeared to be instruments of torture, including hangers and a corkscrew, and then she heard the girl screaming. Eventually, the screams stopped and the men brought the girl's corpse out of the basement in a box. She said nothing to officials until after these same three men broke into her house on August 5, about a week after the incident, and tortured her and a friend with heated wire hangers, apparently to intimidate them. Scared for her life, the witness finally went to the police, and her report precipitated a search for the body.

The girl's decomposed remains were found inside an old cemetery storage vault. A detective noticed a piece of chewing gum on the vault's dirty floor, so he collected it, just in case. Dr. Dennis Asen, a local forensic odontologist, made a cast of the teeth marks left in the gum and awaited the capture of a suspect.

A dental analysis performed on the remains indicated that this was Richezza Williams. She had been burned, poked, and cut with red-hot devices, after which bleach had been poured into her open wounds. However, the remains were too badly decomposed for the pathologist to provide an accurate cause of death.

It turned out that the victim had been involved with a gang known as the Cash Money Boys, Easton's leading drug dealers, and that her crack addiction had driven her to steal from them. They apparently tortured and murdered her as both a punishment and a warning to anyone else considering such a theft.

The witness identified the men responsible, and on August 12, one of them, Corey Maeweather, age nineteen, was arrested and charged with homicide, kidnapping, aggravated assault, and conspiracy. Asen made a cast of Maeweather's mouth and found that one of his teeth fit the mold from the gum "like a lock and key." Maeweather soon offered a confession and pled guilty. The police also knew the identities of his accomplices, one of whom was subsequently arrested and convicted.

ISSUES IN THE COURTROOM

Since 2000, according to statistics from the Innocence Project, at least seven people in five states have been falsely convicted using bite mark evidence. Some members of the legal community question whether bite mark analysis can present itself in court as a science. In 2009 the National Academy of Sciences included bite mark analysis as among those highly subjective forensic disciplines that require close scrutiny. Guidelines for court testimony, in terms of how an expert should offer an analysis of bite mark comparisons, are set forth by the American Board of Forensic Odontology. The identification can be declared positive, probable, possible, not possible, or insufficient as evidence to make a definitive statement. The highest standard is "reasonable medical certainty," wherein for all practical purposes, the expert confidently identifies the perpetrator as the person who made the bite mark in question.

Forensic dental experts must be prepared for cross-examination that emphasizes the art of interpretation over the hard science of more precise identification processes such as DNA analysis. No error rate has been reported for bite mark comparison. This has been a major area of questioning by attorneys since 2002, when a certified odontologist in one case matched a bite mark on a victim to the suspect, only to find that the DNA profile (which did not come from the victim) excluded that same suspect. Most defense attorneys attempt to persuade a jury that the interpretation is highly subjective and thus should not be used to convict. If an impression analysis is the only evidence, the case may be weak.

While bite mark comparisons do have a history in the courtroom, whether such analysis constitutes more than junk science is still under debate, primarily because some "definitive" identifications have helped to convict innocent people. One such example is the case of Ray Krone. Krone, who lived in Phoenix, Arizona, was a regular customer at the CBS Lounge. On December 29, bar manager Kimberly Ancona was found raped and murdered in a restroom, and Krone became a suspect. There were bite marks on Ancona's body that bore an irregular shape, and since dental work from childhood accidents had given Krone an unusual bite, he seemed a possible source. Although Krone had an alibi, his fingerprints did not match those suspected to be the killer's, and his shoe size failed to match the footprints found near the body, someone said that a man named "Ray" had been in the bar at closing on the night of the murder, so he was arrested and tried.

Krone was asked to bite into a piece of Styrofoam and later a cast was made of his teeth. The press dubbed him the Snaggletooth Killer. During the trial, an odontologist said that based on his analysis he was 100 percent certain that Krone had bitten the victim. Krone was convicted primarily on this testimony and sent to death row. In 1996 Krone received a second trial, because a DNA analysis on the bite mark saliva indicated he was not the killer, but once again he was convicted on the bite mark evidence, despite contrary testimony for the defense from three forensic odontologists. This time he received life in prison.

In 2001 the DNA was matched to another man in the FBI's database and Krone was finally freed. He had served more than ten years for a crime he did not commit, and the episode placed forensic odontology in a negative light. A subsequent study by the American Board of Forensic Odontologists, while controversial, indicated that the accuracy rate of this type of interpretation was poor.

In 1994 Ricky Amolsch went to jail over a mistake that a forensic dentist made in a murder case. On August 23 in a mobile home park in southern Michigan, Jane Marie Fray, Amolsch's girlfriend, was found dead. She had been stabbed twenty-two times and an electrical cord was wrapped tightly around her neck. The knife used to kill her was left in her mouth, and she had been bitten near her left ear.

Amolsh was arrested, photographed, and fingerprinted. After one night in jail, he was released, although police had taken blood and hair samples and searched his home and van. He willingly submitted to a dental impression. Dr. Alan Warnick, the chief forensic odontologist for Wayne and Oakland counties, took photographs, made molds, and devised charts of Amolsh's teeth to make a comparison to the bite wound on the victim. Amolsch was soon under arrest once again.

The odontologist claimed that Amolsch's teeth were "highly consistent" with the bite mark on the victim, which persuaded the district judge to sign a murder warrant. During the trial, the odontologist testified that no one else in the metropolitan area would be as good a match to the bite mark as Amolsch was. The only other testimony was that of an ex-convict named Anthony Walker, who said he had spotted Amolsch's van outside the victim's home that morning and had overheard an argument in her trailer.

Then one of the odontologist's other murder cases was challenged, which prompted officials to reexamine the evidence against Amolsch. Dr. John Kennedy gave a second opinion, concluding that it was Walker, not Amolsch, who had bitten Fray's face. Two other dentists agreed. Amolsch was released on bond, and months later the charges were finally dropped, but a great deal of damage had been done: He suffered from depression and had lost his home and family. The county prosecutor's office no longer recommended warrants based on bite mark identification.

Researchers at Marquette University in Wisconsin claim they have developed a computer program that can precisely measure bite mark characteristics. They say it will give more scientific weight to odontological analysis, because—assuming an individual's dentition is as unique as her fingerprints—it could help build a database that could be used by investigators all over the country to narrow down suspect pools. To develop the program, Dr. L. Thomas Johnson and his colleagues collected 419 bite impressions from soldier volunteers. They digitally catalogued such characteristics as tooth width, spaces between teeth, and wear patterns, and set up the program to calculate how frequently each characteristic appeared. They are continuing to collect impressions, hoping their database will eventually assist expert testimony on such items as how often certain dental characteristics occur. Using their system, a rare impression would have more weight than a common one. The use of this system has had mixed success to date.

BACKGROUND AND TRAINING

Forensic dentistry can be a highly valuable forensic discipline in the identification of human remains. It may be helpful for dentists to become familiar with various forensic disciplines, such as DNA analysis, entomology, tool mark examination, and crime scene procedures, if they will be involved in identifications related to criminal investigations. In addition to extensive medical dentistry training, to become board certified, forensic dentists must work with medical examiners, law enforcement, insurance companies, and similar organizations to gain appropriate experience in this process. To become proficient in the documentation and study of dentition, dentists must devote extensive study in this area, completing a minimum of twenty identification cases prior to becoming certified. The study and comparison of bite mark evidence requires additional case examinations and study. Two of the bite mark cases must be submitted to the American Board of Forensic Odontology for review. Dentists who qualify to be certified after these reviews must pass both written and oral examinations.

Chapter Eleven

QUESTIONED DOCUMENTS

M any readers may remember when Clifford Irving forged the letters of the reclusive Howard Hughes to get a significant publishing contract for Hughes's life story. As many in law enforcement know, it can be difficult to detect an expert forgery. Irving was unmasked partly by an announcement from Hughes himself and partly by the analysis made by a document examiner in the US Postal Service. The identification of Irving's style lay in the form of certain letters and the manner in which certain strokes ended—evident to experts despite the extremely close likeness to Hughes's known signatures, which Irving had practiced over and over.

Dr. Henry Lee has come across questioned document examination in a number of cases. He knew that many instrumental techniques were available to analyze paper, ink, and other materials used in documents, but the comparison of handwriting still relied primarily on the training and experience of skilled examiners. Many forged documents had been identified by handwriting comparison.

233

Sometimes, however, results were not so conclusive. One case in particular he will always remember.

On December 26, 1996, at 5:52 a.m., Patsy Ramsey called 911 and shouted that her six-year-old daughter, JonBenét, had been kidnapped and a ransom note left on the staircase in her home. In response to questions, she read different parts of the three-page letter and begged for help. The police dispatcher in Boulder, Colorado, sent Officer Rick French to the fifteen-room home on 15th Street, in a posh community not far from the university. Patsy met him at the door with her husband, John. They had another child in the home, nine-year-old Burke, whom they had said was still asleep. John admitted he had not set the burglar alarm the night before.

Patsy told French that she had gone into JonBenét's second-floor bedroom to prepare her for a holiday trip, but the child's bed was empty and she was nowhere else in the house. Patsy had gone down a back staircase to the kitchen, and on the third step she had found the ransom note, written in black felt-tip ink on white legal paper and laid out with the pages side by side. The writer addressed "Mr. Ramsey" and in exchange for his daughter's life demanded certain conditions, including that he not call the police and that he prepare to pay $118,000. This note went straight to FBI agents who arrived to assist.

More police arrived, as did four of the Ramseys' friends, who were allowed to tramp through the house. A crime-scene evidence team was directed to the home and a trace was put on the phone line for incoming calls, with the expectation of a scheduled call from the kidnapper that morning between 8 and 10 o'clock. There was no sign of forced entry, and no footprints in the melting snow outside, although when a family acquaintance, Fleet White, went on his own into the basement for a cursory inspection, he noticed a broken window and a suitcase placed beneath it. John Ramsey said he had broken it a few months earlier when he forgot his key; he had yet to fix it. There was a grate over the window that appeared to be undisturbed. John called his attorney to discuss getting the ransom money moved into the local bank. He also left the house to pick up the mail. The deadline for the kidnappers' call came and went with no communication. No one seemed to know what to do.

Detective Linda Arndt directed John to take White with him to search the house again from top to bottom, just in case. At 1:00 p.m., the two men started searching in the basement. John opened the door of the so-called wine cellar—a darkened, windowless room within another room and behind the furnace. As he turned on the light, he discovered his daughter's body on the floor, lying on her back under a white blanket. She was cold to the touch, her arms bound over her head with a cord, and another cord was wrapped tightly around her neck and a small piece of black duct tape was over her mouth. Although she was dressed in the clothing she had worn the evening before, close by her body lay her favorite pink nightgown.

John ripped off the duct tape, removed the blanket, and tried to take off the binding. When he could not, he carried his daughter's body upstairs. Arndt took the corpse and laid it on the floor, placing a blanket over it. Hours later, the body was moved to the morgue. Several observers noticed what they would later describe as odd behavior: Patsy cried without tears and John seemed aloof and distant. They also left the child's body before it was removed, although no one instructed them to leave the house. The crime scene had been irreparably damaged.

The autopsy found a ligature around the neck, tightened with a short stick that was broken off a paintbrush from an art kit in the basement. Abrasions were present on the right cheek, the left side of the neck, the right shoulder, and the left lower leg. A ligature bruise was on the right wrist. There were also dotted pattern injuries to the cheek and torso, which some investigators believed could be bruises from a stun gun. A spot of blood was found inside the panties, and there were petechial hemorrhages, or tiny burst blood vessels, on the eyelids, lungs, and neck, indicating asphyxiation. In addition, there was a large hemorrhage on the right side of the skull, over an eight-inch fracture and a bruised area of the brain. The cause of death was determined to be asphyxiation by strangulation, but the child had also suffered blunt force trauma to the head.

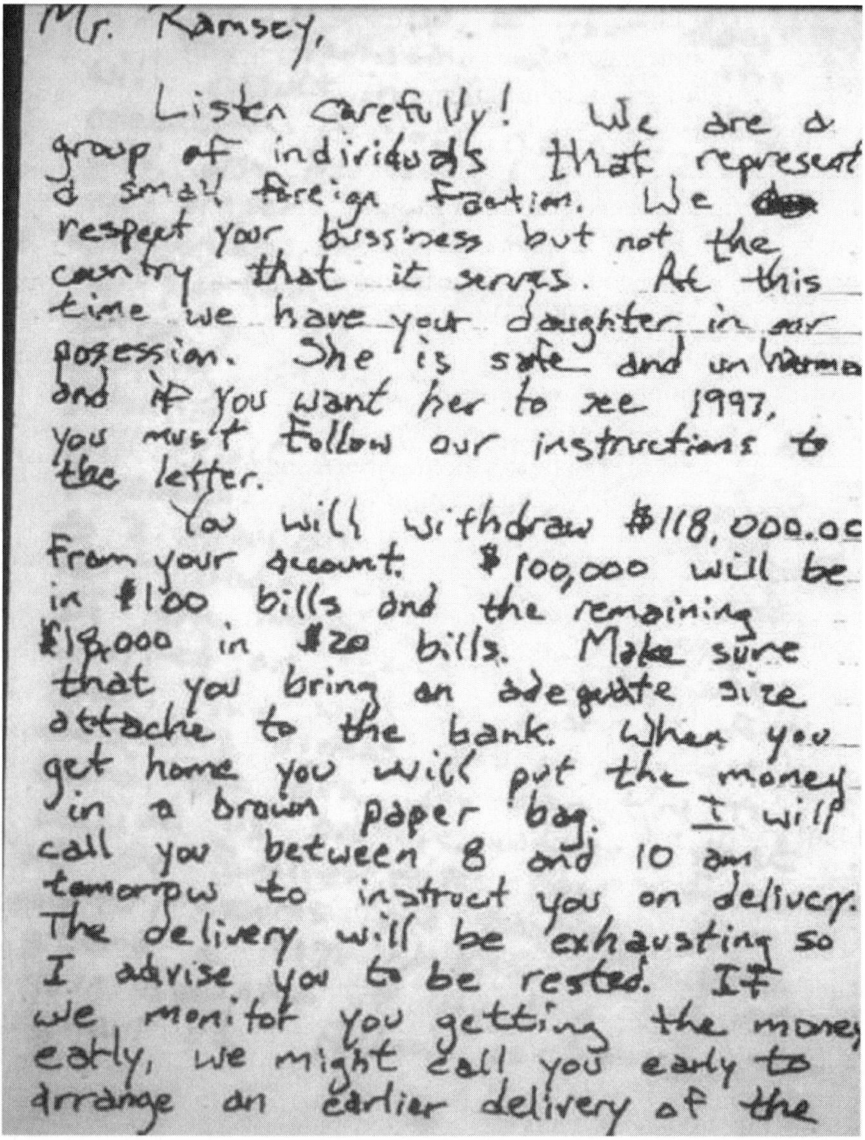

Mr. Ramsey,

Listen carefully! We are a group of individuals that represent a small foreign faction. We do respect your bussiness but not the country that it serves. At this time we have your daughter in our posession. She is safe and unharmed and if you want her to see 1997, you must follow our instructions to the letter.

You will withdraw $118,000.00 from your account. $100,000 will be in $100 bills and the remaining $18,000 in $20 bills. Make sure that you bring an adequate size attache to the bank. When you get home you will put the money in a brown paper bag. I will call you between 8 and 10 am tomorrow to instruct you on delivery. The delivery will be exhausting so I advise you to be rested. If we monitor you getting the money early, we might call you early to arrange an earlier delivery of the

Fig. 11.1. A portion of the ransom note found at the scene in the JonBenét Ramsey case.

and you stand a' 100% chance
of getting her back. You and
your family are under constant
scrutiny as well as the authorities.
Don't try to grow a brain
John. You are not the only
fat cat around so don't think
that killing will be difficult.
Don't underestimate us John.
Use that good southern common
sense of yours. It is up to
you now John!

Victory!

S.B.T.C

The ransom note became a crucial piece of evidence. It was written on a tablet found in the Ramsey home, with a pen from inside the home that was put back in its container. Three pages of writing paper were recovered from the garbage in the home. There was evidence that the letter writer had made a few false starts on the tablet Patsy normally used. The note, shown in figure 11.1, said:

Mr. Ramsey,

Listen Carefully! We are a group of individuals that represent a small foreign faction. We ~~do~~ respect your bussiness but not the country that it serves. At this time we have your daughter in our posession. She is safe and unharmed and if you want her to see 1997, you must follow our instructions to the letter.

You will withdraw $118,000.00 from your account. $100,000 will be in $100 bills and the remaining $18,000 in $20 bills. Make sure that you bring an adequate size attache to the bank. When you get home you will put the money in a brown paper bag. I will call you between 8 and 10 am tomorrow to instruct you on delivery. The delivery will be exhausting so I advise you to be rested. If we monitor you getting the money early, we might call you early to arrange an earlier delivery of the money and hence a earlier ~~delivery~~ pick-up of your daughter.

Any deviation of my instructions will result in the immediate execution of your daughter. You will also be denied her remains for proper burial. The two gentlemen watching over your daughter do not particularly like you so I advise you not to provoke them. Speaking to anyone about your situation, such as Police, F.B.I., etc., will result in your daughter being beheaded. If we catch you talking to a stray dog, she dies. If you alert bank authorities, she dies. If the money is in any way marked or tampered with, she dies. You will be scanned for electronic devices and if any are found, she dies. You can try to deceive us but be warned that we are familiar with law enforcement countermeasures and tactics. You stand a 99% chance of killing your daughter if you try to outsmart us. Follow our instructions and you stand a 100% chance of getting her back. You and your family are under constant scrutiny as well as the authorities. Don't try to grow a brain John. You are not the only fat cat around so don't think that killing will be difficult. Don't underestimate us John. Use that good southern common sense of yours. It is up to you now John!

Victory!

S.B.T.C

The opening paragraph included misspelled words, while more sophisticated words were spelled correctly, and the amount of the ransom demanded suspiciously matched that of John Ramsey's bonus that year. The author also referred to him in both a formal and a familiar manner. Yet while the offender seemed to know the layout of the house, he had come unprepared. He wrote the ransom note in the house, over a period of time, even writing a practice note.

Some investigators believed evidence pointed to a stranger. A boot print found in the wine cellar did not match any of the Ramseys' shoes, there was an unidentified fingerprint on a basement door, and the marks on the child indicated the possible use of a stun gun—something investigators would not expect parents to have used. One neighbor reported hearing a piercing scream during the night from the Ramsey home, although no one from the Ramsey family recalled hearing it.

Fifty-three-year-old John Ramsey was a successful and wealthy CEO, running a computer distribution company called Access Graphics. The neighborhood where the Ramseys lived was an affluent, low-crime area, populated by luxury homes and estates. Patsy was a homemaker and JonBenét participated in children's beauty pageants. The home had been part of a showcase of area homes for the Christmas season, and a number of friends and workers had keys. Yet they all had viable alibis. Despite strong suspicions and a lengthy grand jury hearing, no one was charged in this murder. Eventually Patsy succumbed to cancer and died. In 2007 a man named John Karr was arrested in Thailand. He confessed to involvement in the JonBenét Ramsey case, but later recanted his confession. In 2008 low copy number DNA testing was conducted on JonBenét's clothing, and scientists concluded that male DNA from someone other than the Ramseys was present.

The ransom note has been the subject of intense scrutiny and interpretation, in terms of the materials used for it, the handwriting analysis, and even the linguistic content. One psychologist even claimed to see the evidence of "thoughtprints," or patterns of the writer's thoughts, in it. Handwriting analysts had differing views. Some eliminated both John and Patsy as the author, while others claimed with certainty that Patsy had written it.

Yet obvious information is provided by this note. Written on a white, lined 8x10 tablet that originated in the house, with a pen belonging to the Ramseys, it was much longer than a typical ransom note. Containing 368 words, it lacked a date and asked for an odd sum of money that coincidentally was the amount of John Ramsey's bonus that year. It seemed to have been authored by someone who knew John. It was also a paltry amount, considering what he was worth. That the writers would refer to themselves as a "foreign faction" is odd, because they are not foreign to themselves. It also contains a number of insults against John, clearly derived from personal grudges.

The text is clearly printed and appears to be the work of a meticulous and educated individual. Only one person wrote it. The errors seem contrived rather than ignorant, and there are several internal inconsistencies in the content, as if the author was not quite certain what to say. Kidnappers generally come with a note already prepared, but even if the note was an afterthought, why would any kidnapper leave the body in the house, where it would eventually be found, possibly before the delivery of any money?

Since the murder remains unsolved and no one yet knows who wrote the ransom note, no interpretation can be shown to be correct. However, many people have claimed to have *the* answer—arriving at it with science—and yet they contradict one another. That raises issues for investigators and the courts about the subjective areas of questioned document analysis.

THE HISTORY OF QUESTIONED DOCUMENTS EXAMINATION

For all practical purposes, any written, typed, or printed material is a document; if its authorship or authenticity is unclear, it is a questioned document. The work of a document examiner generally involves probing different aspects of a questioned document with various types of scientific analysis in hopes of revealing its originating source. Examiners need to be proficient in microscopy, photography, and methods of document alteration. Additional instrumental analysis may also be required. The types of documents submitted for analysis typically include ransom notes, suicide notes, poison-pen letters, altered records, business records, forgeries, extortion notes, and disputed wills, contracts, identification cards, and other records. Among the approaches to the analysis of questioned or forged documents are handwriting/typing comparisons, alteration analysis, reconstruction of damaged or obliterated products, document origination, attributional evidence through linguistic analysis, and analysis of the materials used (generally paper and ink).

The first publication associated with questioned documents was a treatise by François Demelle of France, who made a systematic study of handwriting analysis in 1609. In a forensic context, however, one of the earliest cases of a legal document examination based on handwriting occurred in 1868, before this discipline was formally established. When Sylvia Ann Howland died in 1865, she left a considerable estate to be divided among a number of people, including her niece, Henrietta Howland Robinson. However, Robinson contested the will, producing another will that her aunt had supposedly made at an earlier time, with directions attached in a note to ignore any subsequent wills. Howland's executor rejected this note as a forgery, so the case went to court. Charles Sanders Peirce made a mathematical comparison of forty-two separate examples of Howland's signature, testifying that each signature had thirty downstrokes, and that, on average, one in five overlapped. Pierce's statistical calculation convinced the jury how unlikely it was that all thirty downstrokes of two examples of a signature would match perfectly, and yet they did. The implication was that the signature on the disputed note had been traced.

One of the most famous cases in which questioned documents were a central feature, coming two decades after Albert S. Osborn wrote the groundbreaking text *Questioned Documents*, was the kidnapping and murder of Charles Lindbergh Jr. Osborn was the first person to systematically study the characteristics of handwriting in such a way as to identify authorship, and his expertise was acknowledged by courtrooms across the country. The second edition of *Questioned Documents* was published in 1929, seven years after Osborn's second book, *The Problem of Proof*, and just before the Lindbergh kidnapping. Osborn founded the American Society of Questioned Document Examiners in 1942, becoming its first president.

As noted in chapter 2, on March 1, 1932, twenty-month-old Charles Lindbergh Jr., the son of legendary aviator Charles Lindbergh, was taken from his crib. His nurse discovered him missing and asked Anne Morrow Lindbergh, the child's mother, if she had him. Upon hearing that she did not, the nurse asked Lindbergh. Startled, he ran to look in the crib, whereupon he exclaimed, "Anne! They have stolen our baby!"

The first officers to arrive after the kidnapping found footprints outside the nursery window that led to a ladder in three sections. Police also found a chisel and some tire tracks, along with the same kind of mud found tracked through the nursery. On a windowsill in the room was a ransom note in an envelope, which said:

Dear Sir!

Have 50000$ redy with 25 000 $ in 20 $ bills 1.5000 $ in 10$ bills and 10000$ in 5 $ bills. After 2–4 days we will inform you were to deliver the Mony.

We warn you for making anyding public or for notify the Police the child is in gut care.

Indication for all letters are singnature and 3 holes.

At the bottom right-hand corner of the sheet of paper was a drawing of two interlocking blue circles, each an inch in diameter. The penny-sized area where the circles intersected had been colored red, and three small holes had been punched into the design, at the left, right, and center, about an inch apart. There were no fingerprints on the note or in the nursery.

Two years passed before notes from the ransom money, specially marked, turned up on September 15, 1934, at a gas station in New York. The person passing the bill was a carpenter from the Bronx named Bruno Richard Hauptmann. A search of his home turned up more than fourteen thousand dollars of the ransom money. Although he claimed to have received it from a man who had since died, he was arrested.

Central to Hauptmann's conviction—and still controversial—was an analysis of the handwriting in the notes, fourteen of which had been received over the course of the investigation. All were signed with the same symbol and often contained the same misspellings and grammatical errors. The handwriting also looked the same.

The notes were sent to several analysts, who all concluded that the notes had been written by the same person. The misspellings were consistent, as were the odd inversions of some letters, like *g* and *h*, and some referred to earlier notes or events. The same instrument had been used to punch the holes in the symbol, and the letters had been written on the same kind of paper with the same ink. The nationality of the author, inferred from the phraseology, was determined to be German. Osborn composed a paragraph for police to use to get suspects to write out certain words that could be compared with the notes, using words like "our," "place," and "money." The paragraph, he said, must be dictated, not copied. This method allowed investigators to determine whether the suspect's writing made the same sorts of errors as the author of the original note.

Hauptmann was asked to provide samples of his handwriting and to copy the ransom notes as closely as possible. He was made to write over and over, for hours, until he fell asleep at the table from exhaustion. He wrote his statement seven times, and nine sheets of dictated writing were taken to Osborn's son, Albert D. Osborn. Hauptmann had been required to write with three different pens, with some samples written upright and some slanted. The end result was that there were more discrepancies among some of his writing samples than there were between his samples and the ransom notes.

According to the resulting analysis, Hauptmann had a peculiar way of writing *x* and *t*. He also wrote "not" as "note," using an open *o* and an uncrossed *t*, and wrote "the" in a strangely illegible manner. The most telling evidence is a diagnosis that Hauptmann suffered from agraphia—the peculiar tic of adding unnecessary *es* onto various words, such the word "not," evident in the notes and at times in his own letters. Interestingly, samples of Hauptmann's handwriting found in his home showed many of the same peculiarities found in the ransom notes. He protested the verdict to the end, but he was executed in 1936.

Another complicated case that put document examination to the test involved the supposed discovery in the 1980s of Adolf Hitler's secret diaries. The German publishing company Gruner and Jahr paid $2.3 million for sixty handwritten notebooks and a third unpublished volume of *Mein Kampf*. The publishers were told that the papers had been taken out of Berlin toward the end of World War II aboard an airplane that had crashed. A farmer found them and sold them to a document collector, Konrad Kujau, via an unnamed general in East Germany. Kujau had taken them to a journalist on the staff of *Stern*, a newspaper owned by Gruner and Jahr. *Stern* quickly began serializing the diaries, selling publication rights to *Newsweek* in the United States and to the *Times* in the UK.

The owner of the *Times* insisted that tests be performed to establish the authenticity of the diaries. Three experts—Max Frei-Sultzer, the former head of the forensic science department for the police in Zurich, Switzerland; Ordway Hilton, a specialist in document verification, and a third man who worked with the German police—compared samples of handwriting authenticated as Hitler's to the handwriting in the alleged diaries. All three agreed that the texts had been written by the same person, and that person's handwriting was the same as that in the comparison samples. Handwriting analysis confirmed the Hitler diaries as authentic.

However, forensics tests on the paper and ink contradicted this. Looking at the paper under ultraviolet light, the West German analysts found that it contained an additive that had been put into paper only since 1954. The threads attaching the seals contained material manufactured only after the war, and the type of ink used was not available at the time the diaries were purportedly written. A test of the ink that involved the evaporation of chloride later proved that the documents had in fact been written within the past year.

In addition, content analysis revealed historical inaccuracies directly copied from *Hitler's Speeches and Proclamations*, written by former Nazi federal archivist Max Domarus, which were apparently overlooked in the magazine's attempt to keep the scoop a secret until publication. One distinguished historian of Hitler's regime, Hugh Trevor-Roper, had even vouched for their authenticity, but he was clearly in error.

Kujau's own background provided some further clues. As a child he had sold forged autographs of famous politicians, and later he manufactured so-called Nazi mementos, including an introduction to a sequel to *Mein Kampf* and poems by Hitler. As it turned out, Kujau had forged the samples believed to be authentic. He was arrested, gave a full confession, and was sentenced to three years in prison.

One of the techniques Kujau had devised for making the diaries appear authentic was smashing them with a hammer and staining the paper with tea leaves. Using Gothic script, he wrote out Hitler's daily thoughts into black notebooks, each sealed with special seals and a black ribbon. By the time he was finished, the diaries ran from 1935 until 1945. Unfortunately for Kujau, his lack of care in choosing the materials that composed the diary and the seals led to the uncovering of this elaborate forgery scheme.

When Mark Hofmann forged several hundred important Mormon documents during the 1980s and was arrested for two fatal bombings, Special Agent George Throckmorton, a questioned documents examiner from the attorney general's office, performed a number of tests on several of Hofmann's most skillful forgeries. The ink was tested with microspectrophotometry to determine the absorption spectrum and thin layer chromatography to reveal its composition. It was then compared to the database of more than three thousand ink profiles at the US Bureau of Alcohol, Tobacco, and Firearms.

Using one of Hofmann's inspirations, Throckmorton figured out the method used for making the iron gallotannate ink that had defied many tests for determining its age. Using a control group of non-Hofmann documents, he noticed that unique to all Hofmann-handled documents were two characteristics that showed up under microscopic and video spectral comparator ultraviolet examination: the ink ran in a single direction and cracked like alligator skin. This was the effect of artificially aging homemade ink. The downward running of the ink was explained by the fact that the document was hung to dry. To reproduce the effect, Flynn made quill pens from turkey feathers and duplicated some of the handwriting on both modern and aged paper. He oxidized the ink in an oven, using a fuming method for another sample. He found that when iron gallotannate ink was used on old paper and aged, there was no way to determine that it was not as old as claimed. A chemical reaction on the ink, if it was on paper of the right time period, showed no difference from ink of that age. Throckmorton realized that this was how Hofmann had managed to dupe so many document experts.

MATERIALS ANALYSIS

The materials analyzed in a questioned document are the surface and the medium used for inscribing. Analysis most often involves examination of the paper, which is classified according to the materials in its composition. This can differ according to additives, the presence or absence of watermarks, and the surface treatments used. Specialists can usually determine from its composition the date when a particular type of paper was introduced, because some components are more modern than others.

Examining ink means knowing the history of its development. Modern ink can be one of four basic types: iron salts in a suspension of gallic acid, with dyes, carbon particles suspended in gum arabic, synthetic dyes with a range of polymers and acids, and synthetic dyes or pigments in a range of solvents and additives. Inks are analyzed for chemical composition and dyes, usually using various instrumental techniques. In the past, thin layer chromatography was often used to separate the colored and other components of inks.

If the document has been printed or copied on a photocopier, microscopic analysis can often link it with a specific machine, especially if there is a characteristic that individualizes the way it prints or copy machine defects. The type of ink or powder used can assist in this process, and databases exist for this purpose.

HANDWRITING ANALYSIS

Although handwriting analysis is often erroneously compared to graphology (which purports to see personality traits in a person's handwriting style), the science of handwriting examination is a strongly peer-reviewed forensic discipline. Sometimes graphology is called handwriting analysis, and the popular media often confuse the two, but it is not based in science and is not acceptable for use in court. The process of forensic handwriting comparison actually involves the stepwise examination of the formation of the writing and its individual characteristics.

Most people learn to write by imitating a certain style taught in schools in their country or region, usually the Palmer or Zaner-Blosser method in the United States, but eventually idiosyncrasies develop in the way letters are joined or formed, which derive from education, artistic ability, physiological development, degree of meticulousness, and personal preference. Experts contend that no two people write exactly alike, which makes it possible to distinguish one person's writing samples from another's. Repeated usage over a long period of time crystallizes a specific style that will show only slight variation over the years. Nevertheless, something like a signature will never be exactly the same, which makes it possible to detect when handwriting has been traced as a forgery.

Handwriting experts study the variations in writing samples to try to determine whether two (or more) different documents were written by the same person and thereby to identify the known author of one sample with the author of a similar document. The same odd characteristics—spelling, a particular slant, spacing, or the manner of forming certain letters—are expected to show up across samples written or printed by the same person. These are evident even during attempts to alter one's handwriting.

When conducting an examination, analysts look at class characteristics, which are formed from the specific writing system the author learned, and individual characteristics or features that are not common to any group. The latter play an important role in forensic investigation. A known specimen written by an identified person is called the "standard" or "exemplar," and it should be as similar as possible to the questioned writing, specifically containing similar words or letter combinations. In other words, in the Lindbergh case, a letter or diary written by Bruno Hauptmann should contain some words or phrases common to the ransom notes. The more samples available of both types, the better. If more than a signature or common words are desired, experts recommend that exemplars be obtained by reading the appropriate wording to a suspect and have him write it out.

The primary factors for analysis are divided into four categories:

1. *Form.* The elements that comprise the shape of the letters, proportion, slant, angles, lines, retracing, connections, and curves.
2. *Line quality.* The results from the writing instrument used, the amount of pressure exerted, and the flow and continuity of the script.
3. *Arrangement.* The spacing, alignment, formatting, and distinctive punctuation.
4. *Content.* The spelling, phrasing, punctuation, and grammar.

In some cases, aspects of the handwriting will be quite unique, which gives them evidential value. If there are significant dissimilarities between an exemplar and a questioned document, then it's likely there are two different authors, unless the differences can be accounted for, such as when the author has had an accident between writing the two items or when she is taking medication or drugs that might alter her coordination. However, similarities are not necessarily a sure indication, since even the most unique factor in a person's handwriting may show up in someone else's. Ultimately, the handwriting analyst may reach one of several conclusions when comparing two documents: the documents were written by the same person; it is likely the documents were written by the same person; it is unlikely the documents were written by the same person; the documents were not written by the same person; or no conclusion is possible (inconclusive). Expert handwriting analysis takes into account a wide variety of factors and a repetition of numerous similarities. Figure 11.2 shows one of the steps in the examination of a questioned document.

The goal in handwriting analysis is to collect samples that have been written within two or three years of the questioned document, since an adequate collection of samples is critical to a successful identification. Known exemplars are the primary source, but if they are not sufficient in number, the suspected author may be asked to sit down and write, a procedure that has its own protocol. Unlike in

Fig. 11.2. The laboratory examination of a questioned signature.

the Lindbergh case, when Hauptmann was asked to copy sentences directly from the ransom notes, the accepted procedure is to sit the subject at a table where there will be no distraction and invite an objective witness to watch or use a videocamera to film the proceedings. The suspect should not be shown the questioned document or be instructed how to spell certain words or to use certain punctuation. She should use materials similar to those in the document, and dictated text should match some parts of the document. The dictation should be repeated several times, and when the procedure is finished, the subject should be asked to sign and date the text, including the time. Handwriting samples lie outside the protection of the Fifth Amendment and therefore can be acquired without a violation of privacy.

As in other forensic science fields, expertise in questioned document analysis develops as a result of years of exposure. Today there are many automated techniques that can be used in making an analysis, such as the Forensic Information System for Handwriting (FISH), but careful and experienced interpretation is still necessary.

In the case of a document written on a typewriter (usually an older document, since these days most documents are written on computers that do not have machine-specific idiosyncrasies), a different method for comparison is used. This method involves attempting to identify the make and model of the typewriter used, and then identifying a suspect's particular machine. Usually the specific identification factors derive from typeface defects, mechanical failures, or damage. Examination of the ribbon may also be helpful.

Attempts to alter a document generally show up on the medium's surface as erasure, sandpapering, or razoring. Alterations made by using different inks may be detected by infrared lighting techniques, as shown in figure 11.3, which can also assist in determining the contents of a document that has been damaged by fire. A spectral comparator provides a source of additional wavelengths of light with which the scientist can examine the document for variations in ink, alterations, and other characteristics.

Sometimes a questioned document is merely the indentation on the top page of a tablet left by writing on the sheet above it, which has since been removed. In these cases the paper can be examined under oblique lighting or processed with toner powder and an electrostatic charge to clearly see and duplicate the impressions. (Incidentally, examiners would never rub a pencil over the surface of the

Fig. 11.3. An alternate light examination of a check shows that the amount has been changed using an ink with different fluorescent properties.

paper, as seen in many detective movies, since that may actually destroy portions of the indentations!)

LINGUISTIC ANALYSIS

Also called forensic stylistics or attributional analysis, linguistic analysis involves making a detailed analysis of the content of a questioned document to compare what was written to what a suspect reads or generally writes. The basic premise is that no two people use language in exactly the same way—similar to the idea that no two people form their letters or numbers in exactly the same way. The pattern of unique differences in each person's use of language, along with repetition of those traits throughout his writing, provide evidence that links a specific person to the questioned writing. Forensic sytlistics is challenged by some attorneys as unscientific and too subjective to be used as evidence during trial.

This technique is used by linguistic experts all over the country. When examining a questioned sample, such as a letter, experts may search text databases that might contain similar language habits. The language used by an unknown author can help establish the writer's age, gender, ethnicity, level of education, professional training, and ideology. The key features are vocabulary, spelling, grammar, syntax, and punctuation habits. Other kinds of textual evidence may include borrowed or influential source material, document formatting, and the physical document itself. This information may provide investigative leads to law enforcement.

Carole Chaski is a linguist and criminal justice instructor at Delaware Technical and Community College in Georgetown. Her method—syntactic analysis—is based on generative grammar, a touchstone in linguistics for the past five decades. Generative grammar originated in the work of Noam Chomsky, and this approach analyzes the rules of grammar in a particular language to form an algorithm with which to predict which combinations of words will form grammatical sentences. Chaski utilizes a standard statistical test to develop her expert opinion. Syntax is the unconscious and automatic way in which a person combines words to create phrases and sentences; Chaski analyzes a questioned document for distinct syntactic patterns—combinations of nouns, verbs, adverbs, and prepositions—and each is counted statistically.

After confessions validated several of Chaski's analyses, she won a research fellowship at the National Institute of Justice. There she created a database of known authors' writing samples and ran experiments. She tested hundreds of linguistic variables with several different statistical procedures, claiming that she achieved 95 percent accuracy for author attribution from blind samples using her method. She developed a computer program based on her statistical analysis that examines specific types of words in relation to all the others used in a document. In 1998 she founded the Institute of Linguistic Evidence as a nonprofit agency to support research on the validity and reliability of language-based author identification.

In 1992, after twenty-three-year-old computer programmer Michael Hunter was found dead in his bed, Chaski was asked to analyze his supposed suicide note. Joseph Mannino, Hunter's roommate, had made the emergency call. An autopsy indicated that Hunter had died from a mixture of several over-the-counter drugs and an overdose of the anesthetic lidocaine. But when the pathologist found an injection mark on his arm—with no sign of a needle in or near him—the police opened an investigation.

They soon learned that Hunter had lived with two men: Mannino, age twenty-six, and Garry Walston, age thirty. Walston was a landscape architect and Mannino a medical student. Since Mannino could have gained access to lidocaine, it was surmised that he might have killed Hunter in a jealous rage. Walston confirmed that Mannino and Hunter had been angry at each other, and that he had sided with Hunter. Mannino had been in the process of moving out when Hunter was found dead.

Manino denied any wrongdoing, but admitted he had given Hunter lidocaine for migraine headaches. He revealed that Hunter had recently discovered he was HIV-positive and suggested he had probably used the lidocaine to kill himself. Mannino then offered a computer disk that appeared to contain several suicide notes to friends and relatives. Since they were typed, there was no way to do handwriting analysis, but content analysis was plentiful.

Chaski took on the challenge. She received numerous samples of both Hunter's and Mannino's writing. Then she applied her computer program to the samples and the alleged suicide notes, and offered statistical information about grammar and phrasing. None of Hunter's known exemplars exhibited certain key syntactical items in the suicide notes, so Chaski concluded that he had not written the notes. However, there was reason to believe that Mannino might have written them, since he was the one who turned the disks over to the police. An HIV test also showed that Hunter was not HIV-positive. Mannino was arrested, and at his trial he admitted that he had written the suicide notes. He was found guilty of involuntary manslaughter.

ISSUES IN COURT

Linguistics is a social science, and, like the behavioral and natural sciences, it is subject to the *Daubert* or *Frye* standard. However, many judges fail to understand the requirements of science, especially elements such as error rate and objective methodology, so some people who falsely claim to be offering a scientific method may be allowed to testify. Understandably, this bothers experts who do base their methods and interpretations on science.

The social sciences seem to be especially vulnerable in this regard, because their approach does not generally meet the standards of something like DNA profiling or toxicology analysis. Nevertheless, verification is possible. The more rigorous the demands by the court, the more reliable the testimony from these experts will be. Red flags for the court should be self-proclaimed experts who use the term "forensic linguistics," but have not applied actual linguistic methods. Experts who offer personal opinion or gut intuition without statistical backup are also suspect—real numbers, not just vague descriptions of probability, are required for real analysis. These people offer no limits in terms of the amount or type of text needed. Those who make the statement that new data will not change the conclusion are not engaged in science.

Forensic document examination has been challenged as pseudoscience since the *Daubert* decision. The majority of courts have found the study of handwriting sufficiently scientific in the identification and comparison of characteristics; however, the statistical basis to prove the significance of a handwriting conclusion is still lacking. Even ink and paper comparisons raise eyebrows because the actual number of modern writing materials produced is so large; the significance of a positive comparison between a questioned document and materials found in a search of the suspect's home, for example, may be highly overestimated by the trier of fact. As noted above, the handwriting analyst may reach one of several conclusions when comparing documents. Because of the "likely" possibilities and the lack of objective standards to arrive at a particular conclusion, some attorneys believe that this discipline is too subjective for use during trial.

QUALIFICATIONS OF THE DOCUMENT EXAMINER

Document examiners may be certified by the American Board of Forensic Document Examiners, which was formed in 1977. This helped to establish its presence in other courts. Applicants for certification must meet seven standards, including integrity, appropriate education, completion of a specified training program, evidence of a practice in document examination, and a record of appropriate professional activity in the field. There is also a comprehensive exam, with written, practical, and oral components. The renewable certification is valid for five years at a time, with continuing education requirements. In addition, good eyesight is a must, and candidates must be able to pass a "form blindness" test to prove they can distinguish between similarly shaped items. There is no federal licensing of document examiners, but in 1987 the court considered the reliability of handwriting comparisons in *United States v. Buck* and denied a motion to prevent its use.

Forensic document examiners must be well trained in photography and other documentation methods. An awareness of other areas of forensic science, such as DNA analysis and latent fingerprint analysis, is important for proper handling and to avoid contamination of evidence. Few institutions provide formal training, but self-education and working alongside an experienced mentor can assist aspiring examiners to learn and improve. Extensive training in various aspects of document examination and hands-on study may take more than two years. Besides being able to establish the authenticity of a document or its authorship, forensic document examiners must be able to testify in court and compose written reports of their analysis and findings, so they must be knowledgeable about the *Daubert* factors, understand the limitations of the science, and be able to testify in a truthful and unbiased manner.

Chapter Twelve

EMERGING FORENSIC DISCIPLINES

When Dr. Henry Lee started the computer forensics laboratory in Connecticut in 2000, there were few labs in the country conducting tests on electronic evidence. Many investigations at that time centered on the use of the Internet by predators to meet potential victims. This discipline also included analysis of many types of electronic evidence, white-collar crime, and other types of fraud using computers. New software was regularly created, and analysts had to stay abreast of these technical developments. The computer crime and electronic evidence case backlogs in most states were enormous.

With the tragedy of September 11, 2001, homeland security became a national focus. Many forensic science disciplines played a critical role in maintaining national safety. Other techniques contributed to the identification of victims of mass disasters.

As the interest in forensic science increased, many professions focused on their potential contributions to the field. In early 2000 Lee worked with a local university to develop a forensic nursing program. He is regularly asked to provide training for various groups, ranging from journalists to morticians, all of which found their membership interacting with crime scenes, evidence, or legal proceedings. Not only have contributions from nontraditional forensic areas grown, but new areas keep emerging. One example of nontraditional areas playing an important role in a case was the input of psychologists in evaluating the activities and background of Connecticut's serial killer.

Wendy Baribeault was on her way to a convenience store. In broad daylight on June 13, 1984, the seventeen-year-old girl walked along Highway 12 in Lisbon, Connecticut, doing what many teenagers do on a hot summer day to buy a cold drink or some ice cream. However, she did not reach the store, and she never returned home. There was no reason to suspect she had run away, but no one knew where she could have gone. Two days passed before her body was found on the other side of a stone wall on the road on which she had walked. She had been raped and strangled. Her body was buried under a pile of rocks.

It seemed impossible that no one had seen the person who attacked her, but she was among eight young women from the area over the previous three years who had been similarly assaulted. Detective Michael Malchik was assigned as investigator, and state police officers questioned area residents and made a public appeal for information. The police soon received a report from a motorist who had seen a thin white man sporting glasses and driving a late-model blue Toyota following a girl on Highway 12 on the day Baribeault disappeared. The driver was apparently talking with her. The witness could not have known that as soon as the area was clear, this man would act quickly, pulling the young woman over the wall to rape and kill her.

The witness report provided a good lead, and investigators acquired a list from the Department of Motor Vehicles of all the late-model Toyotas registered in the local area, which amounted to about thirty-six hundred. The State Police Major Crime Squad then made a list of white male drivers with vision correction in the right age range. One of the first Toyota owners Malchik and his partner interviewed—to start the potentially tedious process of eliminating possibilities—was a young man named Michael Ross. While there was nothing overtly suspicious about Ross, he kept saying and doing things that made Malchik believe he was about to admit something, so the detective kept thinking up more questions to ask him.

Meanwhile, Henry Lee, Sergeant Robert Mills, and Elaine Pagliaro examined evidence collected from the scene. Laboratory scientists also went back to the scene to reexamine each piece of rock that was used to cover Baribeault's body. Superglue fuming techniques to develop for latent fingerprints had just been introduced in the United States. The investigators used this technique on the rocks, hoping to find suspect's fingerprints. Pagliaro was able to type the semen found on the victim: The suspect was found to be a type-B secretor (meaning a specific blood antigen shows up in all of this person's biological fluids) with a PGM type of 1–1. In addition, a Caucasian-type pubic hair was recovered from Baribeault's clothing.

Malchik went back to ask Ross about his blood type and to collect hair samples. Eventually, Ross admitted to killing Baribeault, so he was taken into custody for a focused interrogation. Later Ross confessed to other murders he had committed, telling police about attacks on five more young women. He claimed he had poor memory about the details.

One victim from his list was Robin Stravinsky, age nineteen, who had disappeared while hitchhiking in November 1983. Her remains were found a week later, and the fatal sexual assault was linked to a double homicide in the area. On Easter Sunday in 1984, April Brunais and Lesley Shelley were hitchhiking home on Highway 138 after seeing a movie in Griswold, Connecticut, when Ross offered them a ride. Instead of taking them to their destination, he kept driving. Brunais, who had a knife, threatened him with it, but he quickly disarmed her. Then he drove the girls to Rhode Island, where he raped one and then strangled both. He took the bodies back to Connecticut and dumped them in a culvert.

In 1994 Ross did an interview with the BBC in which he also claimed to have killed two women in New York. One incident involved sixteen-year-old Paula Perrera, a friendly girl who was active in her church youth group. She suffered from depression and had begun to hitchhike to avoid kids who teased her. Ross picked her up on March 1, 1982. Her body was found in Wallkill, New York State eighteen days later; she had been raped, sodomized, and strangled. DNA testing confirmed Ross's involvement, and in 2000 he was charged with her murder. Police had a suspicion that his second New York victim was twenty-five-year-old Dzung Ngoc Tu, but Ross was never charged in that killing for lack of evidence.

Ross presents an unusual background for a serial killer. Born in 1959, he grew up to become an Ivy League graduate with substantial ambitions. Yet he had a difficult upbringing: His mother was mentally unstable and reportedly neglected and abused him and his three siblings. She abandoned her family, and upon her return she was institutionalized. When Ross was eight, his fourteen-year-old uncle committed suicide; there was speculation among relatives that he might have abused Ross while babysitting him. But Ross, who had no recollection of abuse, showed few of the symptoms typical of children subjected to abusive behavior. He excelled in school and went on to study agricultural economics at Cornell University. With an IQ of 122, he planned one day to own his own farm. No loner, he was socially active, joining clubs and having several girlfriends. He even got engaged. But in secret, he was spinning violent sexual fantasies that resulted in stalking and raping, especially after the engagement ended. In 1981, after he graduated from college, Ross was arrested for sexual assault. He received probation. He soon killed his first victim in New York State, believed to be Dzung Ngoc Tu.

Over the next three years Ross, who claimed his fantasies compelled him to commit these violent acts, raped and killed seven more women. In most of these cases, he was never a suspect. He was arrested in another nonfatal assault, but after serving a four-month sentence and paying a fine, he was allowed to go free.

In July 1987 Ross went on trial for the murders of Deborah Taylor and Tammy Williams. He pled guilty and received a sentence of 120 years. Then, after a trial, a jury found him guilty of four other murders and he received a combined punishment of two life sentences and four death sentences. Among the items of physical evidence against him were blood group typing of semen, hair comparisons, cloth found near a victim that matched the slipcovers in his apartment, and a ligature used on a Rhode Island victim that matched materials in his car. While admitting guilt, Ross was annoyed that the court seemed disinclined to take into account his mental illness. His psychiatrist, Dr. Robert Miller, was not allowed to testify at the penalty phase, which Ross believed would have spared him the death penalty. He petitioned for a new trial, filing numerous appeals, and while the Connecticut Supreme Court upheld the convictions, it overturned the death sentences and ordered a new penalty hearing.

Ross was apparently obsessed with making women love him—perhaps, as some mental health experts surmised, because he was so uncertain of his mother's love. As a teenager, he molested several neighborhood girls, adding details of these assaults to his fantasies; these assaults also made him bolder. By the time he had developed an adult sex drive, he was thinking constantly about rape and murder. Perhaps he was angry, perhaps he was experiencing a yearning for power and control, or perhaps he had a physiological condition that motivated him. Psychology has not yet reached a point to be able to make a definitive diagnosis.

He wrote an article from prison about how his urges never left him. Despite the pleasure he received while raping a woman, he claimed he felt disgusted afterward, growing depressed and suicidal. He said that the female hormonal contraceptive Depo-Provera, which was given to him in prison, had reduced his urges and allowed him some relief, but then liver problems forced him to abandon this treatment. Directly afterward, the urges and fantasies returned full-force.

Then Ross received another hormonal medication that he said helped to clear his mind. For the first time, he said, he became aware of the horrific nature of what he had done to his victims. He decided to give closure to the families and himself by volunteering to be executed. It was a controversial decision, since the state had not executed anyone since 1960, and it necessitated a competency evaluation. The process took about four years, and in 1998 Ross signed a ten-page "death pact" with the prosecutor, C. Robert Satti. However, a superior court judge quickly invalidated this pact as unconstitutional. Another penalty phase hearing was scheduled, this time to allow for more psychological testimony. Ross had hoped to avoid this scenario, so as to spare the victims' families. Nevertheless, the hearing remained on the schedule, but just as it was set to begin in April 1999, Ross had an about-face: He decided he did not wish to be executed, and his defense attorneys prepared to bring the issue of his mental illness to center stage.

During the hearing, the prosecutor used investigators, relatives of the victims, and Ross's BBC interview to emphasize how the victims had suffered and needlessly died for no purpose other than to fulfill a deviant fantasy. However, Dr. Stanley Kauchinski testified on Ross's behalf, showing with records of his treatments that a hormonal imbalance had likely caused his criminal behavior; thus, he could not control himself. Ross's father urged the jury to see his son's value as a specimen for scientists; keeping him alive would allow them to learn more about the psychopathology of a sexually sadistic serial killer. Miller was also allowed to speak this time, and he detailed Ross's mental illness as a mitigating factor in his crimes. Apparently the jury disagreed, as they once more gave Ross death sentences for four of the murders, including that of Wendy Baribeault. In 2001, while this death sentence was being appealed, Ross was extradited to New York, where he also pled guilty to the murder of Paula Perrera, two full decades after he had killed her. His sentence for this crime was eight to twenty-five years.

Ross stopped the appeals process in 2004, accepting the sentence, and was nearly executed in January 2005, but his attorney requested a delay for another competency hearing. Two psychiatrists said that Ross suffered from narcissistic personality disorder, which compelled him to choose to die to avoid looking like a coward, while two others disputed this and said he was truly remorseful and believed he should be punished. A judge decided Ross was competent to determine his own fate. Attempts by the Office of the Public Defender to continue appeals on Ross's behalf were denied. A female correspondent begged Ross to reconsider, promising to marry him if he elected to live. He thanked her, but opted for death. On May 13, 2005, when he was forty-five years old, Michael Ross was executed at the Osborn Correctional Institution in Somers, Connecticut. He offered no last words, although he sent a letter to Dr. Stuart Grassian, a psychiatrist who had argued that he was incompetent to waive an appeal. The letter said, "Check, and mate. You never had a chance!"

The discussion about the exact nature of Ross's mental disorder and his inability to control his actions still continues today. While the focus in forensic investigation is most often on the sciences that analyze direct physical evidence, there are other areas that contribute to understanding or reconstructing a crime, such as the knowledge gained from studying Ross's activities and condition. Among them are psychology, engineering, computer science, and nursing, each of which has a forensic specialty.

FORENSIC PSYCHOLOGY

The discipline of forensic psychology concerns any arena in which the legal system requires services or testimony from a psychiatrist or psychologist. While most practitioners are clinicians with knowledge of forensic issues, this discipline involves a range of specialties in both the civil and criminal arenas. These include consulting on criminal investigations, assessing threats of violence, determining the fitness of a parent for guardianship, developing specialized knowledge of crimes and motives, evaluating the effects of sexual harassment, consulting on sentencing guidelines, developing prison programs, and conducting research that has forensic implications.

For the courts, forensic psychologists are usually hired to evaluate a defendant's present psychological state for competency to participate in some area of the legal process, or to assess a defendant's mental state at the time of a crime in which she was allegedly involved. In addition, psychologists appraise behaviors such as malingering, confessing, deception, hallucinations, or acting suicidal. As consultants, psychologists may assist forensic artists to get a facial reconstruction of a John or Jane Doe right, help with finding a motive for an incident, or advise an attorney in selecting jury members. They can use negotiation or risk assessment to defuse a potentially violent situation or aid death investigators with psychological information about a victim that can reduce ambiguity in a confusing manner-of-death determination. Some forensic psychologists work for police departments to screen for fitness for duty, teach stress management, or determine the need for trauma counseling, while many others are employed in prisons or psychiatric hospitals. Quite a few are therapists in private practice and consult or perform assessments on the side.

To be effective, forensic psychologists must know the workings and expectations of the court, in order to offer information that will facilitate the decision making of the trier of fact (judge or jury) regarding the issue to be decided. They need to be aware of landmark cases in their field and learn proper courtroom protocol to be qualified as experts. They must also be fully prepared to explain to a jury how they arrived at their findings. This most often involves a firm grasp of psychological assessment instruments, procedures for making a standard diagnosis, and methods of statistical analysis in the behavioral sciences

Psychological assessment is central to a broad spectrum of areas. Assessments can be done for the court, the government, schools, military, insurance companies, or any other decision-making fact finders involved in legal issues. In general, psychologists present results from test data and clinical interviews. Forensic assessment instruments measure intelligence, personality traits, motor skills, neurological conditions, potential for deception, and inclination for criminal behavior. The most common battery of tests includes the Wechsler Adult Intelligence Scales (WAIS), the Minnesota Multiphasic Personality Inventory (MMPI-2), the Rorschach test, and the Thematic Apperception Test, and, when organic damage is suspected, the Bender-Gestalt and Halstead-Reitan neuropsychological tests. An important function tested when a defense attorney wishes to use a diminished mental capacity or insanity plea is that of malingering—the faking of symptoms for amnesia, dissociative disorders, or psychosis.

Competency examinations are performed in both criminal and civil cases, most often concerning the defendant's competency to stand trial—whether or not she understands the legal process and its consequences—and can contribute to her defense. However, there are other competencies that can affect the criminal process at different stages: competency to waive one's Miranda rights (right to silence and to legal counsel), to confess, to understand the nature of the crime committed, to testify, to refuse an insanity defense, and even to be executed. In civil cases, competency screenings cover such things as capacity to parent (in child custody suits), appointing guardians, and the consent to have treatment.

In *Dusky v. United States* (1960), the Supreme Court set standards for defining competency. Accordingly, to be judged competent, a defendant must show a rational and factual understanding of the charges; she must possess sufficient present capacity to understand the criminal process, to function in that process, and to consult with counsel. In other words, a defendant must clearly understand the roles played by the various participants and be able to plan or assist in the planning of her defense. A judgment of incompetency prompts the court to transfer the defendant to treatment facilities charged with restoring competency. Sometimes competency can be restored with education about the legal process, but more often treatment involves psychoactive medication.

Besides present mental state, mental health experts often assess a defendant's state of mind during the commission of a crime, referred to as the mental state at the time of the offense (MSO). For example, while competency issues might delay a trial—even indefinitely—insanity is generally about getting an acquittal that will send the defendant to a mental institution rather than to prison. It can also be about mitigating a sentence. The legal system recognizes that responsibility for committing a crime depends on two things: *actus reus*, or evidence that the accused engaged in the act, and *mens rea*, the mental state required to have intended to commit the act and foreseen its consequences. The standard for determining criminal responsibility varies by state, but in the concept of a trial, insanity is not a diagnostic concept; it is a legal concept related to, but not synonymous with, mental illness. One can be psychotic and also be judged sane, because he understood that the nature of the act was wrong. One can also be judged temporarily insane while having no mental illness. There is no uniform standard for determining insanity, and a person found sane in one jurisdiction might be considered insane in another.

To make a determination about the defendant's MSO, the clinician must examine the defendant's actions, circumstances, and perceptions leading up to the crime and coordinate these findings with police and medical examiner reports, as well as with documentation from witnesses and other informants about the presentation and progression of a condition. Mental health defenses to crime include insanity, automatism (sleepwalking), diminished capacity, battered-spouse syndrome, delirium from medical conditions, and involuntary intoxication. The MSO evaluation invariably appraises the motive behind a crime; the more absent a rational motive, the more readily an examiner may consider an irrational motive that might herald impaired appreciation of wrong, inability to conform conduct, or impaired appreciation of the nature and consequences of one's actions.

In some states, defendants can give evidence of reduced mental ability without having to claim insanity, instead claiming they did not purposely or knowingly commit the crime or that they could not have meaningfully premeditated it, and this could win a lesser verdict and sentence.

Outside the courtroom, some psychologists have a presence in emergency service fields such as fire control, corrections, emergency or crisis management, and law enforcement. They may be asked to consult with police departments on hostage negotiations; assist with family crisis interventions; provide assessment on preemployment exams for police officers, fitness for duty evaluations, and special unit (SWAT, Tactical Response Team) evaluations; or offer investigative assistance with unsolved crimes. They might also assist in mass disaster training and counseling.

Among the most popular arenas of forensic psychology is profiling, the method the FBI's Behavioral Analysis Unit utilizes to link serial crimes and to discern motive and offender personality issues. (Private psychologists may also consult on the behavioral analysis of crime scenes.) A profile is an educated attempt to provide investigative agencies with parameters regarding the type of person who committed a certain crime or series of crimes, based on the idea that people will behave according to their psychological makeup and will inevitably leave behavioral evidence. From a crime scene, forensic psychologists can assess whether the perpetrator is an organized predator or an individual who committed an impulsive crime of opportunity. They may also evaluate whether the perpetrator possesses criminal sophistication, pays attention to details, or is acting out a particular type of sexual fantasy.

The basic idea is to get a body of data yielding common patterns in order to develop a general description of an unknown offender. Profiling involves expertise in human behavior, motivation, and patterns of pathology to create a multidimensional report. Some serial offenders leave a "signature"—a behavioral manifestation of a personality quirk, such as the act of biting certain areas of the body or staging the corpse for the most shocking exposure. This helps to link crime scenes and predict future possible attacks, as well as the most likely pickup or dump sites and victim types. Assessing an unknown offender's age range, race, sex, occupation, educational level, social support system, modus operandi, possible military background, type of employment, and other sociological factors is just as important as finding evidence of a personality disorder or deviant fantasy life.

Psychologists may also participate in risk assessment, which can be part of a variety of situations, ranging from a parole hearing to a potentially explosive situation at a workplace or school. This area of the discipline has improved over the past two decades, although it is still quite tricky to know just how great a risk an individual may be to society. There must be a balance between recognizing when threats are just "blowing off steam" versus when they might be rehearsals for a likely dangerous scenario. When assessing whether an offender who has already served time for a crime might commit a similar crime once released, psychologists examine the subject for certain types of personality disorders known to make repeat violence more likely.

The field of neuropsychology has also made a contribution to forensics, not just in terms of testing for neurological disorders in an offender, but also in the area of lie detection. Applications of brain scan devices such as MRIs are currently being refined, with the goal of achieving a high level of accuracy via neurological records. The controversial "brainprint" has already been used successfully as an investigative tool in several murder cases. To conduct a brainprint, the scientist shows a suspect a picture of the scene or other evidence. If the person recognizes something familiar, the brain produces a wavelike response known as a memory and encoding-related multifaceted electroencephalographic response (MERMER). Detection of a change in physiological activity is the basis of the lie detector. In fact, lie detection was among the earliest areas of psychological research, going back to the early part of the twentieth century, although psychologists were not as accurate as they often believed in simply spotting a liar. Technology has improved considerably in this area; nevertheless, lie detectors and other similar devices are currently not admissible as evidence in court.

To participate in the legal arena as a forensic psychologist or psychiatrist, one must obtain the highest degree available in that field (PhD or MD, respectively) and also receive training about courtroom protocol. Clinical psychologists must be licensed and trained in forensic assessment, and, while not yet a requirement, it is useful to be board certified in forensic psychology or forensic psychiatry. Psychologists without a license but with research credentials in specific subject areas, such as eyewitness memory or false confessions, may also participate as experts in a trial. However, the majority of cases are handled by licensed clinical psychologists or psychiatrists.

FORENSIC ACOUSTICS/PHONETIC SCIENCE

Another subdiscipline that has made contributions to criminal investigation is speech or voice recognition. Speech recognition deals with acoustic evidence and involves training in linguistic analysis, human anatomy, decoding procedures, phonetics, and even physics. Phonetics deals with speech production, transmission, and perception. Forensic linguistic experts must train their ears to make fine distinctions and learn to understand how sounds or voiceprints are displayed visually as a spectrograph. Phonetic science involves speech enhancement and decoding, tape authentication, speech analysis, sound identification, and the identification of speakers. Including acoustic analysis broadens the discipline to include such things as gunshots, the impact of machines in an accident, and musical sounds.

Bell Telephone Laboratories developed voiceprint technology in 1941 for intelligence operations during World War II, and it was first used in a forensic context in the early 1960s for bomb threats against major airlines. Senior Bell Labs employee Lawrence G. Kersta, a physicist with extensive experience analyzing more than fifty thousand voices, believed the technique was 99.65 percent accurate in identifying the source of a voiceprint. He was one of the first people to recognize that qualities unique to each person's voice can be processed and charted on a graph, because physical vocal mechanisms create differences that make each person's voice unique. The size and shape of the vocal cavity, tongue, and nasal cavities contribute to these differences, as do the way a subject coordinates her lips, jaw, tongue, and soft palate to make speech. Kersta insisted that voices remain stable over a lifetime, although this notion was initially theoretical. His test case in 1971 made national headlines.

As noted in chapter 11, in 1970 a writer named Clifford Irving claimed he had a manuscript that was Howard Hughes's autobiography and said he was authorized by Hughes to make a deal with a publisher. He had letters from Hughes, he said, which he freely offered for authentication. Handwriting experts believed that Hughes had written them, so McGraw-Hill paid Irving a large sum for the rights to the manuscript. However, the experts were wrong: The manuscript was a fraud. Irving had taken a gamble, hoping the reclusive billionaire would remain in his shell, but Hughes surfaced and renounced the project. He agreed to be interviewed by reporters by phone, and stated he had never met Irving. The call was recorded.

Irving insisted the man on the phone was a fraud, but NBC hired Kersta to make a voiceprint analysis of the recording, initially attempting to support Irving's claims. He compared the pitch, tone, and volume to that of a recorded speech Hughes had made in 1947. Despite the twenty-five-year time difference, Kersta compared the spectrographic patterns and found that the voice was indeed that of Howard Hughes. Irving was arrested and convicted of forgery, and Kersta's theory about the stability of the human voice was confirmed.

Voice and noise analyses are done on a sound spectrograph. The human voice begins in the vocal folds and ends at the lips. The vocal folds provide a closed end that amplifies the sound, and the tension of the vocal folds determines the frequency of the vibrations. Changes in the shape of the mouth, the throat, and the lips will also change the frequency. The spectrograph converts the sound frequency and amplitude into a visual graphic display, a voiceprint. An example of a voiceprint can be seen in figure 12.1.

With an analog spectrograph, a high-quality magnetic tape is placed on a scanning drum, which holds a measured segment of tape. As the drum revolves, an electronic filter allows a specified band of frequencies to get through, and these are translated into electrical energy. A stylus records the energy signature onto special paper. As the process continues, the filter moves into increasingly higher frequencies and the stylus records the intensity levels of each range. The horizontal axis on a voiceprint registers how high or low the voice is; the vertical axis registers the frequency. The degree of darkness within each region on the graph illustrates intensity or volume.

For most forensic purposes, comparisons are made between known and questioned samples. When sufficient similarity exists between the patterns both voice samples make on the graph, analysts can draw various conclusions about the probability of the voice samples originating from the same person. To make a "positive identification," the highest standard when testifying in court, requires the identification of similarities among twenty distinct speech sounds.

Since courts evaluate the methods of interpretation, as well as

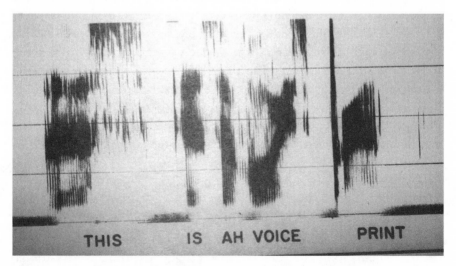

Fig. 12.1. An example of a voiceprint recorded on a spectrograph.

the actual accuracy and reliability of the spectrographic instrument, it is important that any spectrograph technician who testifies in court be highly qualified. Technicians must complete a course of study on spectrographic analysis, successfully analyze a certain number of voice comparison cases under the supervision of an expert, and pass an examination devised by a board of experts in the field. The skills involved in aural and visual voice interpretation include critical and sensitive listening, an ability to check for tape tampering, experience reading magnetic tapes, capability to operate the spectrograph equipment, and the ability to work with an investigative team. However, voiceprint analysis has been challenged as junk science in recent years and courts have varied in their acceptance of voiceprint technology. The National Academy of Sciences has also questioned this method, noting the differences in accuracy and error rate among cases. Nevertheless, all studies on spectrographic accuracy, including a 1986 FBI survey, show that properly trained experts who use standard aural and visual procedures get highly accurate results. Those who do the recordings for analysis must also be competent to operate the recording device, because the quality of the tape has great bearing on the interpreter's results. The use of voice analysis in many investigations, such as for homeland security, has proven very successful.

Speech enhancement and decoding involves the elimination of interference in order to clarify the questioned speech or sound. For this procedure, the analyst uses filtering tools and listens repeatedly to every detail. If the voice is anonymous, such as with a bomb threat or ransom demand, the voice recording can nonetheless offer information about the caller, such as age, race, gender, and country (or region) of origin. In addition, background noises that occur during the call can be isolated and subject to the process of identification. If a suspect is being considered, her voice can be recorded and compared to the questioned sample.

In addition to voices, other types of sounds can be key factors in a forensic investigation. In 2008, acoustic analysis by experts Philip Van Praag and Robert Joling turned up new evidence regarding the assassination of Senator Robert F. Kennedy on June 5, 1968, at the Ambassador Hotel in California. While Sirhan Sirhan did lift a pistol and took several shots at Kennedy, the new theory indicates that not only did Sirhan possibly conspire with someone else, he did not actually cause the fatal wounds.

Kennedy and his entourage went through the hotel's pantry area, where he was hit four times after he shook hands with two of the hotel staff. Three bullets entered his body, including one into his brain, and one lodged in a shoulder pad in his suit. He was taken to a hospital, where he died the next day. Sirhan, a Palestinian refugee, was arrested and taken into custody. He admitted he shot Kennedy and claimed it was for the cause of exploited people. Witnesses who wrestled with him at the scene confirmed that he was the shooter. Yet Sirhan had been in front of Kennedy, and the autopsy indicated that the bullets that hit Kennedy had come from behind him at close range. Sirhan had only eight bullets in his revolver, but fourteen bullets were lodged in walls around the room and in five other victims (all of whom survived).

A journalist recording Kennedy's appearance captured the shooting incident on tape, which was available for analysis. Joling and Van Praag went to work. The recording quality was poor, but during the course of five seconds, the two investigators counted thirteen separate shots. Two pairs of double shots occurred so close in time that it was impossible for a single shooter, even an expert marksman, to have gotten them off. Five of the shots had unusual acoustic characteristics, and the scientists proposed that they came from a different type of gun, pointed at a different angle. Their analysis might eventually inspire a new investigation, which may clear Sirhan and implicate someone else.

FORENSIC ENGINEERING

Forensic engineering is the discipline of checking buildings, bridges, and other structures for safety and understanding the behavior of structures under catastrophic loads or after collapse. Engineers are responsible for determining why a building collapsed or was damaged from a bomb or impact—in other words, why it was compromised. Engineers must understand the various technical disciplines involved in construction so that a whenever a failure or catastrophic incident occurs, they can analyze it from every angle. They must understand the design, the composition of the materials used, the reputation of the engineers and building companies engaged in the construction, the types of errors that could have occurred at different stages in construction, and even the geological surveys for the area.

After extensive examination, using mathematical calculations and computer simulation, engineers can see specifically how a building failed and determine whether there was intentional criminal damage, criminal malpractice, or an unforeseen failure. Forensic engineers analyze structures after fires, explosions, collapse, damage from natural disasters, and damage due to neglect or poor construction. When analyzing damage from an act of terrorism, as with the Pentagon and World Trade Center on September 11, 2001, they utilize the physics of explosions to determine the extent and pattern of the damage, as well as the precise reason for the building's failure.

Forensic engineers were instrumental in the investigation of the most destructive act of domestic terrorism on American soil, the 1995 bombing of the nine-story Alfred P. Murrah Federal Building in Oklahoma City, Oklahoma. Timothy McVeigh loaded a five-thousand-pound ammonium nitrate–based homemade explosive into a Ryder rental truck and left it parked on the north side of the building on the morning of April 19, 1995. When the bomb exploded at 9:02 a.m., one-third of the building collapsed, killing 168 men, women, and children and injuring another 800.

The resulting crater on that side of the building was thirty feet wide and eight feet deep, as shown in figure 12.2. The blast also damaged more than three hundred other buildings in the general area. Once the dust was clear and the scene secured against other possible explosives and imminent collapse, forensic engineers went to work to help determine which areas were still unsafe and what was the full extent of the bombing. Working with the FBI Explosives Unit, they had to evaluate the way the building had collapsed to determine the type of explosive used, where it was placed, and whether there was more than one.

In such investigations, an initial step is to interview the building engineer of record to learn about the building's design and construc-

Fig. 12.2. The Murrah Federal Building in Oklahoma
City after it was bombed by a domestic terrorist.

tion, and then conduct a comprehensive visual inspection. Although the building had been designed and constructed twenty years earlier and the project involved several companies, investigators managed to locate the chief structural engineer, the general contractor, and even the 1974 drawings. While the building met state codes for wind resistance and normal loads from office use, there was no consideration in the design for extreme conditions such as earthquake or explosion. The collapse appeared to have been initiated when two or more bomb-damaged columns on the north side failed.

The Federal Emergency Management Agency (FEMA) assembled a Building Performance Assessment Team (BPAT), which included civil, government, and US Army engineers. Together they photographed and investigated the results of the blast, creating 157 architectural drawings from which to work and collecting samples from different areas of the blast site. In such incidents, forensic engineers look for ground zero—the point of origin of the collapse—and the BPAT found that in the exploded truck. They learned that an audiotape existed from a meeting conducted in a building across the street at the time of the blast, with which an acoustic analysis could be performed. Construction Technology Laboratories in Illinois analyzed sections of concrete and structural bars to provide information about the building's physical properties. In essence, the building was ordinary reinforced concrete framing with reinforced columns, girders, and beams, well designed and properly built.

After the investigation, experts used the data from forensic engineers to develop a plan for a new building that could reduce a future progressive collapse by 95 percent, thereby reducing fatalities and other collateral damage. When the investigation was completed, the building was demolished.

In other types of cases, engineers might use a dialectrometer to locate imperfections inside walls. This instrument uses an electronic impulse and records the absorption of energy to indicate significant changes in parts of the structure that are not readily visible. From sophisticated calculations in any crimes involving a building, the engineers can estimate potential damage from different distinct forces, which means they can supply a prosecution team with accurate information in cases where the attempt to damage a building was thwarted. They can also advise on how to protect new buildings against future attacks.

COMPUTER FORENSICS

Computer forensics (also known as cyberforensics, digital forensics, or forensic informatics) is the application of analytical methods to electronics and computers for the purpose of developing evidence or assisting an investigation. In this field, investigators must have specialized knowledge about computers, the Internet, and other digital evidence, and they must keep up on innovations in the electronic world. Computer forensics has many subspecialties, any of which can involve gathering, storing, classifying, manipulating, and retrieving information. Investigators may develop crime scene simulation/animation, enhance images or filter noises, recover digital evidence, track identity theft, decoy and ambush child predators online, and prove computer fraud. Evidence can come from computer hard drives, cell phones, black boxes, RFID tags, digital cameras, memory devices, and other digital instruments. Some examples of digital evidence awaiting analysis are depicted in figure 12.3. Investigators must apply techniques for searching databases quickly and effectively, without distorting the information, as once altered, it's often impossible to detect the change or to recover the data's original state. Proper analytical procedures discourage analysis of the original electronic evidence for this reason, so analysts will make an exact copy of the hard drive or other stored data and work with this copy.

One of the most famous cases involving computer forensics was the apprehension and arrest of Dennis Rader, aka the BTK Killer. He had eluded law enforcement in Wichita, Kansas, since 1974, eventually killing ten people, including a family of four. He taunted police with letters describing his crimes between 1974 and 1991, and then was silent for many years. However, when he resurfaced in 2004,

Fig. 12.3. Various types of computer crimes and electronic evidence awaiting laboratory analysis.

instead of sending a note or manuscript, he sent a computer disk. The document on the disk contained metadata, or embedded information, that allowed experts to trace it back to the computer on which it was created. Once the computer was identified, it was a simple matter of acquiring proof that Rader was the long-sought offender. He was stunned that technology had foiled him, and he pled guilty and offered a full confession in exchange for a life sentence.

Forensic computer specialists learn ways to access a computer and uncover whatever the user has done on it. They can recover deleted data, decode encrypted files, and restore corrupted files, as well as determine which Web sites a person has visited to acquire information or make contacts (as was done with the Washington, DC, homicide investigation of intern Chandra Levy). This can be used as circumstantial evidence in court. Yet in terms of evidence gathering, the role of the computer as a repository and organizer of information can be tricky. The major dangers when retrieving data are the potential loss of information and data distortion or alteration. To be admissible in court, computer data must be handled following proper protocol, with the information-gathering method and chain of custody invulnerable to challenge. (The process of "cherry-picking," or retrieving just the information that supports a particular position, has recently been challenged by defense attorneys, who now realize how easy it is to string together possibly unrelated cyberdata to make a case, as in the untimely death investigation of Hollywood actress Lana Clarkson. In that case, an expert testified for the defense that a search of stored e-mails for the words "suicide" and "depression" produced an important result—an e-mail expressing how worn out Clarkson was from her deep depression. (On cross-examination, however, it was pointed out that the word "suicide" never appeared.)

Computer operating systems use virtual memory for retrieval and speed. Cyberspecialists in law enforcement rely on equipment that can duplicate whatever is on a computer's hard drive without having to turn the computer on, so as to prevent loss of data from programs that may activate to erase it. If investigators follow proper protocol and seize a machine, they can work on encrypted data without the risk of destroying it. However, they might be faced with a "live system"—a machine that is still on. Investigators have been trained to work on live systems, because turning the computer off may erase evidence of an attack that did not register on the hard drive and destroy keys to unlocking cryptographic storage that exist only in a computer's temporary memory.

For use in court, the tools used to gather the data must be accepted as standard by the forensic informatics community; they must also be capable of producing replicable results. Chain-of-custody standards require the investigator to prove that the evidence is an accurate representation of the data on the computer.

Computer crime, which began with pranks and simple theft, has progressed into much more sophisticated crimes. During the early 1970s, offenders simply tried to gain unauthorized access to computers, stealing time for which others had paid. Lawmakers soon realized the need for formal regulations and penalties, but initially these measures were weak and ineffective. However, as serious criminals realized the potential of the World Wide Web—as well as how ill equipped investigative agencies were to detect and stop them—the crimes grew more dangerous. Pedophiles looked for children, child pornographers established international rings, thieves upped the stakes with substantial monetary scams, hackers violated government records and corrupted corporate networks, and terrorists developed better methods of communication—to name just a few. Law enforcement finally caught up, instituting training sessions for federal and state agencies and establishing regional centers for digital evidence processing, as well as local ones for those areas with greater demand. Investigators have grown more adept, with some acquiring expertise in collecting digital evidence and analyzing it for its relevance to a case. Around the country, predator sting operations have netted numerous child molesters.

Among the fastest-growing cybercrimes is identity theft, or the use of someone else's personal records—from bank accounts, to social security numbers, to home addresses—in order to purchase large items, reappropriate debt, or divert law enforcement. Image Data, an electronic data protection service, reports that one out of five Americans were themselves or were related to someone who was a victim of identity theft. The figures continue to climb, although, as the media alerts the public, more people have taken steps to protect themselves from this type of crime. Unfortunately, many companies investigate only if the monetary damage exceeds a certain figure— and the thieves know this. Crimes like this have a high probability of going cold, in part because the criminals can be difficult to catch and in part because victimized individuals are reluctant to report it. Identity theft is the primary way in which terrorist groups targeting the United States have managed to get professional training, driver's licenses, banks accounts, and access to sensitive information.

Another area of computer forensics involves digital imaging and crime simulation. Computer simulations assist investigators in constructing different possible scenarios for an incident, based on raw data input and ease of manipulation. For example, a reconstruction expert might devise a simulation of an apartment where a shooting occurred, adding blood spatter, bullet trajectory data, and other evidence to help reconstruct just how the incident developed and to locate the shooter's position. With such devices as the Scansphere laser 3-D program, investigators can create a 360-degree view of the entire room and examine it from different perspectives. An arson program re-creates a fire in a specific type of building when the investigator enters a point of origin and other data about the actual fire. If the result fails to match the scene, another point of origin can then be designated.

FORENSIC NURSING

Another field that is showing considerable promise for improving investigations is forensic nursing. Nurses trained in forensic procedures combine nursing skill and clinical practice with knowledge of the legal system, acting as liaisons between health care and the legal system. Forensic nurses apply the biopsychosocial education of the registered nurse in the scientific investigation and treatment of trauma and/or death of victims and perpetrators of abuse, violence, criminal activity, and traumatic accidents. In 1992 a group of sexual assault nurse examiners formed an association to focus on the interaction between nursing and the law; thus began the International

Association of Forensic Nurses (IAFN). Since that time, the IAFN has grown into an organization with thousands of members, and, with the support of the American Nurses Association (ANA), it has developed forensic nursing standards of practice. The American Academy of Forensic Sciences formally recognized this specialty in 1991.

Although the IAFN was founded by a group of sexual assault nurse examiners, forensic nursing today includes more than just this subspecialty. Forensic nursing is multifaceted, and nurses may be found working with victims or perpetrators of domestic violence, sexual abuse and sexual assault, elder abuse, and other forms of physical trauma. Forensic nurses work in a variety of public health and public safety settings as well as in the private sector. The scope of practice is broad and can include product tampering, environmental hazards, medicolegal death investigation, sexual assault examination, and epidemiological issues. Clinical roles include emergency and trauma care, corrections, nurse investigators, evidence collectors, psychiatric/mental health evaluators, sexual assault nurse examiners, and nurse coroners. In another role, legal nurse consultants specialize in forensic practice and providing expertise in legal matters. Forensic practitioners often care for living clients and train other nurses to assess and care appropriately for these victims. As members of an interdisciplinary team, forensic nurses must possess expertise in normal anatomy and physiology, assessment skills, determination of causative factors of injuries, and use of therapeutic communication.

The founders of the IAFN recognized the unique ability of nurses to understand the causes of domestic and sexual violence and needs of victims of these crimes. The holistic approach reflected in the extensive training forensic nurses receive provides the necessary support for victims while their health care needs are addressed. Studies have shown that the public puts great trust in nurses, which allows forensic practitioners opportunities for care that are not easily available to other investigators or members of the community. When a patient arrives at the emergency room suffering from injuries, the forensic nurse assesses the immediate medical needs of the patient. Because of his training, the forensic nurse is also acutely aware of the cycle of violence typically demonstrated in these situations. He can work with the patient to provide a safe environment in which to discuss the options for the future and assistance that may be available. Within the United States, the focus of forensic nursing is primarily in the areas of sexual assault and other interpersonal violence, but in other countries more of the focus is on correctional, mental health, and psychiatric forensic nursing.

Documentation of traumatic injuries is critical. This documentation includes thorough, unbiased recording of the history of injury from the victim and/or caregiver. Accurate notations are important, since, as part of the medical record, these can be used to provide evidentiary support of the victim's testimony. Forensic nurses develop skills in photographic documentation of these injuries.

A large part of any forensic nursing role involves education. Because the victims of trauma and crime often find themselves at health-care facilities, forensic practitioners are vital to the training of emergency room and other hospital personnel in the proper collection and preservation of physical evidence. Their unique background also allows them to provide information about the responses of victims of crime to law enforcement, attorneys, and other members of the criminal justice community. Their understanding of the causes and manifestations of conditions such as post-traumatic stress disorder, battered-spouse syndrome, and rape syndrome is critical for proper treatment of the patient and can be useful to investigators. As expert witnesses, forensic nurses provide education to the trier of fact on these and other aspects of victimology and clinical practice.

Forensic nurses are well suited to be death investigators or coroners. Because of their medical training, these nurses are able to employ medical knowledge when reviewing medical records, medications, and assessing injuries. At the same time, their understanding of the legal requirements for evidence collection, documentation, chain of custody, scene search, and warrants ensures that any evidence is obtained in a proper and admissible manner. Forensic nurses have advanced training in traumatic wound identification, including skills to recognize patterned injuries and injuries that are in various stages of healing.

Forensic nursing is an expanding field in its early stages of development. Job opportunities for nurses educated in forensics continue to grow. In addition to the more traditional roles described above, forensic nurses may serve on child and adult protective service investigation teams, act as members of fatality review boards, develop and run hospital-based violence intervention programs, work for police departments, provide comprehensive sexual assault nurse examinations in hospitals, or provide holistic care at community-based centers.

Chapter Thirteen

FORENSIC SCIENTISTS ON TRIAL

G ood scientists let the chips fall where they may and report conclusions honestly and completely. Most scientists are hardworking and honest. They understand the role of evidence in legal proceedings, but do not let the "side" they are working for influence their conclusions. However, sometimes things go wrong, and even good people may get caught in the traps of ego and greed. When lecturing students, Dr. Henry Lee tells them about some of the forensic examiners who took shortcuts, embellished their résumés, or colored their testimony. He emphasizes to his students that all those who made the wrong choice ultimately lost their honor and professional standing. Ultimately, his students learn the most from the examples of well-known, talented scientists in various disciplines who established reputations by providing unbiased and thorough findings and testimony.

In the early 1990s, a series of robberies and rapes occurred about one block apart from each other in Chicago, Illinois. Based on the modus operandi and witness descriptions, police believed the assaults were committed by the same person. A short time later, John Willis was arrested for these rapes. The first case occurred in a beauty parlor. After the victim in that case was forced to perform oral sex on the attacker, she spit onto a toilet paper wrapper. That paper was later recovered by police. As Willis went to trial in 1991, testing was performed on the wrapper at the Chicago Police Department's Serology Unit. Human semen was detected on the wrapper. The scientist who did the conventional serological testing for ABO blood group reported that her results were inconclusive. She based this statement on what she called a failure in one of the controls, the known ABO stains and unstained paper that were run during the test to show that the procedure was working. She testified that, based on her findings, she could not exclude Willis as the contributor of the semen. At the time, the actual test results were never given to the defense for review. Willis was convicted of this crime in 1992, but continued to maintain his innocence. In 1994 another man, Dennis McGruder, was arrested for a 1992 rape and robbery that displayed an MO similar to Willis's case. Willis pointed out the similarities in the appeal of his conviction, but his request for a new trial was denied. Willis was convicted of a second similar crime in 1993. Although DNA testing was available, DNA tests were not carried out by the crime lab and the defense did not have access to the evidence. Willis even claimed that McGruder admitted his guilt in the two crimes attributed to Willis, but this evidence also was not allowed in court.

Willis's attorneys continued to appeal his cases. Eventually, the original laboratory notes were released and reviewed by other experts. The scientists who reviewed those notes were shocked. The tests for the ABO blood group were not as inconclusive as the scientist led the jury to believe. Willis's blood type was B. That B was not detected at all in the semen stain from the toilet wrapper, which would indicate that Willis could not have left the semen sample. Information about this apparent exclusion had not been given to Willis's defense team prior to his trial. Some wondered whether the jury had been intentionally misled.

As a result of this new information, Willis's defense team was ultimately provided with a glass slide from the beauty parlor case on which sperm remained. DNA analysis was conducted that showed conclusively that Willis was not the source of the semen. In fact, the

DNA profile developed from the sperm matched a convicted felon—Dennis McGruder. In 1999 John Willis was released from prison after spending seven years incarcerated for crimes he did not commit.

As this case demonstrates, the focus of the forensic scientist's work should be the objective evaluation of evidence that will be used in a legal proceeding. Scientists conduct tests and write reports of their findings and conclusions. What is relatively unique is the fact that forensic experts may have to present findings during legal proceedings and explain the significance of those findings as they relate to a specific case, and those explanations should be thorough and not misleading. When this objectivity is lost, the consequences can be drastic.

THE AMERICAN JUSTICE SYSTEM

The justice system in the United States is based on the English system, which is an adversarial system. When we say that the justice system is adversarial, we mean that our system allows for two sides of a question to be heard before a trier of fact (a judge or a jury). Both sides present evidence that supports their arguments. Certain rules help to keep the process fair and to keep questionable facts from being presented. The trier of fact then weighs the information presented by both sides to make a decision as to which side presented the more convincing case. In a criminal case, this means a decision about whether or not the defendant is guilty. The American criminal justice system is also an accusatorial system that assumes the defendant is innocent until and unless guilt is proven. In an accusatorial system the defendant is pointed to as having caused the harm, but the burden to prove the defendant's guilt rests on the accuser (the prosecution).

In a criminal trial, the justice system has developed a series of specific steps that must be followed according to specific rules so that the rights of all are upheld while society attempts to prove the case against a defendant. As everyone who watches television knows, the standard of proof for a criminal trial is "beyond a reasonable doubt." This proof must be in the form of evidence that is obtained in an appropriate manner. The burden of proof in a civil case is "preponderance of the evidence," or, more simply put, "more likely than not." Thus, a person could be found liable in civil court using evidence that does not meet the burden of proof in a criminal case. One of the most prominent examples of this possible difference between a civil and criminal trial outcome are the O. J. Simpson cases. O. J. Simpson was tried for the murders of his ex-wife, Nicole Brown Simpson, and her acquaintance Ron Goldman. After months of highly publicized testimony, O. J. Simpson was acquitted of all criminal charges related to their deaths. Several months later a civil case was held, claiming that Simpson was responsible for the two untimely deaths. The civil jury found Simpson civilly liable and awarded the families $30 million.

THE ROLE OF EVIDENCE

Evidence is defined as any physical, circumstantial, or direct information offered to prove or disprove an issue in dispute. As described earlier, the adversarial system allows each side to present evidence that is most favorable to its side, while allowing challenges to the evidence by the other side. Generally, unless the opposing side objects successfully, that evidence will be considered by the trier of fact. Once evidence is admitted at trial, the jury has sole discretion and responsibility to decide how important a particular piece of evidence is and which evidence is credible.

In general, evidence can be divided into four categories: (1) witness testimony, (2) physical evidence, (3) documents or writings, and (4) demonstrative evidence (visual or audio materials presented to assist the jury). Many types of evidence in many formats are presented during a trial. While the actual form and origin of the evidence may influence the decision, the relevance and reliability of evidence must be considered by the judge before it can be used in a court proceeding. Evidence that is not relevant wastes time and can mislead a jury. Evidence that is not reliable cannot be challenged properly by the opposing side. Neither type of evidence is allowed in a fair trial.

For evidence to be relevant it must pertain to the case and be useful to the trier of fact in making a decision. Relevance is basically a logical evaluation of the evidence as it pertains to the case. If there is a logical relationship between the evidence and the case, the judge will allow its presentation. This rule helps to prevent the admission of evidence that may be misleading or confusing. Relevance functions as the initial filter of evidence, based on the particular case scenario. One example of an evidence rule based on the concept of relevance is the rape shield rule, which disallows the use of a victim's prior sexual history as irrelevant in determining whether a sexual assault took place.

Evidence must also be reliable to be admissible. Reliability of evidence may be established in several ways, depending on the nature of the evidence presented. Witnesses generally may testify to what they directly saw or did. The opposing party has the right to challenge those statements through cross-examination. Witnesses cannot testify to what was told to them, because there is no way to know if what they were told was true. There are some exceptions to this rule, such as allowing a doctor to testify to what a patient said. The reliability of such statements is based on the premise that a person seeking medical assistance would speak truthfully to a medical provider in order to obtain appropriate care.

If physical evidence is collected from a scene, the witness will be asked about the chain of evidence to show its reliability. Chain of evidence identifies where the evidence was found, where it has been, and who has handled it. Questions about how the evidence was handled may be raised. These questions are important if it is possible that mishandling of the evidence could have resulted in contamination or if some important characteristic of the physical evidence has been changed.

SCIENTIFIC AND TECHNICAL EVIDENCE ADMISSIBILITY

Reliability of expert testimony, whether scientific, medical, or technical, must also be established. The current common standards for scientific and other expert evidence are described in the Supreme

Court's decisions in *Frye v. United States* (1923) and *Daubert v. Merrell Dow Pharmaceuticals* (1993). These cases make it clear that the judge must act as a gatekeeper, determining whether evidence is reliable and relevant before any jury can hear it. It is the judge who first rules whether any witness is qualified as an expert and may testify on a particular subject. Even if a witness qualifies as an expert, the judge may determine that a particular subject of the testimony is *not* admissible because it does not meet other criteria for scientific or technical evidence.

1. Frye *standard*. In 1923 the Federal Court of Appeals established the standard for the admissibility of scientific evidence in a case regarding use of a polygraph. This decision established a rule that would continue for seventy years and still remains in effect in several states. In *Frye*, the court refused to allow testimony about a polygraph result, stating that to be admitted into evidence, a scientific procedure must have gained "general acceptance" in the relevant scientific community. Critics of the *Frye* standard claim that this test does not guarantee that evidence is reliable or even that it is good science. *Frye*, they claim, only means that a large number of people use the test and rely on the results. As technology boomed in the 1980s, the question of what actually makes a technical, scientific, or medical result reliable was revisited.

2. Frye-*Plus standard*. As more complex and varied testing was available in the 1970s and 1980s, some states, particularly California and New York, adopted what is sometimes called the *Frye*-Plus or "Super-*Frye*" standard. Under this expanded test, the scientific method or standard applied to the evidence must be generally accepted in the relevant scientific community *and* the accepted procedures must have been followed correctly. In other words, how the test is done or interpreted is as important as what the test is. This ensures that the results are reliable.

3. Daubert *standard*. *Daubert* revolutionized the way courts look at scientific and technical evidence. In a somewhat complicated case involving the effects of certain drugs, the US

Supreme Court overturned a lower court ruling that excluded research evidence because it failed to meet the *Frye* standard. The Court said that general acceptance in the scientific community was an important factor, but other things also should be considered before a judge decides if the evidence is reliable. To admit scientific evidence, the judge should also consider: (1) whether the technique or theory has been tested and validated, (2) whether the procedures or techniques have been reviewed by other scientists in the field or published in a peer-reviewed journal, (3) what the error rate is, and (4) whether standards have been established and if they were applied. Even if all these factors are met, a judge may still exclude evidence if other issues raise questions about the reliability of the evidence. Some courts have held, for example, that while a DNA procedure may generally be accepted, the specific way in which the DNA procedure was applied can make it suspect. In 1999 the Supreme Court held that the *Daubert* standard applied to all types of technical expert witness testimony, not just the traditional sciences and medicine.

Many states have adopted the *Daubert* standard—or some modification—for determining the admissibility of scientific evidence. Some state courts have added additional factors such as the reputation of the expert and the extent to which a protocol previously has been accepted in the court. If there are concerns about a procedure or method of handling evidence, specific questions may be asked about national standards, proficiency testing, certification, and similar topics.

THE FORENSIC EXPERT'S ROLE IN THE JUSTICE SYSTEM

The forensic expert plays a critical role in the investigation of an incident. The well-trained scientist can provide insight into the causes of the incident, the sequence of events, or the nature of the evidence that has been collected. Most of the work done by the expert occurs outside the courts of law. This includes activities such as evidence recognition and collection, evidence examination, consultation with attorneys and investigators to discuss findings, and research into new procedures and applications. The impact the expert can have on a case prior to any legal action is significant. The forensic professional is also involved in training and educating members of the justice system and the community through teaching, lectures, and publications.

As discussed in previous chapters, juries and attorneys often expect that scientific or technical evidence will be presented in a case. It falls on the expert witness to provide the scientific evidence and to interpret the results for the jury. An expert witness is someone recognized by the judge as having knowledge in a particular subject that is greater than the knowledge of the average person. If the topic area is relevant to the case at hand and requires specialized knowledge, an expert can be called on. Consequently, in recent cases in one courthouse alone, expert witnesses were allowed to testify on auto mechanics, heart surgery, manufacturing safety standards, and sports activities. Whether an individual can testify in a court of law or at a legal proceeding as an expert witness is ultimately determined by the judge. Acting as gatekeeper, it is up to the judge to determine who is an expert and what the area of expertise of that person is.

Many forensic experts never go to court, instead providing information and services to attorneys, law enforcement, and others responsible for handling investigations, trials, and hearings. Since this is a very common facet of the expert witness experience, it is important to consider how user groups determine who is a suitable expert in a case. It is equally significant for experts to consider whether a case is suited for their particular skills and temperament. It is extremely important for expert witnesses to discuss their areas of expertise and their limitations prior to accepting any case. One of the biggest mistakes some expert witnesses make is to go beyond their specializations. For example, one forensic dentist was reported as testifying to tool marks made by a knife at the crime scene, even though he had no specific training in that area. Many attorneys are not aware of the different backgrounds and training necessary for some specialties, or they may misunderstand scientific and technical information. So the expert witness must make sure to explain the training in procedures and background a well-trained scientist in that field should possess.

Prior to being qualified as an expert witness by a judge, the attorneys (and possibly the judge) will ask a series of questions regarding the educational background and training of the proffered expert. Witnesses may be asked about writings, publications, or other activities that have a direct relationship to their professional standing. Opposing attorneys may ask questions to point out why a particular witness should not be allowed to testify. In such situations, a witness may be asked about past testimony, experience, employment records, or other factors that may show bias. Bias—tending toward one side over another—could influence how the expert thinks, decides which tests to perform, and interprets data.

THE EXPERT WITNESS GONE WRONG

Being an expert in the justice system is an important responsibility. Forensic scientists who work on criminal cases hold someone else's life in their hands. The majority of forensic scientists are diligent and conscientious. They keep up-to-date on advances in their disciplines and remain proficient in the laboratory. Since most forensic scientists are employed in government laboratories, they tend to be underpaid and working under demand for results to be used as investigative leads or for trial. There seems to be a constant backlog of cases in most labs. However, the rewards of applying the principles of science to matters of the law are many. Most scientists will readily admit that among the greatest moments of their careers is when their results eliminate a wrongly accused suspect.

But, as in every profession, sometimes things go wrong. Among the more than two hundred Innocence Project cases in which the wrongly convicted have been exonerated, 11 percent involved "forensic misconduct." (This percentage does not include cases involving what the Innocence Project calls "limited science," such as ABO blood typing, which was state-of-the-art testing at the time of the original trial.) This misconduct can be intentional (exaggerating the importance of a result, using all of the evidence, laboratory fraud) or negligent (insufficient training, mistakes, loss or contamination of evidence). No matter what the reason, the improper application of forensic science can have devastating effects. Not only is the life of a person potentially harmed, but public trust in the science and the judicial system is affected.

The following are a few of the most notorious examples of scientists who were charged with forensic misconduct:

1. *Fred Zain.* A supervisor in the West Virginia State Police Laboratory, where he spent many years in the serology unit, Fred Zain was the go-to guy—if you had a case and wanted to make sure you got a good result from the evidence, Zain was who you asked for. He was well trained and had attended numerous workshops and symposia, keeping up with the latest developments in forensic serology. He even claimed to have compiled several collections of materials that he used for comparisons in his casework. After Zain retired in 1989 he went to work in Texas. It was then that his misdeeds came to light. Several cases needed to be reexamined for testimony. Scientists at the West Virginia lab discovered that Zain was dry labbing. (Dry labbing is what scientists call it when someone makes up results and does not conduct a test or collect data in the laboratory.) Items he said were tested were in their original condition. Tests he said were done were not completed, or some tests were done on some items but reports were written so it looked like the results applied to all the evidence. By the end of the 1990s, hundreds of cases had been reviewed in West Virginia and Texas. When the West Virginia Supreme Court cleared the way for Zain to be charged with fraud for taking salary while lying about his work, a justice stated that Zain not only cost the state the amount of wages and benefits that were fraudulently obtained, but also subjected numerous individuals to criminal convictions based on false serology evidence. Fred Zain died in 2002, at the age of fifty-two, while some of these cases were still in question.

2. *Joyce Gilchrist*. Jeff Pierce was released from prison in 2001 after serving fifteen years in prison for a crime he did not commit. This started an investigation into the technician whose work put him—and hundreds of other people—behind bars. Joyce Gilchrist had been working for many years when the outrage concerning this incident made her infamous. In Pierce's case, she had testified about hairs in such a way as to imply that her microscopic comparison was truly a "match," even though every well-trained forensic scientist knows that hairs can only be "similar" and never associated with one and only one source. Gilchrist also examined fibers and biological fluids in her lab in Oklahoma City, often getting just the results that were needed in a case. Her ability to provide forensic evidence in critical cases led one defense attorney to describe her as using "black magic"—a nickname that stuck and of which she appeared quite proud. The only problem is that much of her work was incomplete and slipshod. Her findings were not supported by the tests she conducted, and her testimony often went beyond reasonable interpretations. In fact, before the Pierce case, a case was overturned in which the state supreme court said her hair testimony was improper and outside the standards of forensic science. (Yet prosecutors kept having her testify and courts kept allowing it!)

   As a result of the Pierce case, seven of Gilchrist's cases were reviewed by the FBI. Five of those cases were found lacking and the scientific work inferior. The FBI suggested that all cases be reviewed in which Gilchrist's evidence played a significant role. In response Gilchrist noted that she never intentionally did anything wrong in a case she worked. Joyce Gilchrist was fired from her position in Oklahoma City in 2002.

3. *Dr. Brian Meehan*. Brian Meehan was the director of DNA Security of Burlington, a private company that was hired by North Carolina District Attorney Mike Nifong to test samples from a highly publicized sexual assault case in which three Duke University students were accused. Nifong sent

DNA Security twenty-two samples from evidence that had been collected during an examination of the accuser. Three students were charged with the assault. A limited report was issued that did not address complete findings. When the court ordered the state to turn over all laboratory documents to the defense, their review of the DNA results showed that at least four different males were identified in the samples tested by DNA Security. None of those DNA profiles matched the accused students. Meehan admitted in court that in discussions with Nifong he had agreed to provide a report that did not contain all of the DNA results obtained on the evidence. As would be pointed out later, this was against standard company policy. Eventually all charges were dropped against the Duke students and Nifong was brought up on ethics charges before the state bar association. Meehan admitted in a 2007 CBS interview that the report did not include complete results and that this was not the common practice at his laboratory. He stated that the failure was a big error.

4. *Houston Police Laboratory.* In November 2002, a local TV station reported on serious allegations of major problems within the Houston Police Department DNA Laboratory. This led to an external audit of the DNA unit and the suspension of DNA operations shortly thereafter. As the investigation into the operation of the lab continued, it was discovered that two drug examiners created documents to reflect the results of testing that was never conducted. Thus, it appeared that the problems at the lab went far beyond the DNA unit. Eventually the lab was reorganized and a new director was hired. The chief of police created a commission to review the work that had been done in every section of the lab before its reincarnation.

An independent review of cases analyzed between 1980 and the time of the lab reorganization revealed some serious problems in the DNA, serology, and drug sections of the lab. The review committee found that there were significant problems with analysis and reporting of results in a large proportion of the serology and DNA cases. Problems included poor documentation and interpretive errors that led to misleading and incorrect conclusions. Analysts were poorly trained and lacked scientific technique. The team pointed out that there was a significant lack of oversight by the laboratory director and supervisors, which led to many of the problems that developed.

The number of serious problems in forensic science laboratories is unknown. The reported cases of significant errors and wrong-doing are few in relation to the number of practicing scientists. But the occurrence of even one problem requires addressing the topic. What are the causes of such misconduct?

When individual forensic scientists choose to "create" results or heighten the significance of their findings, ego may be the issue. If you are the person who can "save the day," your standing among the investigators and prosecutors is boosted. Sometimes investigators or scientists are convinced that the suspect is guilty, and they dry lab, or create evidence to obtain the results they are looking for. These cases of wanton dishonesty are hard to imagine and abhorrent to all good forensic scientists and ethical people. As noted in the discussion of the independent review team in Houston, dry labbing is a "hanging offense" in the scientific community.

A desire to please might also come into play (which may have been what went on in the Meehan case). In an effort to satisfy the investigators or an attorney, the scientist may begin to push the interpretation of a result a little too far, make the statistic a little better, or word a report in a particular way in an effort to satisfy the attorney trying a case. (Such a response may even be unconscious on the part of the scientist.) Fear of being exposed or having to explain an error or mistake led one DNA scientist to hide a DNA database search that hit on a different suspect than the defendant when he made an error the first time he entered the DNA profile. Some scientists may be loath to abandon a pet theory about a case, even if the data no longer support that interpretation. There also have been cases of individuals presenting false credentials to obtain positions or where forensic scientists have falsely testified to academic credentials when qualifying as an expert witness in court. A scientist might overstate his qualifications in an effort to sound more professional and knowledgeable to the jury, especially in a case where the opposing side has its own expert.

Bias is one of the most common sources of forensic misadventure. Bias against a defendant may not be conscious as scientists do their work, but such bias may influence their evaluation of data—they may interpret results in a light most favorable to the investigation. This can happen with both defense and prosecution experts. The results obtained by other scientists can also bias one's own evaluation of evidence, as seen in the Madrid bombing case in 2004, where several fingerprint examiners at the FBI made an association between a latent fingerprint found on evidence from the scene and a suspect. On careful inspection, that print identification was found to be erroneous, but even the defense expert agreed with the original examiner, since he knew that several examiners at the FBI knew that an association had been made. There is still keen interest in this inherent bias in the verification of matches made by another examiner. Arguments concerning the effect of this unconscious bias have been made in several firearms and fingerprint cases.

One of the most difficult situations involving forensic misconduct happens when a scientist is conducting tests to the best of her ability, but lacks the knowledge or training necessary to perform the analyses properly. Laboratory managers and supervisors who do not conduct technical reviews of the scientist's work contribute to the problem by failing to recognize the need for training or the erroneous results that are obtained when the examiner is unqualified. These were found to be significant factors in the problems at the Houston DNA unit; neither the supervisor nor the bench technicians had the knowledge, skills, or ability to produce or evaluate data appropriately. It is the responsibility of every forensic scientist to remain current in the field and to maintain finely honed laboratory skills—otherwise mistakes may not even be recognized. Testimony may be erroneous. Only if an independent expert reviews the results or testimony might the problems be identified.

IMPROVING THE SCIENCE OF FORENSIC SCIENCE

Instances of forensic science misadventure have caused an uproar among attorneys, judges, other scientists, and the public. How can these incidents be eliminated? How can the public trust the science and the scientists? Several steps have been taken by the forensic community to ensure the quality of the scientific services provided by laboratories. Other professionals within the justice community have suggested alternative ways to reassure citizens that casework is completed using generally accepted procedures that meet scientific standards by qualified scientists and technicians. Certification, accreditation, proficiency testing, oversight, and independent operation have all been suggested as solutions. Approaches that may be useful include:

1. *Self-monitoring.* The forensic community must monitor itself. Each scientist is aware of the need to practice in an ethical manner. It is the responsibility of each scientist to maintain proficiency. All work should be technically reviewed by trained scientists who can determine whether the appropriate tests were run and whether interpretations are correct. Many technical errors can be identified in this manner and can then be corrected before the results are released.

2. *Management support.* Managers of forensic services must provide opportunities for examiners to receive appropriate training. Managers should gain as much knowledge as feasible about the operations of each unit in the laboratory. External audits and consultants can assist the manager in evaluating unit procedures and performance. If a person or unit is deficient, casework must stop until such time as the individual or unit demonstrates proficiency in case-type samples.

3. *Quality assurance/quality control programs.* Quality assurance (QA) is a planned set of actions that provide confidence that a product or service will be of the desired quality. Quality control (QC) involves the measures taken to implement QA. All good laboratories, from environmental labs to clinical lab-

oratories, have a QA program; forensic science laboratories are no exception. Using quality standards, checking the quality of reagents and chemicals used in the procedures, and having procedures that have been shown to meet scientific standards are all part of QA/QC. Because QA concerns all matters that directly affect the quality of the "product," a comprehensive program includes adequate training, proficiency testing for lab scientists, and peer review.

4. *Laboratory accreditation or certification.* National and international accrediting and certifying bodies exist that publish QA/QC standards. Each laboratory must meet the criteria laid out in the standards and possess documentation of its compliance. For example, there must be a record of who made a solution, the source of chemicals contained in the solution, when it was made, and that it reacted appropriately before scientists can use each chemical solution that is critical in a test. Both self-audits and external audits by a team of recognized experts in the discipline(s) being examined are conducted regularly as part of an accreditation or lab certification program. If there is noncompliance, the laboratory must make appropriate changes that meet the approval of the accreditation board. Forensic laboratories are typically accredited by the Association of Crime Laboratory Directors Laboratory Accreditation Board or by other organizations granting certification through the International Organization for Standardization (ISO). Medical examiners' offices may be accredited by the National Association of Medical Examiners. The American Board of Forensic Toxicology certifies toxicology laboratories. Adherence to these standards protects the public from laboratories that use outdated or improper procedures. Audits may also identify individual wrongdoing, depending on its nature and the type of individual error or misconduct.

5. *Individual certification.* Certification can also apply to individuals. When an analyst is certified, the certifying organization is saying that the person meets the criteria of a knowledgeable, proficient scientist. Most certification pro-

grams require both a written test, demonstrating the scientist's understanding of the theory and methods applied in a discipline, and a hands-on proficiency test that requires the scientist to use laboratory procedures to arrive at an acceptable predetermined answer. This qualification applies only to the examiner and does not reflect on the laboratory operation or procedures. In the United States, certification may be earned in various forensic disciplines by the American Board of Criminalists, the International Association for Identification, the Association of Firearm and Tool Mark Examiners, the American Board of Forensic Document Examiners, the American Board of Forensic Odontology, and the American Board of Forensic Toxicology.

6. *Commission oversight.* Some states have established independent commissions to oversee forensic operations within the state. Advocates encourage formation of oversight commissions to develop and enforce quality standards for forensic science laboratories, to monitor policies and procedures that ensure scientific methods are being applied appropriately, to ensure that policies are being followed that prevent bias in testing, and to help ensure that all scientists receive proper training. These commissions should include experts who understand the needs of both the forensic community and the criminal justice system. Some advocates have suggested that the system should go beyond mere commission oversight and that forensic labs should operate independently of other organizations.

No matter what approaches are chosen to maintain high-quality scientific standards in forensic science, part of the answer lies in the actions of each forensic scientist. All forensic scientists must always be on guard against possible instances of negligence, incompetence, bias, and fraud—both their own and that of others. Above all, forensic scientists, members of the justice system, and the public should recall former US Attorney General Janet Reno's comments at the 2008 meeting of forensic laboratory directors: "The truth is that the overwhelming majority of forensic scientists are ethical, thoughtful, competent practitioners who increasingly subject themselves to rigorous professional oversight through accreditation and certification. Most are underpaid and overworked."

Chapter Fourteen

THE FUTURE OF FORENSIC SCIENCE

Forensic science has come a long way. During the 1960s, although basic science informed investigative strategies, there was little concern about using gloves to avoid contamination or about preserving biological evidence. For the technology of the times these were not grave issues. When Dr. Henry Lee began his career, laboratories were sparse at best, with little funding for equipment or technology. Investigators relied on fingerprints and other traditional forensic identification techniques to provide leads. The mounting war against drugs in the 1970s inspired more federal funding. Money was spent on better-trained personnel and modern police procedures, including forensic technology. Instrumentation, such as gas chromatography, was at the forefront of the new weapons against crime. Computerization and miniaturization in the 1980s and 1990s made equipment portable and affordable. This was also the time of the DNA revolution, when forensic science took advantage of the latest developments in biotechnology. Now, with further advances in instrumentation and artificial intelligence, techniques have been refined and many more have become automated.

In the future, forensic innovation will continue to develop and expand in five primary areas:

1. *Teleforensics.* The crime scene will come to the expert. With satellite images and better digital rendering, crime scenes will be linked through online formats to forensic experts or laboratories. Techniques developed at NASA for outer-space exploration will be able to be used with items such as semen, bloodstains, and gunpowder residue and mapped in high resolution on a 3-D digital chart, including zooming in on specific items or areas. Cyclovision or similar programs will assist in these efforts by capturing a 360-degree image of the scene. This projective technology will help to reduce contact contamination and crime scene traffic, speed up investigations, and provide a better courtroom presentation. Forensic scientists at a laboratory will offer preliminary expert opinions concerning the nature of the evidence or patterns, provide guidance about what other evidence to look for, and determine possible sources of the evidence for investigators. They will provide information about the most appropriate ways to collect and preserve evidence. In addition, more experts at many different locations will examine the real-time images and consult by phone or conference call, even directing the ongoing investigation. Future improvements will include better encryption for wireless data and projecting accurate images at greater distances. More images, such as fingerprints and firearms evidence, will also be searchable against databases.

2. *Data mining or informatics.* Data mining is the process of sorting through large caches of information to retrieve needed data efficiently. It is also the process of looking for patterns to aid in decision making or prediction. In the future, there will be more and faster databases for evidence searching. There will also be more databases for criminal profiling. Faster, more readily available access to these databases may provide the information before the detective even leaves the crime scene. Among the databases currently available are those for

bullet and cartridge casings, chemical composition of automotive paint, tire tread patterns, glass types, textile fibers, shoe prints, ink, narcotics, prescription drugs, ignitable liquids, DNA, vehicle identification, and fingerprints.

3. *Digital documentation of the crime scene and 3-D reconstruction.* Traditional photos on film are currently being replaced in many contexts with digital images. Documentation at a crime scene—from notes to diagrams and photographs in digital format—can be made on palm-size devices. These images can then be quickly transmitted electronically to the laboratory, which makes crime scene reconstruction—especially 3-D reconstruction—easier. When the entire crime scene can be reproduced to capture every angle and provide close-ups, it can be projected onto a screen or sent to many computers simultaneously for better brainstorming sessions. Digital images also provide a quick way for scene investigators and scientists to determine that they have accurate and complete documentation of a scene. Several significant challenges to digital images in court have addressed the ability to fake or alter an image. These issues, which are also a concern with standard photography, will continue to be raised as the technology improves. Digital technology has also led to the development of a global alert map operated by the National Association of Radio-Distress Signaling and Infocommunications in Hungary that provides a real-time recap of international events. Using this map, forensic scientists in certain specialties can be alerted almost immediately if they are needed in some far-away area after a flood or other natural disaster. Experts can be in one country but participate in consulting on a real-time investigation in another country, as well as get immediate updates.

Global positioning systems (GPS) have revolutionized the way investigators locate both individuals and evidence such as automobiles and cell phones. Tracking devices provide useful information to investigators, helping to find stolen vehicles or follow a suspect, and have been known to save victims of kidnapping and assault. Systems are being developed that use

GPS to document the location of physical evidence and incorporate this information into a computerized file, relieving crime scene technicians of tedious measurements that can lead to errors and consume valuable time at a scene.

4. *Expert system modeling.* Detectives who have questions about how to collect trace or biological evidence will be able to search an expert database for complete instructions, including what packaging to use for collection, how to use it, and how to best preserve the sample. Expert databases will also provide the contact information for individuals who can assist local scene personnel with difficult evidence or scene reconstruction. This will be a considerable benefit to smaller jurisdictions that have little experience with major crimes, because expertise will be readily available to prevent evidence loss or contamination.

5. *Portability.* Just as computers went from enormous mainframes that took up an entire city block to handheld devices, so other analytical products have become smaller and easier to take to crime scenes. The development of DNA testing on microchips is in its final stages. The day is coming when on-site DNA analysis will be done on biological samples found at a scene, eliminating the need to wait for results from a lab. Scientists are also developing portable systems to conduct preliminary DNA profiles on biological samples so that only evidence with significant possibilities for advancing the investigation will be sent to the laboratory for extensive testing. This will also bring new challenges, however, in the efforts to prevent contamination and consumption of samples. It will be necessary to train more scientists so that testing can be done by appropriately trained persons.

Portable instrumental analysis, such as gas chromatography or Raman spectroscopy, is available for identification of unknown substances in homeland security and other investigations. The cost of these miniaturized systems is now within the budgets of many investigative and forensic units. As this equipment becomes more affordable, small gas chromatographs will be used at fire scenes to collect and analyze potential evidence for accelerant use. Other gas detection systems will be used to protect personnel in industrial environments and at incident scenes. Affordable portable Raman spectroscopy will provide scientists with handheld devices that contain a library of spectra of known substances, and which can be added to by scientists or scene personnel. Raman spectroscopy can also be used to identify unknown contents in a container and maintain the integrity of the evidence without exposing personnel to the sample. The advantage of such scene identification is obvious—dangerous materials can be handled appropriately for the protection of the community and the investigators, while other materials can be packaged and collected as evidence in false complaints or other cases. They might also be used in the future to intervene in acts of terrorism.

ON THE HORIZON

With science working hand in hand with cutting-edge technology, the future is quickly opening up. Nanotechnology, the science of tiny things, is one of the most widely discussed areas of biology. Nanotechnologists manipulate minute structures—so small that they must be magnified 1,000 times with an optical microscope to make them visible. Their size allows them to be injected into the bloodstream or absorbed through skin, and carbon nanotubes offer the potential for creating biomechanical computers. This technology could enter into cases of intentional poisoning (via bloodstream examinations) or even provide difficult-to-detect miniature sensors for security systems.

Innovative virtual imaging produces 3-D images that are already exploited by forensic pathologists for a limited type of noninvasive autopsy, using a combination of CT scans and magnetic resonance imagining (MRI). The digitized images can easily be stored or sent via the Internet to other pathologists for consultation; they can also be made into exhibits for use in the courtroom. As this technology is improved, it will be increasingly utilized, especially internationally.

New methods are also on the horizon for biometric identification, such as palm-vein recognition technology. In this procedure, a machine shoots a beam of light through a person's hand; the blood absorbs the light, casting shadows that can be accurately mapped. Individuals can then be identified according to their personal "vein maps." This technology is currently being eyed in Japan as a way to stem identity theft and prevent fraudulent bank transactions.

In the area of digital forensics, Logicube, Inc., has produced CELLDEK, an information extraction device that can be used, without altering data, on cell phones and PDAs. Reportedly, it can access data from 90 percent of all North American devices. Using this device, trained investigators can process cell phones and PDAs at a crime scene rather than sending them to labs to await data extraction. CELLDEK offers information on calls made and received, the time and date, the internal phonebook, lists and memos, and even deleted material, such as previously stored phone numbers. Obviously, guidelines will need to be developed and enforced so that this technology will not be abused.

Electronic Sensor Technology has developed the zNose, a gas chromatograph that captures and analyzes odors using surface acoustic wave technology. One model is portable, and three other types are in development. This device will work well for homeland security, with units installed in buildings as early warning alarms for chemical or biohazardous threats.

Scientists at the Institute of Environmental Science and Research (ESR) in New Zealand view soil and its resident insects as a means for developing a "soil fingerprint" that will make investigating and solving crimes easier. Environmental scientist Jacqui Horswell developed a way to use DNA to analyze bacteria, so that a soil sample from an offender's shoe or car might be matched to a particular site. The scientists extract DNA from the sample to look at a gene, 16S rRNA. Then they make copies via polymerase chain reaction amplification. Once DNA profiles are developed, biologists can enter the data into a computer program that will make comparisons and determine a match. Because scientists can code the entire community of bacteria in a soil sample, they can compare one soil sample with another. The ESR researchers hope to develop a database for bacterial profiles so they can determine the statistical significance of a "match" and determine the provenance of unknown soil samples. In addition to soil samples, the sequencing technology used by Horswell has potential applications for other types of evidence, such as seeds, hair, and vegetation, as well as other mixtures where biological substances are components of the sample.

Aside from soil comparison, bacterial analysis has another important forensic function. Dr. Arpad Vass, a research scientist at Oak Ridge National Laboratory, has been working for years on the analysis of microbial measurements from decomposition found in soil beneath corpses. These data have assisted in narrowing estimates of the postmortem interval (PMI)—the period between the time a person dies and the time his body is discovered. In addition, insects that live in the soil go through developmental stages, and as they die and decompose they leave an imprint that helps with forming a PMI time line, as discussed in chapter 4. During decomposition, bacteria evolve, and knowing more about those changes and being able to compare them against a database, can help investigators answer many questions about the circumstances of a suspicious death.

Forensic biologists are always working to do more analysis using less sample material in a shorter amount of time. Some of the procedures currently used to identify the type of body fluid in a stain, for example, were developed in the early part of the twentieth century. Researchers are working to develop new applications of ribonucleic acid (RNA) analysis and real-time PCR DNA techniques to gain information about the source of biological materials, while using small amounts of sample and minimizing the potential for contamination. RNA is a chemical similar to DNA that is involved in protein synthesis and cell expression. The type of tissue that is the source of RNA can be identified using molecular biology techniques. These techniques should streamline testing, consume less of the sample, and provide a more conclusive determination of the type of body tissue or fluid analyzed.

In forensic psychology and psychiatry, the technology used to study the brain will offer more precise analysis in such areas as deception detection, the nature of violence, and the effects of drug ingestion and treatment. While the meaning of brain scans is still controversial, they will increasingly come into play in trials, especially for the defense. Cases in which brain scans have been used to show differences between the adolescent and the adult brain have initiated many discussions about the status of the juvenile offender. Scans have shown that the brain is not fully developed until well into the twenties, and consequently, impulse and emotion direct activities in juveniles more than in adults. This physiological difference has been used as a defense in juvenile cases, where attorneys claim poor decision making and impulsive actions must be considered when assessing guilt of or sentencing youths. Psychopathy has already been evaluated in some cases as a genetic anomaly rather than evidence of an "evil character," and certain results from "brain fingerprint" scans discussed in chapter 12 have shown promise as a way to determine whether someone was present at a crime scene. Advances in the prediction of risk for violent recidivism should make great advances in the near future, given how much research is currently being undertaken in this area. Similarly, the treatment of sex offenders, currently a dire issue, will likely be improved.

MASS DISASTERS

With the increase in mass murders and the impending threat of large-scale terrorism, the science of identification has rapidly advanced. After the incidents in the United States on September 11, 2001, with some twenty thousand pieces of human remains from the estimated 2,749 killed at the World Trade Center, a number of innovations assisted in the efficient identification of remains that once would have been beyond state-of-the-art processing.

Until that time, medical examiners typically thought in terms of fingerprints, dental records, X-rays, and personal effects for identifying victims of mass disasters. But few such incidents had fragmented and commingled so many human remains to the extent effected by the collapsing twin towers. New York City's DNA lab at the office of the medical examiner, along with several private labs around the country, responded to the immediate and critical need.

The primary lab initially lacked a laboratory information management system to keep track of processed samples, but with the assistance of many dedicated scientists, the complex work became manageable. At first, scientists established a system of extracting DNA to send to another lab for traditional analysis, while the state police lab in Albany, with the assistance of analysis teams from other parts of the country, extracted DNA from the personal effects of the missing, given to them by the victims' relatives. This lab also collected DNA swabs from relatives to establish kinship connections. Bode Technology, a private lab, modified procedures used to extract DNA from bones, and the FBI established a stand-alone CODIS system for computerized matching. But as the DNA degraded and the fragments became less workable, new methods were necessary.

In September 2001, crime labs across the country used short tandem repeats as biological markers in nuclear DNA. If a sufficient number of markers from the World Trade Center remains matched known DNA samples, scientists were able to make an identification. Eventually, they used mitochondrial DNA and or single-nucleotide polymorphisms (genetic variations at a single DNA location) to identify many of the remains collected from the debris. While "mitotyping," forensic mitochondrial DNA testing, has been used on degraded samples and forensic casework, especially at the Armed Forces Laboratory, SNPs are a relatively new technology, and no laboratory to date has used this method for routine forensic work. In the end, DNA analysis of one kind or another played a part in 89 percent of all identifications of remains from the World Trade Center and was the sole method of identification in 86 percent. In the event of future mass disaster, this statistic should offer some measure of solace.

Forensic scientists are also seeking ways to expand into countries around the world, especially those with few or no resources. The FBI assists internationally with setting up computerized databases and teaching programs in countries that lack resources. Federal agencies and professional organizations are working in several countries to establish forensic services where none currently exist. Specially trained teams of scientists and medical examiners arrive after natural or human-made disasters to assist with the identification of the dead. The identification of victims of plane crashes, natural disasters, and in mass gravesites is a slow and meticulous process that requires careful work by the forensic scientist and the investigator. DNA technologies combined with databases will make the process more timely.

CHALLENGES WITHIN THE JUSTICE SYSTEM

The work of forensic scientists is intimately associated with the justice systems of the world. Whether they are civil or criminal evidence experts, forensic practitioners must be able to satisfy the demands for reliable evidence and make clear the significance of forensic findings. Among the most important challenges that face forensic scientists today is the need to educate other members of the justice system—attorneys, judges, and investigators. Most judges—who are responsible for making decisions about admitting evidence into court—have only a rudimentary science background. Where are those judges going to learn the science? It is important that forensic practitioners provide objective, accurate information concerning the science behind any forensic testing, make clear the limitations of that testing, and provide sufficient basis outside forensics to support scientific claims. This knowledge can be expanded by forming partnerships with researchers and educators in related fields. Such teams can expand the understanding of forensic science to the justice communities, helping to explain the fundamental concepts to them and to other nonscientists.

It is no longer sufficient for forensic examiners to obtain on-the-job-training and nothing else. Science and technology are changing daily, and forensic scientists must keep up with new developments and new ideas. Forensic scientists can help the cause of justice only when they educate themselves and others in these new technologies. Knowing that such changes occur at a rapid pace, the forensic community must continue to find ways to safeguard the rights of both victims and those accused of crimes by preserving evidence whenever possible for future developments in testing. One need only to look at the revolution in individualization that took place with the development of DNA to understand why this is important. Initially, large amounts of DNA were necessary for profiling; within a few short years 1/1000 of the amount of DNA used for DNA "fingerprinting" were giving conclusive, reliable results. Because of some highly publicized cases and the exoneration of falsely imprisoned people by the Innocence Project, some attorneys and members of the public have already lost faith in the scientific integrity of some forensic procedures and scientists. Keeping this in mind, each scientist should look at procedures, technologies, data, and conclusions with a critical eye as if someone else's life depends on it—because it does!

.

During almost fifty years as a forensic scientist, Dr. Henry Lee has seen remarkable changes in the field. Interesting work is currently being done in every major discipline. Some changes in the way forensic scientists did and will do things were inevitable. However, Lee knows that the bottom line will never change—good forensic science will always provide facts that can be used to achieve justice for both the victims and the accused.

SOURCES

CHAPTER 1. THE CRIME SCENE AND THE SCIENTIST

Aisne, A. "C.S.I. Effect Put under the Scope," *Ann Arbor News*, May 18, 2007.

Herzog, A. *The Woodchipper Murder.* New York: Henry Holt, 1989.

Hooper, R. "Television Shows Scramble Forensic Evidence." *New Scientist*, September 9, 2005. http://www.newscientist.com/article/mg18725163 .800-television-shows-scramble-forensic-evidence.html (accessed March 18, 2008).

Lee, H. C., and T. O'Neil. *Cracking Cases: The Science of Solving Crimes.* Amherst, NY: Prometheus Books, 2002.

Lee, H., T. Palmbach, and M. Miller. *Henry Lee's Crime Scene Handbook.* San Diego, CA: Academic Press, 2002.

Tyler, T. "Viewing CSI and the Threshold of Guilt." *Yale Law Journal* 115 (2006): 1050.

Willing, R. "'C.S.I. Effect' Has Juries Wanting More Evidence." *USA Today*, August 5, 2004.

CHAPTER 2. FORENSIC SCIENCE IN HISTORICAL PERSPECTIVE

Becker, P., and R. F. Wetzell. *Criminals and Their Scientists: The History of Criminology in International Perspective.* Cambridge: Cambridge University Press, 2006.

Cole, S. A. *Suspect Identities: A History of Fingerprinting and Criminal Identification.* Cambridge, MA: Harvard University Press, 2001.

Evans, C. *The Casebook of Forensic Detection.* New York: John Wiley and Sons, 1996.

———. *The Second Casebook of Forensic Detection.* Hoboken, NJ: John Wiley and Sons, 2006.

Field, K. S. *History of the American Academy of Forensic Sciences, 1948–1998.* Conshohocken, PA: American Society for Testing and Materials, 1996.

Fridell, R. *Solving Crimes: Pioneers of Forensic Science.* New York: Grolier, 2000.

Horn, D. G. *The Criminal Body: Lombroso and the Anatomy of Deviance.* New York: Routledge, 2003.

Lee, H. C., and F. Tirnady. *Blood Evidence: How DNA Is Revolutionizing the Way We Solve Crimes.* Cambridge, MA: Perseus, 2003.

Levy, H. *And the Blood Cried Out: A Prosecutor's Spellbinding Account of the Power of DNA.* New York: BasicBooks, 1996.

Snyder Sachs, J. *Corpse: Nature, Forensics and the Struggle to Pinpoint Time of Death.* Cambridge, MA: Perseus, 2001.

Thorwald, J. *The Century of the Detective.* New York: Harcourt, Brace & World, 1964.

———. *Crime and Science.* New York: Harcourt, Brace & World, 1966.

Vidocq, F. E. *Memoirs of Vidocq: Master of Crime.* Edinburgh: AK Press, 2003.

Wambaugh, J. *The Blooding: The True Story of the Narborough Village Murders.* New York: William Morrow, 1989.

Wilson, C., and D. Wilson. *Written in Blood: A History of Forensic Detection.* New York: Carroll and Graf, 2003.

CHAPTER 3. THE SCIENTIFIC METHOD IN FORENSIC EVIDENCE EXAMINATIONS

Fisher, B. *Techniques of Crime Scene Investigation*, 7th ed. Boca Raton, FL: CRC Press, 2003.

Gaensslen, R. E., H. Harris, and H. Lee. *Introduction to Forensic Science and Criminalistics*. New York: McGraw-Hill, 2007.

Kiely, T. *Forensic Evidence: Science & the Criminal Law*, 2nd ed. Boca Raton, FL: CRC Press, 2005.

Lee, H., ed. *Crime Scene Investigation*. Taipei, Taiwan: Central Police College, 1990.

Lee, H., and H. Harris. *Physical Evidence in Forensic Science*. Tuscon, AZ: Lawyers and Judges, 2006.

Lee, H., G. Taft, and K. Taylor. *Forensic Science Today*. Tuscon, AZ: Lawyers and Judges, 2006.

Hammer, R., B. Moynihan, and E. Pagliaro. *Forensic Nursing: A Handbook for Practice*. Sudbury, MA: Jones & Bartlett, 2006.

CHAPTER 4. DEATH INVESTIGATORS

"Appeals Court Refuses to Overturn Murder Conviction of Novelist Michael Peterson." CourtTV, September 19, 2006. http://www.courttv.com/trials/novelist/index.html (accessed April 22, 2008).

Baden, M., with J. A. Hennessee. *Unnatural Death: Confessions of a Medical Examiner*. New York: Ivy Books, 1989.

Baden, M., with M. Roach. *Dead Reckoning: The New Science of Catching Killers*. New York: Simon & Schuster, 2001.

Bass, B., with J. Jefferson. *Death's Acre*. New York: G. P. Putnam's Sons, 2003.

Benedict, J. *No Bone Unturned*. New York: HarperCollins, 2003.

Dix, J., and R. Calaluce. *Guide to Forensic Pathology*. Boca Raton, FL: CRC Press, 1999.

Ewinger, J. "Jurors Sort Out Two Accounts of Nun's Killing." *Cleveland Plain Dealer*, May 11, 2006.

———. "No Proof of Priest at Scene of Killing." *Cleveland Plain Dealer*, April 28, 2006.

———. "Priest's Trial in Death of Nun Will Include Talk of Rituals, Cults." *Cleveland Plain Dealer*, April 12, 2006.

————. "Three Witnesses Recall Seeing Priest at Murder Scene." *Cleveland Plain Dealer*, May 8, 2006.

Fanning, D. *Written in Blood*. New York: St. Martin's, 2005.

Fridell, R. *Solving Crimes: Pioneers of Forensic Science*. New York: Grolier, 2000.

Goff, M. L. *A Fly for the Prosecution: How Insect Evidence Helps Solve Crimes*. Cambridge, MA: Harvard University Press, 2000.

Haglund, W. D., and M. H. Sorg. *Advances in Forensic Taphonomy: Method, Theory and Archaeological Perspectives*. Boca Raton, FL: CRC Press, 2002.

Lee, H. C., and T. O'Neil. *Cracking Cases: The Science of Solving Crimes*. Amherst, NY: Prometheus Books, 2002.

MacDonell, H. L. *Bloodstain Patterns*. Corning, NY: Laboratory of Forensic Science, 1993.

Manheim, M. H. *The Bone Lady*. New York: Penguin, 1999.

Noguchi, T., with J. DiMona. *Coroner at Large*. New York: Simon & Schuster, 1985.

North Carolina v. Michael Peterson, 2003. http://www.courttv.com/trials/novelist/index.html (accessed March 22, 2008).

Randall, B. *Death Investigation: The Basics*. Tucson, AZ: Galen Press, 1997.

Seewer, J. "Letter Opener, Bloodstains Key to Prosecutor's Case," Associated Press, May 1, 2006.

————. "Prosecutor Says Priest Wanted to Humiliate Nun in Her Death," Associated Press, May 11, 2006.

————. "Twenty-six Years Later, Jury Convicts Priest of Nun's Slaying," Associated Press, May 12, 2006.

Snyder Sachs, J. *Corpse: Nature, Forensics and the Struggle to Pinpoint Time of Death*. Cambridge, MA: Perseus, 2001.

The Staircase Murder. Paris: Maha Productions, 2004.

Ubelaker, D., and H. Scammel. *Bones: A Forensic Detective's Casebook*. New York: M. Evans, 1992.

Wecht, C. *Mortal Evidence*. Amherst, NY: Prometheus Books, 2003.

Wonder, A. Y. *Blood Dynamics*. San Diego, CA: Academic Press, 2001.

Yonke, D. *Sin, Shame, Secrets*. New York: Continuum, 2006.

CHAPTER 5. FINGERPRINT EVIDENCE

Beavan, C. *Fingerprints*. New York: Hyperion, 2001.

Dimeo, L. "Vacuum Metal Deposition: Its Value in Developing Archival Prints." Southern California Association of Fingerprint Officers, October 3, 2002. http://www.scafo.org/library/100302.html (April 29, 2008).

Lee, H., and R. E. Gaensslen. *Advances in Fingerprint Technology*, 2nd ed. Boca Raton, FL: CRC Press, 2001.

Lee, H. C., and H. A. Harris. *Physical Evidence in Forensic Science*. Tucson, AZ: Lawyers and Judges, 2000.

Lee, H. C., and T. O'Neil. *Cracking More Cases*. Amherst, NY: Prometheus Books, 2002.

McMenamin, J. "Judge Bars Use of Partial Prints in Murder Trial." *Baltimore Sun*, October 23, 2007.

Mnookin, J. "Fingerprints: Not a Gold Standard." *Issues in Science and Technology* (Fall 2003).

Newman, A. "DNA Leads to Arrest in '73 Slaying in New Haven." *New York Times*, June 25, 1999.

Tuohy, L. "Killer Asks for New Look at Case." *Hartford Courant*, January 9, 2008.

CHAPTER 6. FIREARMS EVIDENCE

Hamby, J. E., and J. W. Thorpe. "The History of Firearms and Toolmark Identification." *AFTE Journal* 31, no. 3 (1999).

Kieley, T. *Forensic Evidence: Science and the Criminal Law*. Boca Raton, FL: CRC Press, 2001.

Lee, H., and J. Labriola. *Famous Crimes Revisited*. Southington, CT: Strong Books, 2001.

Lee, H., T. Palmbach, and M. Miller. *Henry Lee's Crime Scene Handbook*. New York: Academic Press, 2001.

Schehl, S. "Firearms and Toolmarks in the FBI Laboratory." *Forensic Science Communications* 2, no. 2 (2000). http://www.fbi.gov/hq/lab/fsc/backissu/April 2002/research/2002_02_research02b.htm (accessed May 8, 2008).

Schwartz, A. "A Systematic Challenge to the Reliability and Admissibility of Firearms and Toolmark Identification." *Columbia Science and Technology Law Review* 6 (2004): 1–42.

Scientific Working Group for Firearms and Tool Mark Evidence. *Guidelines for the Analysis of Firearms and Tool Mark Evidence.* http://www.swggun.org/guidelines/htm (accessed July 15, 2008).

Wecht, C. *Mortal Evidence.* Amherst, NY: Prometheus Books, 2003.

CHAPTER 7. TRACE EVIDENCE AND CHEMICAL ANALYSIS

Deedrick, D., and S. Koch. "Microscopy of Hair Part I: A Practical Guide and Manual for Human Hairs." *Forensic Science Communications* 6, no. 1 (2004). http://www.fbi.gov/hq/lab/fsc/backissu/jan2004/research/2004_01_research01b.htm (accessed August 8, 2008).

————. "Microscopy of Hair Part II: A Practical Guide and Manual for Animal Hairs." *Forensic Science Communications* 6, no. 3 (2004). http://www.fbi.gov/hq/lab/fscbackissu/july2004/research/2004_03_research02.htm (accessed August 8, 2008).

Gaensslen, R. E., H. Harris, and H. Lee. *Introduction to Forensic Science and Criminalistics.* New York: McGraw-Hill, 2008.

Houck, M., ed. *Mute Witness: Trace Evidence Analysis.* New York: Academic Press, 2001.

Lee, H., and P. DeForest. "Forensic Hair Examination." In *Forensic Science*, edited by C. Wecht. Boca Raton, FL: CRC Press, 1984.

Lentini, J. *Scientific Protocols for Fire Investigation.* Boca Raton, FL: CRC Press, 2005.

Lewis, P. "Walter McCrone, Debunker of Legends, Is Dead at 86." *New York Times*, July 26, 2002.

Reffner, J. "Remembering Walter C. McCrone." *Journal of Forensic Sciences* 49, no. 2 (March 2004).

Saferstein, R., ed. *Forensic Science Handbook, Vol. 1.* Upper Saddle River, NJ: Prentice Hall, 2001.

Scientific Working Group on Materials Analysis. *Guidelines for Forensic Fiber Analysis. Forensic Science Communications* 1, no. 1 (1999). http://www.fbi.gov/hq/lab/fscbackissu/april2005/standards/SWGMAT_fiber_training_program.pdf (accessed July 18, 2008).

Stauffer, E., and J. Lentini, "ASTM Standards for Fire Debris Analysis (E1387 and E1618): A Review." *Forensic Science International* 132 (2002): 63–67.

CHAPTER 8. DNA EVIDENCE

Conners, E., T Lundgregan, N. Miller, and T. McEwen. *Convicted by Juries, Exonerated by Science: Case Studies in the Use of DNA Evidence to Establish Innocence after Trial* (NCJ 161258). Washington, DC: National Institute of Justice, US Department of Justice, 1996.

Coyle, H. M. *Forensic Botany*. Boca Raton, FL: CRC Press, 2004.

"DNAPrint Genomics Helps Boulder Police Solve 10-Year-Old Rape/Murder Case Using Cutting Edge DNA Technology." Reuters, January 30, 2008. http://www.reuters.com/article/pressRelease/idUS145130+30-Jan-2008+MW20080130 (accessed July 6, 2008).

Federal Bureau of Investigation. *Quality Assurance for Forensic DNA Testing Labs and Quality Assurance Standards for DNA Databasing Labs*. Washington, DC: US Department of Justice, 2007.

Gaensslen, R. E. *Sourcebook in Forensic Serology, Immunology and Biochemistry*. Washington, DC: US Government Printing Office, 1983.

The Innocence Project. http://www.innocenceproject.org (accessed July 3, 2008).

Jeffreys, A., J. Brookfield, and R. Semeonoff. "Positive Identification of an Immigration Test-Case using DNA Fingerprints." *Nature* 317 (October 3, 1985): 818–19.

Lee, H., and C. Ladd. "The Use of Biological Evidence and DNA Databanks." In *Forensic Nursing: A Handbook for Practice*, edited by R. Hammer, B. Moynihan, and E. Pagliaro. Sudbury, MA: Jones & Bartlett, 2007.

Lee H., and F. Tirnady. *Blood Evidence: How DNA Is Revolutionizing the Way We Solve Crimes*. New York: Perseus, 2003.

National Commission on the Future of DNA Evidence. *What Every Law Enforcement Officer Should Know about DNA Evidence*. Washington, DC: National Institute of Justice, US Department of Justice, 1998.

Rudin, N., and K. Inman. *Introduction to Forensic DNA Analysis*, 2nd ed. Boca Raton, FL: CRC Press, 2001.

Seigel, R. "Interview of Sir Alec Jeffreys." National Public Radio, July 15, 2005. http://www.npr.org/templates/story.php?storyed=4756341 (accessed July 6, 2008).

Thompson, W. C. "Tarnish on the 'Gold Standard': Understanding Recent Problems in Forensic DNA Testing." *Champion* (January/February 2006): 14–20.

US Congress, Office of Technology Assessment. *Genetic Witness: Forensic*

Uses of DNA Tests (OTA-BA-438). Washington, DC: US Government Printing Office, 1990.

US Department of Justice. *Principles of Forensic DNA for Officers of the Court*. Washington, DC: National Institute of Justice, 2006.

Wambaugh, J. *The Blooding*. New York: William Morrow, 1989.

Wulff, P. H. "Low Copy Number DNA: Reality vs. Jury Expectations." *Silent Witness Newsletter* 10, no. 3 (2006). http://www.denverda.org/DNA_Documents/LCN%20DNA%20NDAA%20Silent%20Witness%20Article.pdf (accessed April 13, 2008).

CHAPTER 9. FORENSIC DRUG ANALYSIS AND TOXICOLOGY

American Board of Forensic Toxicologists. *Procedures for Certification*. http://www.abft.org/Specialist.asp (accessed July 6, 2008).

Cravey, R. H., and R. C. Baselt. "An Introduction to Forensic Toxicology: The Science of Forensic Toxicology." Society of Forensic Toxicologists, 2008. http://http://www.soft-tox.org/default.aspx?pn=Introduction (accessed August 11, 2008).

Gaensslen, R. E., H. A. Harris, and H. Lee. *Introduction to Forensic Science and Criminalistics*. New York: McGraw-Hill, 2008.

Hayes, A. W., ed. *Principles and Methods of Toxicology*, 5th ed. Boca Raton, FL: CRC Press, 2008.

Klaassen, C. D., and J. B. Watkins III, ed. *Casarett & Doull's Essentials of Toxicology*. New York: McGraw-Hill, 2003.

LeBeau, M. A. "Toxicological Investigation of Drug Facilitated Sexual Assaults." *Forensic Science Communications* 1, no. 1 (April 1999). http://www.fbi.gov/hq/lab/fsc/backissu/april1999/lebeau.htm (accessed August 2, 2008).

Middlebury, R. A. "Forensic Toxicology in the Fore . . . and Aft." *Forensic Magazine* (June/July 2008). http://forensicmag.com/Article_Print.asp?pid=210 (accessed August 2, 2008).

Negruz, A., M. Juhascik, and R. Gaensslen. "Estimate of the Incidence of Drug Facilitated Sexual Assault in the United States." *NCJRS Report*, June 2, 2005.

Rape, Abuse and Incest National Network. http://www.RAINN.org (accessed July 16, 2008).

Scheck, A. "Using Sensitive Forensic Testing, Lab Cracks the Dr. Death Case." *Emergency Medicine News* 23, no. 2 (February 2001): 51–52.

Scientific Working Group for the Analysis of Seized Drugs. "SWGDRUG Recommendations," http://www.swgdrug.org/approved.htm (accessed August 3, 2008).

Society of Forensic Toxicologists. *Forensic Toxicology Laboratory Guidelines*, SOFT/AAFS Lab Guidelines, 2006. http://www.soft-tox.org/docs/Guidelines%202006%20Final.pdf (accessed August 2, 2008).

United States of America v. Michael J. Swango, U.S. District Court, Eastern District of New York, Fed # 99R00496 indictment filed July 11, 2000. http://www.vamalpractice.info/Adobe%20pdf/Swango/Swango%20Indictment.pdf (accessed April 23, 2009).

U.S. Department of Veterans' Affairs. The Case of Dr. Michael Swango, 2008. http://www.vamalpractice.info/dr_swango1.htm (accessed August 3, 2008).

Westveer, A. E., J. P. Jarvis, and C. J. Jensen III. "Homicidal Poisoning—The Silent Offense." *Law Enforcement Bulletin* (August 2004): 8–11.

CHAPTER 10. FORENSIC ODONTOLOGY

Baden, M., and M. Roach. *Dead Reckoning: The New Science of Catching Killers*. New York: Simon & Schuster, 2001.

Bowers, C. M. "A Statement Why Court Opinions on Bite-Mark Analysis Should Be Limited." *American Board of Forensic Odontology Newsletter* 4 (1976).

Bowers, C. M., and R. Johansen. "Forensic Dentistry: An Overview of Bite Marks." In *Human and Animal Bitemark Management*, edited by C. M. Bowers. Forensic Mailing Services, 2000. http://www.forensic.to/webhome/bitemarks (accessed April 2008).

"Can the Teeth Tell All?" *York Daily Record*, May 15, 2008.

Kiely, T. F. *Forensic Evidence: Science and the Criminal Law*, 2nd ed. Boca Raton, FL: 2006.

Lee, H. C., and H. A. Harris. *Physical Evidence in Forensic Science*. Tucson, AZ: Lawyers and Judges, 2000.

McRoberts, F., and S. Mills. "From the Start, a Faulty Science." *Chicago Tribune*, October 19, 2004.

Miller, R. "Torture Killing Shook City." *Easton (NJ) Express-Times*, June 1, 2003.

Saferstein, R. *Criminalistics: An Introduction to Forensic Science*, 5th ed. Englewood Cliffs, NJ: Prentice Hall, 1995.

Sperber, H. D. "Chewing Gum—An Unusual Clue in a Recent Homicide Investigation." *Journal of Forensic Sciences* 23 (1978): 792. http://astm.org/JOURNALS/FORENSIC/PAGES/4825.htm (accessed April 2008).

State v. Swinton. 268 Conn. 781, 847 A.2d 921 (2004).

Stout, D. "Runaway Girl Is Found Dead after Torture, Police Say." *New York Times*, August 16, 1996.

Swickard, J. "Freed Suspect Asks Justice." *Detroit Free Press*, August 25, 1999.

CHAPTER 11. QUESTIONED DOCUMENTS

Berg, A. S. *Lindbergh*. New York: Putnam, 1998.

"Ex JonBenét Ramsey Murder Suspect John Mark Karr Arrested for Domestic Violence." Associated Press, July 7, 2007.

Fisher, J. *The Lindbergh Case*. Piscataway, NJ: Rutgers University Press, 1994.

Harris, R. *Selling Hitler*. New York: Penguin, 1986.

Lee, H., and J. Labriola. *Famous Crimes Revisited*. Southington, CT: Strong Books, 2001.

Lee, H. C., and T. O'Neil. *Cracking More Cases*. Amherst, NY: Prometheus Books, 2004.

Murray, M. "Forensic Linguist Studies Syntax as a Signature." *Sussex (DE) News Journal*, November 16, 2002.

Nickell, J., and J. Fischer. *Crime Science: Methods of Forensic Detection*. Lexington: University Press of Kentucky, 1999.

Ramsland, K. *The CSI Effect*. New York: Berkley, 2006.

Robinson v. Mandell. 20 F. Cas 1027 (C.C. D. Mass. 1868. No. 11959).

Schiller, L. *Perfect Murder, Perfect Town: The Uncensored Story of the Jon-Benet Murder and the Grand Jury's Search for the Final Truth*. New York: Harper, 1999.

Sillitoe, L., and A. Roberts. *Salamander: The Story of the Mormon Forgery Murders*, 2nd ed. Salt Lake City, UT: Signature Books, 1989.

Thomas, S., and D. A. Davis. *JonBenét: Inside the Ramsey Murder Investigation*. New York: St. Martin's, 2000.

Worrall, Simon. *The Poet and the Murderer*. New York: Dutton, 2002.

CHAPTER 12. EMERGING FORENSIC DISCIPLINES

Arrigo, B., and S. Shipley. *Introduction to Forensic Psychology*, 2nd ed. New York: Elsevier, 2005.

Bonadiman, Joseph S. C. "Causes of Failure: What a Forensic Engineer Looks For." *Forensic Examiner* 12, nos. 11 & 12 (November/December 2003): 23–27.

Bosela, P. A., and N. Delatte, eds. *Forensic Engineering*. Reston, VA: American Society of Civil Engineers, 2006.

Brancik, K. *Inside Computer Fraud*. Sarasota, FL: CRC Press, 2008.

Brewer, N., and Kipling D. W. *Psychology and Law*. New York: Guilford, 2005.

Casey, E. *Digital Evidence and Computer Crime: Forensic Science, Computers and the Internet*, 2nd ed. San Diego, CA: Academic Press, 2004.

Corley, W. G., and R. Sturm. "Forensic Engineering: Lessons Learned from the Oklahoma City Bombing, Parts I and II." *Forensic Examiner* 10/11, nos. 1–4 (2001): 17–19, 31–34.

Dusky v. United States. 362 U.S. 402 (1960).

Elliott, M. "Michael Ross: Why a Killer Offers to Die." *Connecticut Law Tribune*, April 29, 1996.

Evans, C. *The Casebook of Forensic Detection*. New York: John Wiley & Sons, 1996.

Hammer, R., B. Moynihan, and E. Pagliaro, eds. *Forensic Nursing: A Handbook for Practice*. Sudbury, MA: Jones & Bartlett, 2006.

Hollien, Harry. *The Acoustics of Crime: The New Science of Forensic Phonetics*. London: Springer, 1990.

"Indefinite Reprieve for Ross." *New York Newsday*, February 1, 2005.

Kersta, L. G. "Voiceprint Identification." *Nature*, December 29, 1962.

Marcella, A., Jr., and D. Menendez. *Cyber Forensics: A Field Manual for Collecting, Examining, and Preserving Evidence of Computer Crimes*, 2nd ed. Sarasota, FL: CRC Press, 2008.

McCrary, G., with K. Ramsland. *The Unknown Darkness: Profiling the Predators among Us*. New York: Morrow, 2003.

Melton, G. B., J. Petrila, N. G. Poythress, and C. Slobogin. *Psychological Evaluations for the Courts*, 2nd ed. New York: Guilford, 1997.

Nickell, J., and J. Fischer. *Crime Science: Methods of Forensic Detection*. Lexington: University Press of Kentucky, 1999.

Ramsland, K., with D. DiVito. "Nurses Who Kill." *Nursing Malpractice*, 3rd ed. Tucson, AZ: Lawyers and Judges, 2007.

Randerson, J. "New Evidence Challenges Official Picture of Kennedy Shooting." *Guardian*, February 22, 2008.

Ressler, R. *Whoever Fights Monsters*. New York: St. Martin's, 1992.

Welner, M., and K. Ramsland. "Forensic Psychology." In *Foundations of Forensic Science and Law: Applications in Criminal, Civil, and Family Justice*, edited by C. Wecht and J. Raggo. Sarasota, FL: CRC Press, 2006.

CHAPTER13. FORENSIC SCIENTISTS ON TRIAL

American Society of Crime Laboratory Directors Laboratory Accreditation Board. ASCLD/LAB Objectives, 2008. http://www.ascld-lab.org/dual/ aslabdualobjectives.html (accessed August 10, 2008).

Collins, J., and J. Jarvis. "The Wrongful Conviction of Forensic Science." *Crime Lab Report* (July 18, 2008): 2–16.

Conners, E., T. Lundgren, N. Miller, and T. McEwen. *Convicted by Juries, Exonerated by Science: Case Studies in the Use of DNA Evidence to Establish Innocence after Trial*. National Institute of Justice Research Report NCJ161258. Washington, DC: US Department of Justice, 1996.

Final Report of the Independent Investigator for the Houston Police Department Crime Laboratory and Property Room. June 13, 2007. http://www.hpdlabinvestigation.org/reports/070613report.pdf (accessed August 10, 2008).

Hodel, M. B. "Crime Lab Chemist Goes on Trial in W. Va. for Alleged Fraud." *Athens (GA) Banner-Herald*, September 4, 2001.

Huber, P. *Galileo's Revenge: Junk Science in the Courtroom*. New York: BasicBooks, 1993.

The Innocence Project. http://www.innocenceproject.org (accessed July 3, 2008).

Kiely, T. *Forensic Evidence: Science and the Criminal Law*, 2nd ed. Boca Raton, FL: CRC Press, 2005.

Peterson, J. L., J. Ryan, P. Houlden, and S. Mihajlovic. *Forensic Science and the Courts: The Uses and Effects of Scientific Evidence in Criminal Case Processing*. Final Report, National Institute of Justice Grant 82-IJ-CX-0064. Chicago: Chicago Center for Research in Law and Justice, University of Illinois at Chicago, 1986. http://www.ncjrs.gov/pdffiles1/ pr/102387.pdf (accessed July 2008).

Schorn, Daniel. "The Duke Case: Lesley Stahl Talks to Parents of Accused, Prosecution Forensic Expert." CBS News/*60 Minutes*, January 14, 2007. http://www.cbsnews.com/stories/2007/01/11/60minutes/main 2352512.shtml (accessed August 11, 2008).

"Under the Microscope." CBS News/*60 Minutes II*, July 24, 2002. http://www.cbsnews.com/stories/2001/05/08/60II/main290046 (accessed March 14, 2008).

William Daubert v. Merrell Dow Pharmaceuticals, Inc. 113 S. CT 2786 (1993).

CHAPTER 14. THE FUTURE OF FORENSIC SCIENCE

Bowen, R., and J. Schneider. "Forensic Databases: Paint, Shoe Prints, and Beyond." *NIJ Journal* 258 (October 2007).

Conti, T. "Body Fluid Stain Identification Using qPCR." Paper presented at the Green Mountain DNA Conference, Burlington, VT, August 6, 2008.

Eckenrode, B., E. Bartick, S. Harvey, M. Vicelick, B. Wright, and R. Huff. "Portable Raman Spectroscopy Systems for Field Analysis." *Forensic Science Communications* 3, no. 4 (October 2001). http://www.fbi.gov/hq/lab/fsc/backissu/oct2001/eknrode.htm (accessed June 12, 2008).

Kanable, R. "Modern Forensic Science Today and Tomorrow." *Law Enforcement Technology*, July 2005.

Mennell, J. "The Future of Forensic and Crime Scene Science—A U.K. Perspective." *Forensic Science International* 157, no. 14 (March 2006): 1–12.

Mitchell, C. "Tech 2010: #13 Feel Secure: The Detective that Every Jury Believes." *New York Times*, June 11, 2000.

Rappeport, J. R. "The Present and Future of Forensic Psychiatry." *Journal of the American Academy of Psychiatry and the Law* 33, no. 2 (2005): 263–64.

Robertson, J. "The Future of Forensic Science." In *Proceedings of the Asia Pacific Police Technology Conference*, edited by J. Vernon and D. Berwick. Canberra: Australian Institute of Criminology, 2000.

Shaler, R. C. *Who They Were: Inside the World Trade Center DNA Story.* New York: Free Press, 2005.

US Fire Administration. *Hazardous Materials Response Technology Assessment.* Washington, DC: Federal Emergency Management Agency, 1996.

Williams, M. "Forget Fingerprints and Eye Scans: The Latest in Biometrics Is in Vein." *Computerworld Security*, June 29, 2005.

INDEX

hydroxyzine, mass spectrum of, 203
hypothesis formation (as step in
scientific method), 55, 57, 89

IAFN. *See* International Association of Forensic Nurses
IAI. *See* International Association
for Identification
IBIS. *See* Integrated Ballistics Identification System
ICP-MS. *See* inductively coupled
plasma mass spectrometry
identification
  biometric identification, 306
  of human remains, 99, 221–24
  of victims of disasters, 308–10
  See also Bertillonage; fingerprints
identification and compar-
ison/individualization (as step in
forensic method), 57, 58
identity theft, 278–79
Image Content Technologies, 215
immunology, 58, 79
Imperial Criminological Institute
(University of Graz), 40
inclusion (interpretation of DNA
analysis), 186
inconclusive (interpretation of
DNA analysis), 186
individualization/identification and
comparison (as step in forensic
method), 57, 58
inductively coupled plasma mass
spectrometry, 205
informatics, forensic. *See* computer
forensics
infrared lighting and document
analysis, 250

Innocence Project, 189–91, 228,
291
inquests, 89–90, 91
insects, study of. *See* entomology
instrumental analysis, 158–59
Integrated Ballistics Identification
System, 135
International Association for Criminal Identification. *See* International Association for Identification
International Association for Identification, 51, 114, 125
International Association of
Forensic Nurses, 279–80
Internet and cybercrime, 278
interpretation
  interpretation and testimony
  (as step in forensic method),
  57, 59
  interpretation as a part of
  DNA analysis, 185–86
Interstate Commerce Act (US), 48
*Introduction to Forensic Science
and Criminalistics* (Lee), 22
investigative leads, 75
iodine-benzoflavone, 119
Irving, Clifford, 233, 269
isoenzymes, 174–75
Izmailov, N. A., 44

Jackson, Stonewall, 131–32
Jefferson, Thomas, 183
Jeffreys, Alec, 171, 173, 175, 177
Jennings, Thomas, 114
  (case against), 125
Jesserich, Paul, 41
John Jay College of Criminal Jus-
tice (JJCCJ), 21